3/0

Gilbert Before Sullivan

Gilbert
Before Sullivan

SIX COMIC PLAYS

BY W. S. GILBERT

EDITED AND WITH AN INTRODUCTION BY

Jane W. Stedman

THE UNIVERSITY OF CHICAGO PRESS

Library of Congress Catalog Card Number: 67–16778

THE UNIVERSITY OF CHICAGO PRESS, CHICAGO 60637

Routledge & Kegan Paul, Ltd., London

The University of Toronto Press, Toronto 5, Canada

FOR PROFESSOR NAPIER WILT

maître

Preface

THE GERMAN REED ENTERTAINMENTS of W. S. Gilbert are often referred to by biographers and historians of the Victorian Stage, but seldom read. In the present collection, I have undertaken to make their texts accessible, to re-create their theatrical background, and to indicate their relationship to Gilbert's libretti for the Savoy Operas. I have tried, too, to present Mr. and Mrs. German Reed "in their habit as they lived." I hope, therefore, that this book will be of interest and use both to the student of the theatre and to the general reader.

I should like to thank the Theatre Collection of The New York Public Library, Astor, Lenox and Tilden Foundations, for permission to quote from Boucicault's letter to Bancroft; the Victoria and Albert Museum for permission to use quotations from reviews, programs, and pictures in the Enthoven Collection, as well as its copy of *Ages Ago* as printed by Mallett; the Trustees of the British Museum for permission to reprint the Joseph Williams texts of the Entertainments, the typescript of *Our Island Home*, the score of *Ages Ago*, material from the Gilbert papers and the manuscripts of plays in the Lord Chamberlain's Deposit, and examples of the entertainments of Charles Mathews and Howard Paul; Simon and Schuster, Inc., for permission to reprint Captain Bang's song from Isaac Goldberg's *The Story of Gilbert and Sullivan*, originally published by them in 1928; and Mr. Barry Duncan for the copy and history of Gilbert's *carte de visite* photograph, originally in a scrapbook belonging to the Marryat family.

I am particularly grateful to Mr. Reginald Allen, whose conversation saved me from at least two erroneous suppositions (I leave it to him to decide which), who collated the two Joseph Williams texts of *A Sensation Novel* for me, and whose unparalleled Gilbert and Sullivan Collection furnished me with the Mallett libretti for Gilbert's five printed Entertainments, a manuscript copy of *Eyes and No Eyes*, illustrations, and playbills. For permission to quote from these, I am further indebted to Mr. Allen and to the Pierpont Morgan Library, New York.

I must also thank Mr. F. B. Cockburn for allowing me to print hitherto unpublished material from the Gilbert Papers and the License Copies of the Entertainments. I am sorry to have been unable to discover the present holder of Sir Francis Burnand's copyrights, but I hope that he (or she) will not object to my quoting from *Cox and Box* and *Records and Reminiscences.*

My gratitude to Mr. Herbert Cahoon of the Pierpont Morgan Library; to Mr. Colin Franklin of Routledge & Kegan Paul, Ltd; and to my former students, Mrs. Mary Ann Steiner, Mrs. Gloria Cohen, and Mr. Jerry Fitzgerald, all of whom have, with kind celerity, aided and abetted.

Finally, I acknowledge my great and affectionate indebtedness to the encouragement and criticism of George C. McElroy, husband, wit, sounding board, and proofreader.

J. W. S.

Roosevelt University
Chicago

Contents

Illustrations

Line drawings on the title page and scattered throughout the plays are Gilbert's own.

It is to a thoroughly careful carrying out of this style of entertainment on an enlarged scale that Messrs. GILBERT AND SULLI-VAN owe their success with such pieces as The Sorcerer (*which was eminently a GER-MAN REED style of entertainment, like the same Author's* Ages Ago), *and* The Pinafore. *The Opera Comique performance is only the GERMAN REED'S entertainment 'writ large'. . . .*

Punch, *January 10, 1880*

Note.—In A.D. *1969, Mr. and Mrs. German Reed hope to have the pleasure of continuing the history of these interesting portraits.*

Book of the lyrics of Ages Ago, *1869*

Introduction

IN 1854 MR. AND MRS. GERMAN REED (Priscilla Horton before her marriage and for more than a decade after) toured the provinces; he played the piano while she imitated European singing styles in a magnificent contralto. Early the next spring they brought "Miss P. Horton's Illustrative Gatherings" to St. Martin's Hall in London and began a family entertainment which lasted until 1895.

The first Gatherings heard brief musical sketches in which both the Reeds acted, and for which Mr. Reed again supplied the accompaniment. But with their move to the Gallery of Illustration in Regent Street (1856) and the acquisition of a third performer (John Parry in 1860), they began to elaborate their programs and casts until "Mr. and Mrs. German Reed's Entertainment" became an English equivalent of the *Bouffes Parisiens*, but "quite free from coarseness" as the *Athenaeum* pointed out.[1] Eventually, the Reeds employed and helped to shape the talents of most mid-Victorian comic librettists and composers, conspicuously those of William S. Gilbert and Arthur Sullivan, both in the Gallery's stable of the sixties, but not yet teamed.

Priscilla[2] and Thomas German Reed[3] were singularly suited to be the godparents of the Savoy Operas. Both had been in the theatre since the

---

[1] *Athenaeum*, November 2, 1872, p. 571.

[2] Born January 1, 1818, at Birmingham; died March 18, 1895. David Williamson, *The German Reeds and Corney Grain: Records and Reminiscences* [London: A. D. Innes & Co., 1895], p. 3.) The *Dictionary of National Biography* gives her birthday as January 2. They also differ on the date of her retirement from the Gallery, Williamson giving 1879, the *DNB* 1877. Both in these sources and in others there often are variations in dates, especially for the Reeds' early careers. In each case, I have taken the one which seemed most probable.

[3] Born June 27, 1817, at Bristol; died March 21, 1888. His middle name, which he used more or less as a first name, came from his mother: Frances German. Reed's name offered endless amusement to comic journalists, as in the following paragraph of filler from the second number of *Mirth*: "Somebody speaking of Corney Grain, observed that he could write French fluently. 'Yes,' said another, 'and he can German read.' This person is still at large." There is even a pun on his name in one of German Reed's own pieces.

age of ten and had had a wide variety of practical experience. Reed began as a concert entertainer and soon added juvenile roles at the Haymarket, where his father was musical conductor. He managed a season of opera at Sadler's Wells in 1836 and became musical director of the Haymarket five years later. Like most mid-nineteenth century theatre musicians, Reed could turn his hand to almost anything: every instrument in the orchestra; adaptations of Auber's operas; scoring, arranging, and even — if necessary — composing "original" music for the stage. For the Gallery of Illustration he set such librettists as Burnand and Gilbert; and that his talent was real although minor is suggested by the *Athenaeum*'s review of *Our Island Home*, where Reed's music is described as "not only strictly appropriate to the far-fetched fun of the piece, but . . . written in genuine artistic fashion," displaying "talent which under more favourable circumstances might have done credit to our native school of composers."[4] Reed also seems to have had the analytic ear requisite for a Victorian adapter, as witness his observation to Burnand that Offenbach's "*Voici le sabre*" was basically similar to "The Keel Row." Later, aided by a nose which could be set trembling at will, Reed became a fair, although not versatile comedian.

When this musician married Miss P. Horton in 1844, and indeed during their whole married life, her fame decidedly outshone his. Like him, she had begun her stage career in childhood, playing the Gipsy Girl in *Guy Mannering*. As an adolescent she sang in Vauxhall concerts ("that clever little creature Horton," Dickens' Theatrical Young Gentleman called her). She debuted at Covent Garden as Mealy Moth in the 1830 pantomime *Harlequin Pat and Bat*. From moth Miss Horton rose to become the definitive Ariel of her day. Suspended in mid-air for Macready's elaborate *Tempest* (Covent Garden, 1838), she sang "Where the bee sucks" so beguilingly that Alfred Bunn, Macready's sometime manager and long time denigrator, attributed *The Tempest*'s success to Priscilla's aerial music — a not impartial judgment but perhaps an accurate one, for as late as 1871 the *Graphic* could dismiss an actress in the same role as graceful, but "not the Ariel of Miss P. Horton's younger days. . . ."

Miss Horton played a good deal of Shakespeare: Dorcas in a lavishly cast *Winter's Tale*;[5] Celia to Ellen Tree's Rosalind at the Haymarket

---

[4] *Athenaeum*, July 2, 1870, p. 25. The *Graphic* found Reed's music for Gilbert's *Eyes and No Eyes* "as usual extremely lively" (XII [July 10, 1875], 31). In 1896 this work was re-set by "Florian Pascal" (Joseph Williams).

[5] Macready, Phelps, Helen Faucit, the Keeleys, Mrs. Warner, and Mrs. Nisbett.

where German Reed conducted; Hecate in Macready's farewell *Macbeth*; and even Ophelia with Macready and Phelps. This last performance, pronounced the *Athenaeum* of March 21, 1840, approached "very nearly to the wild pathos of the original in one scene, and is touching and beautiful in all." In the same year she created the role of Georgina Vesey in Bulwer-Lytton's satirical comedy, *Money*. More important, she played the Fool in *Lear* when Macready returned Shakespeare's version of that play to a stage which had long known only Tate's foolish and fool-less mutilation.

Miss Horton might have gone on to Lady Macbeth and Lady Teazle had she not appeared in the title role of Planché's Easter extravaganza, *Fortunio and His Seven Gifted Servants*, at Drury Lane in 1843. This was the first Planché extravaganza in which Madame Vestris, the prime exponent of silken breeches roles, did not appear. Priscilla also substituted for Vestris in the Haymarket's 1843 Christmas piece, and thereafter created the principal roles in Planché's Haymarket extravaganzas. These works were fairy tales told seriously but lightly, as distinct from the broad travesty of their close relatives, the mid-Victorian burlesques. Enlightened with whimsical comedy, some of which anticipated Gilbert's, and staged with fantastic elegance, Planché's plots of fairy princes and fortunate peasants fitted Miss Horton's vivacious personality. Her voice, which had already coped with Handel's Acis, embellished the music drawn, as was conventional, from popular and folk songs and from opera. However, this Fortunio's soubrette charm differed radically from that of her predecessor. Madame Vestris coquetted with her audiences as befitted a discreet sex symbol; Miss Horton's appeal was jauntier, unaffected, and cheerful: "filling the stage with sunshine whenever she appeared." [6] Such attractive respectability was highly useful to her as Mrs. German Reed.

For respectability was the keynote of the German Reed Entertainments. From Malvolio onward, puritans had sniffed at the cakes and ale of the popular theatre; and the mid-Victorian sniff was long and loud, even though G. H. Lewes assured his contemporaries that "it is in human

---

[6] John Coleman, of her Fortunio (*Memoirs of Samuel Phelps* [London: Remington & Co., 1886], p. 19). Miss Horton also played transvestite roles in an occasional burlesque. She was Oedipus in the Broughs' wildly inventive *Sphinx* in 1849. In 1858 she left the professional stage completely. At this time she was "no longer the slender golden-haired Ariel of fifteen years since, but . . . a handsome, genial, lively, natural actress, overflowing with animal spirits and mimicry, and with one of the finest contralto voices ever heard in this country." (Unidentified clipping dated June 26, 1859, in the Enthoven Theatre Collection.)

nature to be amused by dramatic representations. . . ."[7] Their attitude remained, as Gilbert put it, "It's human natur', p'raps — if so, / Oh, isn't human natur' low!"[8]

"Good God . . . you have let that child go to a playhouse" was the shocked reaction of Emily Soldene's favorite uncle when he saw the eight-year-old future Carmen dancing innocently with her shadow.[9] Players were particularly suspect. Even a broadminded clergyman who "saw no error in a play" and would have liked to attend one considered it impossible, "as he had a conscientious conviction against the moral character" of actors. William Robertson, the theatre manager who recorded this anecdote, observed bitterly, "They rather like the honey, but the bees must be smothered,"[10] a statement which indicates both the darling Victorian vice of hypocrisy and the dilemma of persons eager for the pleasure of a playhouse but unwilling to go there.

Still, ways could be found. Lewes attributed the Victorian passion for oratorio largely to the religious world's seizing "any flimsy subterfuge" in order to enjoy itself. Let a dramatist stage a biblical play in costume, wrote Lewes, and the pulpits of England would execrate him. "But Saul in a black coat and white waistcoat, singing with unmistakable operatic graces to a Michal in crinoline and flounces, is considered very edifying, if the musical drama be called an oratorio, and be performed out of a theatre!"[11]

The passion for technically innocent merriment, as well as a thirst for instruction, sent mid-Victorians to conjuring performances, to scientific lectures, dissolving views, dioramas and panoramas, to Albert Smith's illustrated "Ascent of Mont Blanc," and especially to minstrel

---

[7] G. H. Lewes, *Selections from the Modern British Dramatists* (new ed.: Leipzig: F. A. Brockhaus, 1867), I, 3–4.

[8] "Babette's Love," *The Bab Ballads. Much Sound and Little Sense* (London: John Camden Hotten, 1869), p. 69.

[9] Emily Soldene, *My Theatrical and Musical Recollections* (London: Downey & Co. Ltd., 1897), p. 5. Phelps's Shakespearean productions at Sadler's Wells were the only theatrical performances which Emily as a child was permitted to attend.

[10] In an unpublished manuscript, "The Actor's Social Position," quoted by T. Edgar Pemberton in *The Kendals: A Biography* (New York: Dodd, Mead and Co., 1900), pp. 28–29. William Robertson was the father of Tom and Madge Robertson (Mrs. Kendal), leading dramatist and actress respectively. In a short piece entitled "Gaslight Fairies," which he did for *Household Words* in 1855, Dickens perhaps best described the clergyman's attitude with the observation that he himself wished "we were not so often pleased to think ill of those who minister to our amusement."

[11] Lewes, *Selections from the Modern British Dramatists*, I, 11.

shows, notably Christy's and later Moore and Burgess' Minstrels — clean, respectable, family entertainments performed in "halls," not temples of dramatic sin.

To attract this public, as well as the more sophisticated playgoers, the German Reeds used a simple but effective subterfuge, based on the Victorian habit, already noted by Lewes and later heavily satirized by Gilbert, of taking the word for the thing. The Reed performances were announced and conducted in completely non-theatrical terms. To the very last, they were "illustrations," not "plays." Acts were called "parts" and roles "assumptions." When the 1856 "gathering" — not audience — assembled, it saw not a set, but an elegant drawing room. A piano and later an eminently respectable, even chapel-like, harmonium comprised the Reed orchestra; a harp, too, was permissible. The atmosphere, as F. C. Burnand, a Reed librettist, described it, was "that you were attending a meeting . . . and that the attendants were somehow not very distantly related to pew-openers, or might even have been pew-openers themselves only slightly disguised. . . ." [12]

So successful was this appeal that upon German Reed's death in 1888 the *Illustrated London News* could describe him as a public benefactor who provided "a special form of refined amusement" for "good people not accustomed to frequent the ordinary London theatres. . . ." These, German Reed had enabled to "taste the delights of innocent stage comedy, gentle, harmless mimicry, and burlesque operatic singing, without risking their consistency. . . ."

Harmless mimicry was the original basis of the Reed programs, and in this respect the Reeds were like many of the entertainers and entertainments which they eventually transcended. Comic monologues and one- or two-man shows with music were, of course, nothing new in the theatre.

The outlines of Victorian "entertainments" had been sketched in the eighteenth century by Samuel Foote, dramatist and mimic, when he evaded the Licensing Act by announcing an Auction of Pictures which turned out to be his imitations of contemporaries. Or he invited, via advertisements, "friends" to drink chocolate with him and allowed them to watch him "instruct" his theatrical "pupils" while the chocolate was a-making. Charles Dibdin, Senior, at his "Sans Souci," gave solo programs of stories, anecdotes, recitations, and songs for which he wrote both words and music, while he also originated small musical comedies

---

[12] Sir Francis C. Burnand, *Records and Reminiscences Personal and General* (London: Methuen and Co., 1904), II, 333.

such as *The Quaker*, which anticipated the German Reed repertory. In his variety programs and in his son's similar "Sans Six Sous," the emphasis was on versatility rather than mimicry. Both appeals were combined in the rapid conversation and patter programs of the elder Charles Mathews. Through rapid exits, lightning changes, and alterations in voice, he might impersonate as many as twenty-five characters in the same evening.[13] He also carried this pluralism into the formal theatre in such farces as Theodore Hook's *Killing No Murder* (1809), during which he impersonated an impecunious actor impersonating an ostler, valet, hairdresser, and cook.

There were also "actresses of all work," such as Fanny Stirling, who played all three title roles in Wilks's *'Tis She! or The Maid, the Wife, and the Widow* (1838). Such combinations were frequent on the Victorian stage, to say nothing of the economic necessity of doubling in Shakespearean casts. Charles Mathews the Younger undertook both Puff and Sir Fretful Plagiary; Farren was Frederick the Great *and* Voltaire in *The Court of Old Fritz*; Dickens dashed through six rapid-change parts, one of them an old woman, in an amateur performance of *Mr. Nightingale's Diary*; and even Samuel Phelps played Justice Shallow and Henry IV in the same production. In such combinations it goes without saying that a serious actor displayed his histrionic powers of creating varied characters, not his virtuoso skill in changing roles rapidly. The serious actor delineated rather than suggested character; he did not discernibly exploit his own personality as the entertainers Dibdin and Mathews did. When Phelps doubled a role he characterized two distinct persons, neither of whom was Phelps himself. When Mathews whirled through twenty-five parts, he played twenty-six characters, for his own clever personality joined and controlled the rest.

The German Reeds retained elements of all these varieties of recitation and characterization in their programs. From first to last they featured a musical-mimetic monologuist, at the beginning, Mrs. Reed herself, who imitated a singing dandy complete with mustache, and on the same bill took both parts of a dialogue between two old women. Her costume differed on each side so that she could change character simply by turning from left to right. Then came John Parry,[14] who

---

[13] For examples, see Appendix B.

[14] John Orlando Parry (1810–1879), baritone, was the son of a Welsh bard who could play three flageolets at the same time. The younger Parry made his debut as an infant prodigy on the harp. His adult career began in 1830; he studied under Lablache, sang comically a famous duet with Malibran: "When a little farm we keep," and played in Dickens' operetta, *The Village Coquettes*.

arrived at the Gallery of Illustration from giving impersonations of an evening party: host, hostess, waiters, male and female guests, and even the supper! Upon Parry's retirement, Corney Grain [15] in 1870 took over the *de rigueur* mimicry of singers, professional and amateur, and of instruments and popping corks as well. Both Parry and Grain worked out gently satiric sketches such as "The County Commissioners" and "Wanted a Governess" (Parry) and "The Fancy Fair; or, Woman's Rights and Man's Wrongs" (Grain).

The Reed company also doubled and re-doubled roles in their one-act farces and operettas, partly because the company was very small, but more often to capitalize on its talent for quick changes. Their authors wrote with this in mind, especially when the cast consisted of only the Reeds and Parry. As Burnand described the pattern, the writers had "to allow the impersonator time to change from one character to another, or to resume an assumption while the two others were diverting the audience and carrying on the plot. If two were changing 'off,' one was 'on' with a song, and with plenty of 'stage business.'"[16]

Thus Mrs. Reed might impersonate a sentimental maiden aunt and "an American fast Lady of the Period," or a German countess and a French landlady; another player could be both an elderly aristocrat and a young artist; while Corney Grain once undertook the quadruple delineation of Good Humour, Care, the Old Year, and Old England in Planché's last stage work, *King Christmas*, at the Gallery in 1871. In most of these "assumptions," versatility of illusion was the great desideratum, and the *Athenaeum* praised Mrs. Reed's ability to take on

---

In 1849 he began his own "entertainment," which he left for the Gallery of Illustration when sustaining a whole evening became too exhausting, physically and nervously, for him. At the Gallery, he did a solo turn and acted in the "illustrations." With no props except a piano, Parry could "bring to the imagination of his listeners, as it were concrete representations of places and people with the accompaniments of time, weather, atmosphere, and detail of circumstance . . . vividly rendered." (*Gossip of the Century* [London: Ward and Downey, 1892], II, 283.) Albert Smith wrote some of Parry's comic ballads. George Grossmith much later said he had taken Parry as his model.

[15] His full name was Richard Corney Grain — Corney being the last name of an aunt. Obviously no right-minded comedian would content himself with "Dick," given an opportunity like this.

Like Falstaff, Corney exploited his size. "Corney's manner was solemnity itself, and his remarks about the inconvenience of his own fatness were made with such serious concern that some ladies near me seemed quite annoyed by my laughing over it." (M. Vivian Hughes, *A London Family, 1870–1900* [London: Oxford University Press, 1946], pp. 160–61.)

[16] Burnand, *Records and Reminiscences*, II, 335.

(or off!) a variety of characters, giving to each a marked physiognomy.[17] But the Reeds also utilized their own identities as if they were simultaneously real and role. For instance, in Robertson's *A Dream in Venice* (1867), German Reed falls asleep after taking hashish for his neuralgia and dreams that he has escaped from a Venetian dungeon, only to discover that his wife has survived him by two centuries and is now Mrs. John Parry.[18] Gilbert's *Our Island Home* (1870) put the entire company on stage as themselves, but then carried them through a wildly fictional plot which involved a rearrangement of their past real lives as well. Yet in these instances the Reeds were not simply capitalizing on their own personalities and idiosyncratic talents as Mathews might have done. Their multiple identities were subordinated to a controlling plot whose comedy combined technical virtuosity with a double view of reality.

This sophistication was generally absent from other monologuists and entertainments of the period. The famous but forgotten Woodin, for instance, was chiefly content with a traditional miscellany, as his titles "Olio of Oddities" and "Carpet Bag" indicate — even though some Reed authors, Gilbert allegedly among them, wrote for him. Perhaps the closest approach to the Reed format was Mr. and Mrs. Howard Paul's Drawing Room Entertainment. Mrs. Paul's versatility matched Mrs. Reed's. Her first London success was Captain Macheath (a breeches role in the nineteenth century), and her last was Lady Sangazure in *The Sorcerer*. She had played Lady Macbeth to Phelps's Thane and was an excellent Grand Duchess of Gerolstein.

Mrs. Paul and her American manager-writer-husband presented programs, the best known entitled "Patchwork," in which Mrs. Paul gave — of course — musical imitations and Mr. Paul comic monologues.[19] Their

---

[17] In its review of *King Christmas*, December 30, 1871, p. 893. In this "Fancy-Full Morality" play Mrs. Reed was Dame Fortune and the Genius of the Drawing Room, the latter certainly type-casting and a pretty compliment.

[18] They also played fictitious personages in the same plot: Parry impersonated an Italian waiter, a German waiter, a French waiter, all recognized as the same man by German Reed, but not as being impersonated by Parry. Mrs. Reed, among other characters, played Dr. Lavinia Sage, in which role she imitated a variety of bedside manners and sang a song in Latinate doubletalk. In the mock opera which formed part of German Reed's dream, Mrs. Reed personified the Adriatic. Robertson's Entertainment was never published; the license copy is part of the Lord Chamberlain's collection now in the British Museum.

[19] Howard Paul enjoyed considerable fame as an American wit, although collections of his jokes show little originality. No doubt his manner improved his matter.

enlarged company at times toured the "parsonic and puritanic" provinces,[20] as the Reeds did, although they lacked a home base like the Gallery. The Paul troupe was a good one, with Rutland Barrington as a regular and George Grossmith as an occasional member,[21] both later rising to comic leads with Gilbert and Sullivan. Yet at Mrs. Paul's death in 1879, just two years after Mrs. Reed's retirement, the *Athenaeum*, which had praised Priscilla Reed's "matured powers," sadly dismissed Isabella Paul with "she sacrificed for second-rate objects an amount of natural vocal endowment rarely combined . . . with such genius for the stage. . . ."[22]

One may reasonably ask why the German Reeds had a splendid success and the Howard Pauls a commonplace one. An important factor was undoubtedly the wider variety of entertainment already discussed, to say nothing of the Reeds' exceptional sensitivity to the public's readiness for change and their well-timed enlargements of company and scope. Furthermore, the Reeds' natural domestic appeal was more consistently and skilfully brought forward, and was enhanced in 1871 by the addition of their son Alfred, who became a deft comedian. But there were other significant causes, some of them repeatedly stressed in contemporary reviews, which gave the Gallery of Illustration its mid-century accolade: "incomparably the best entertainment house in London. . . ."[23]

First among them was the small theatre itself, described by reviewers as "snug" and "bijou."[24] Its stage was clearly visible from every seat in

---

[20] Burnand, *Records and Reminiscences*, II, 336.

[21] Grossmith said that he played at the Gallery of Illustration in 1868 and 1870 (*A Society Clown: Reminiscences* [Bristol: J. W. Arrowsmith, 1888], p. 91), but this was not with the Reeds. On evenings or for matinees when the Reeds were not acting, the Gallery was used by other performers. For instance, an amateur company put on a very creditable *As You Like It* there, and Mark Lemon did his condensed version of Falstaff in 1868. In 1857 Dickens' amateur troupe performed *The Frozen Deep* at the Gallery before Queen Victoria.

[22] See Appendix B for examples of the Howard Paul Entertainments.

[23] *Illustrated Times*, XV (November 27, 1869), 343. This superlative may be Gilbert's; he was a *Times* reviewer, but not given to puffing performances he found wanting.

[24] It was also a firetrap, like most London theatres, according to Hollingshead's Letter to the Editor of the *Daily Telegraph* (March 10, 1875). In 1874 the lease of 14 Regent Street expired, and the Reeds moved the Galley to St. George's Hall, where it remained until 1895. *Fun*'s reviewer objected to the hardness of the seats there, and an anonymous Gallery-goer who wrote to complain about a nail received Mrs. Reed's personal promise that "all future occupants of the seat will be emanci-

the house. There were no fees for checking wraps or for playbills,[25] and tickets cost one to five shillings, less than those at an avowed theatre. Even so, the Reeds employed the best scenic artists of the day — Telbin, Beverley, O'Connor — to create the sets (usually only one per "illustration"). Reed authors were well paid for quality. In a decade when an entire burlesque brought its author not more than one hundred pounds, while the adaptor of a French farce was lucky to get twenty,[26] Gilbert received a hundred and fifty pounds for each of his Gallery of Illustration pieces.[27]

The small scale of the Entertainment also allowed an author to retain greater control over the staging of his work than at the larger theatres where Gilbert had found, in his first and only pantomime, that a dramatist "must set aside anything in the shape of parental pride in his work, and . . . be prepared to see it cut up and hacked about by the stage-manager without caring to expostulate."[28] Badly staged and worse paid, many Victorian writers were forced into unprotesting mediocrity. This is especially clear in the doggerel speeches which tradition cast in decasyllabic couplets replete with puns. The Reeds' use of prose dialogue was in itself a reform, for the rhymed lyrics were more enhanced by contrast and the puns were more effective in prose, as Gilbert pointed out, because the line itself had not been distorted to force a rhyme.[29] In plots, the Reed writer might be somewhat cramped by the necessity of providing and covering quick changes of role, but he possessed another,

---

pated from the obtrusive iron." (Maurice Willson Disher, *Victorian Song from Dive to Drawing Room* [London: Phoenix House Ltd, 1955] p. 170.)

[25] Abolition of fees was a recurrent Victorian battle. Initiation of this reform has been variously attributed to Benjamin Webster at the Adelphi, Madame Vestris at the Lyceum, John Hollingshead at the Gaiety, Albert Smith at the Egyptian Hall, and Richard D'Oyly Carte at the Savoy. Twentieth-century audiences, however, still pay sixpence or a shilling for programs.

[26] Even so, conditions were infinitely better than those a quarter-century before, when a cartoon entitled "Encouragement to Dramatic Literature" could show a manager saying to a timid playwright: "Ha! Yes; I like your piece: good points — strong situations — nervous dialogue. So — well — what will you give me to play it?" (*Man in the Moon*, IV [1848], 150.)

[27] Gilbert stated this sum in a letter to Harold Power, August 8, 1877, a copy of which is now in the Gilbert Papers, British Museum. Gilbert's copies of letters to Mrs. German Reed in the same collection bear out his statement.

[28] W. S. Gilbert, "Thumbnail Studies. Getting Up a Pantomime," *London Society*, XIII (January, 1868), 56.

[29] *Illustrated Times*, XIV (May 1, 1869), 282–83. The review is unsigned, but its style and point of view indicate that it is by Gilbert.

almost unique, freedom in addition to those already described — his words could precede the music.

This was not the case in any other light musical genre. Even Planché, the doyen of extravaganza, who had written an opera libretto for Weber and almost written one for Mendelssohn, had to fit his lighter lyrics to already extant tunes. Prolific burlesque writers such as H. J. Byron and F. C. Burnand too often fell back on nonsense words, Byron ringing an amazing number of jangled changes on the nonsense song "Hoop de dooden do." Drowning out the older folk ballad and operatic borrowings, such music-hall melodies had so dominated the sixties that Gilbert's burlesque of *The Princess* (1870) was heavily praised for drawing its music from Offenbach and Hervé.[30]

There was no Offenbach, it is true, among the English *bouffes*, but there was Sullivan; and there were at various times George Macfarren, James L. Molloy, Alfred Cellier, and Frederic Clay. Often, of course, the "composer" might be merely an arranger, usually German Reed himself, who could equally adapt drawing-room songs or compose concerted music. The Reed composers, unfortunately, were less free than the writers; an orchestra limited to piano and harmonium scarcely gave Sullivan's "eccentric scoring" the scope which his orchestral wit demanded.[31] On the other hand, the forced concentration on melody must have contributed to the tightness of the best productions. The absence of ballet, chorus, and supers eliminated the threat of musical filler and spectacle for its own sake, throwing the emphasis back on literary rather than feminine form. Gilbert among the Reeds never had to find dramatic justification for introducing a Fish Ballet, as the Lyceum had required of him. Respectability gained, too, for ladies of singing and dancing choruses often supplemented their meagre professional wages with those of sin. By limiting themselves to a cast of principals, the Reeds could afford both virtue and something like adequate rehearsals[32] (no Victorian theatre before the Savoy seems to have really had enough).

All these circumstances combined to emphasize coherence of form and neatness of pattern, thereby achieving a kind of comedy which, at its best, depended on more subtle juxtapositions than the *sans culotte*

---

[30] Gilbert had already put verses to music by these composers for his burlesque, *Robert the Devil* (1869).

[31] The *Athenaeum* (April 3, 1869, p. 479) lamented the loss of Sullivan's orchestration when *Cox and Box* was produced at the Gallery.

[32] But not always. The *Athenaeum's* review of Offenbach's *Croquefer* (January 2, 1869, p. 27) as produced at the Gallery of Illustration, says that on opening night the singers "had the manner of second-rate amateurs."

burlesques, on more manipulation of clearly defined characters than the fairy tale extravaganzas, and on more carefully thought out word and idea play than either. Doubly debarred from explicit sex comedy, first by their era and second by their own aura of middle-class morality, the German Reeds substituted the wit of logical absurdities, of paradox and verbal conceit. So did other musical theatres, but the Gallery of Illustration's word sallies were wittier. In short, the Reed Entertainments fostered a kind of comedy which Gilbert was already beginning to develop toward the satirical farce of *Engaged* and the great series of Savoy libretti.

In appealing to that part of the audience not satisfied simply by re-labeling, the Reeds were fortunate that their most stimulating period coincided with a reaction against the by-now stereotyped burlesques which had dominated the sixties. The Theatrical Lounger of the *Illustrated Times* (almost certainly Gilbert) made a widely-shared objection to "the eternal repetition of the same class of strained jocularity, the same class of repulsive comic song, the same old wearisome breakdown. . . ."[33] The *Mask* longed for "Light amusing pieces, too, which come like trifles at the end of dinner, and therefore should be full of spirit and whipped cream, but not dependent on flesh and legs to make it palatable."[34]

Burlesque had become a construction of clichés, almost, indeed, a ritual, in which even H. J. Byron's coruscation of puns palled through familiarity. The perpetual victims — *The Lady of Lyons*, dishonest tradesmen, *Faust, Der Freischütz*, stockjobbers — were parodied in the same old ways, and comedy was declining into ludicrous stage business which passed for wit. Nor had the jaded public clearly recognized what it wanted instead. Dion Boucicault, melodramatist and author of non-musical comedy, wrote bitterly to an actor-manager, "The public pretend they want pure comedy — This is not so — What they want is domestic *drama* treated with broad comic characters. . . . Comedy, — pure and simple — is rejected of 1868."[35] More than twenty years before, Planché, whose wit *did* attract "cultivated persons," attempted to open "a new stage door," as he put it, "by which the poet and the satirist could enter the theatre without the shackles imposed upon them by the

---

[33] *Illustrated Times*, XIV (May 1, 1869), 282.

[34] "A Dream of the Season," *Mask*, I (August, 1868), 215.

[35] MS letter to Squire Bancroft, February 19, 1868, in Theatre Collection, The New York Public Library, Astor, Lenox and Tilden Foundations.

laws of the regular drama. . . ."[36] This was in his 1846 adaptation of *The Birds*, which he hoped would "lay the foundation for an Aristophanic drama, which the greatest minds would not consider it derogatory to contribute to."[37] *The Birds* was a *succès d'estime*, not *d'argent*. But Planché's door was finally set ajar at the Gallery of Illustration, and the audience which the Reeds helped to train followed Gilbert and Sullivan to the Opera Comique and the Savoy.[38]

Almost every important comic dramatist of the day at some time or other worked for the German Reeds: among them William Brough, the most imaginative of burlesque writers; Gilbert à Beckett, who collaborated with W. S. Gilbert on *The Happy Land*;[39] Shirley Brooks, F. C. Burnand, and Tom Taylor, editors of *Punch*[40] (the last also author of *Our American Cousin*); and Tom Robertson, who originated the cup-and-saucer school of Victorian domestic comedy.

Brough supplied "Miss P. Horton's Illustrative Gatherings" with amusing character songs and wrote entertainments for the expanded Gallery. His neat lyrics were at first based on a comic situation more often than on personality, which Mrs. Reed was expected to supply. As a servant girl, she sang:

> The first time he came in to tea, the snow was on the
> ground;
> Next morning master's overcoat was nowhere to be
> found,
> And yet I see'd it on the peg when I sat down to
> tea
> With that young man from the country as kept
> company with me.[41]

---

[36] J. R. Planché, *Recollections and Reflections . . . A Professional Autobiography* (new and rev. ed.; London: Sampson Low, Marston & Company, Limited, 1901), p. 294.

[37] *Ibid.*, p. 294. In this autobiography, Planché said that Gilbert's *Palace of Truth* and *Pygmalion and Galatea* showed that there was at last an audience for this sort of comedy.

[38] *Punch* pointed out that "many persons who have hitherto restricted themselves" to the Reeds were now patronizing the productions of Gilbert and Sullivan (LXXVIII [January 10, 1880], 4).

[39] This was a burlesque of Gilbert's own *The Wicked World*. Produced at the Court Theatre in 1873, it ran into censorship troubles because of its political satire.

[40] Brooks was editor from 1870 to 1874; Taylor from 1874 to 1880; Burnand from 1880 to 1906.

[41] Sheet music, "The Young Man from the Country" by William Brough and

Or, in the role of Pamela Dibbs, she insisted, "Tisn't me breaks the things; it's a fact I never does nothing at all. . . ." Impishly she explained how, with two masters, she avoided work:

> I tell them whichever may call
> I'm with t'other engag'd; so you see
> I never does nothing at all.[42]

Comic servants like these disappear from most German Reed programs of the late sixties and early seventies, probably because the situations they describe could not sustain a full plot, nor was there room in a tightly constructed farce for a minor character merely to fulfil the traditional maid's role of comedy-cum-exposition. The dramatis personae of Reed entertainments were, like their audiences, drawn mostly from the middle class. The autobiographical song describing occupation or revealing character therefore became more important as the Reeds moved from impersonation to plays. Brough's Toy-Woman's Song in *A Peculiar Family* (1865) exemplifies the transition. It is still self-contained and excerptable, but it is also a part of the plot when sung by Mrs. Reed as a countess-spy disguised as a peddler. The words suggest Gilbert's more intricate catalogue for Little Buttercup:

> Come and buy, one and all,
>   I have prime wooden toys;
> I've a trap, bat, and ball,
>   For the good little boys.
> I've a box that plays tunes;
>   I've of lovers a pair,
> That is two wooden spoons,
>   True to life I declare.
> Come and buy, they are good,
>   And of very soft wood,
> Come and buy, come and buy.[43]

T. German Reed (1857), in the Enthoven Theatre Collection of the Victoria and Albert Museum. I have supplied punctuation.

[42] Sheet music, "I Never Does Nothing at All" by William Brough and T. German Reed (1861), in the Enthoven Theatre Collection. The song was part of Brough's *An Illustration on Discords, by Two Rival Composers, . . .* played by Parry and the Reeds. The complete text is in the Lord Chamberlain's Collection.

[43] Book of words of *A Peculiar Family* by William Brough and German Reed, printed by J. Mallett (1865), in the Enthoven Theatre Collection. The license copy gives only this verse, but Mallett prints a second, somewhat satirical one.

Street-sellers' songs were parodied in comic periodicals of the period. In an

The plot of *A Peculiar Family*, like many nineteenth-century farcical plots, both French and English, depends on the contretemps of mistaken identity, a kind of comedy more effective if acted than if narrated in a funny solo. Here, because of an accidental exchange of hats, a conventional British family finds itself mixed up in a political intrigue. The synopsis of one of Burnand's pieces — "Further complications — everybody being perfectly clear as to his own, or her own, line of conduct persistently misunderstands everybody else" [44] might almost be the motto of German Reed authors. Certainly Gilbert's plots, cleverer and crisper than Burnand's, still used problems of identity, misapprehension, and cross-purposes double-crossed.

Gallery of Illustration comedies often had a touch of the fanciful, as in the mock-Oriental *Tale of Old China* (Burnand and Molloy, 1875). Sometimes their fantasy used a convenient dream framework as did Robertson's *A Dream in Venice*, with its time-juggling, or *Our Family Legend*, a dream-play by Tom Taylor. In this precursor of Gilbert's *Ages Ago*, a young man falls asleep in a house in North Wales and dreams that his ancestor's portrait comes to life. Taylor's finale conventionally and awkwardly begs his audience:

> To each beauty take the trouble
> Eyes to use, and see it double —
> Prize our wheat, reject our stubble —[45]

German Reed wheat might contain some mild satire of the "what fools these mortals be" sort, which Gilbert made trenchant; comments on

---

1863 issue of *Fun*, for example, a proto-Buttercup sang to the tune of "I Dreamt I Dwelt in Marble Halls":

> For years have I dealt in brandy-balls,
> In toffy and sweetstuff beside;
> And I will not dissemble, the goods I calls
> I looks on with pleasure and pride.
> For my brandy-balls are well-known, and boast
> A highly popular name;
> And the public, I find, which pleases me most,
> Oh! they loves 'em still the same.

The second verse refers to peppermints, ginger-drops, rose-lozenges, and hard-bake.

[44] *Mildred's Well*, printed by J. Mallett (n.d.), p. 6, Enthoven Theatre Collection. This does not include dialogue.

[45] Quoted in an unidentified newspaper clipping in the Enthoven Theatre Collection. The full form of this finale appears in the license copy of *Our Family Legend* in the Lord Chamberlain's Collection.

contemporary social abuses; and the ubiquitous parody in which the Victorian stage derided what at alternate moments it took seriously. Having commented on the "spooniness" of lovers, Brough's Toy-Woman slyly announces, "I've the Parliament House,/With a lot of queer sticks." *Near Relations* (1871) by Arthur Sketchley shows designing relatives victimizing an old aristocrat; and Planché's *King Christmas: A Fancy-Full Morality* is unusually didactic for an Entertainment. This fantastic piece, "written in passable English, having a rational object," as the author himself put it,[46] concludes with personified Christmas and Fortune crowning Young England King of the Bean for the glory of Old England. Mrs. Reed, appropriately cast as the Genius of the Drawing Room, urged the New Year:

> Give art new life! free it from job and fetter,
> And take my word for it, 'twill soon be better!
> It is not genius that Old England lacks,
> But courage to contend with cant and quacks;
> There's room in all things for much reformation.
> Bid trade revive — check frantic speculation;
> Obtain from Chance a power of attorney,
> To give us safety on a railway journey;
> The prices down of beef and mutton beat for us;
> And don't drive us to eat what isn't *meet* for us;
> . . . .[47]

The lyrics of *King Christmas* were, atypically for the Reeds, set entirely to pre-existing melodies, the enforced habit of Planché's long theatrical lifetime. The tunes ranged from *"Gavotte de Vestris"* and "Cheer, Boys, Cheer" to *"Si vuol ballare"* and *"Va pensiero."* Generally, however, if the Reeds went outside their own collection of composers they turned to early Offenbach, whose ingenuity of rhythm rather than of orchestration transferred satisfactorily to piano. The Gallery produced both *Croquefer, ou le Dernier des Paladins* and *Ba-ta-Clan*, which became *Ching-Chow-Hi* in William Brough's hands. His adaptation of this *chinoiserie musicale* translated the French nonsense verses of the original Halévy libretto into English double talk:

> Booriboo goo! whang ko-too!
> Goori Bang choo! gong tong kitch-kee-koo!

---

[46] Planché, *Recollections and Reflections*, p. 458.

[47] *King Christmas: A Fancy-Full Morality* in *Extravaganzas* (Testimonial Edition; London: Samuel French, 1879), V, 297.

> Hangee-Bam boo! Hi cum loo!
> Slashee clashey skew cum Bang She-loo!

and

> Morto! morto! die! kill-ee oh!
> Strangolly oh! spifflicate oh!
> Smash-ato! off chop pate-oh!
> Te-to-Tum oh! morto![48]

The heroine's Pet-Ping-Sing suggests Gilbert's later "Japanese" baby talk. German Reed's *Too Many Cooks* used music by Offenbach, as did a duologue, *The Happy Result*, in which Reed played Fritschen and Rosa D'Erina, Lischen. *Les Deux Aveugles* turned into Burnand's *Beggar My Neighbor: A Blindman's Bouffe.*

Reed also experimented from time to time with works on a larger scale than the Gallery's pocket musicals. His first attempt was in 1863 with what he called an *"opera di camera,"* an opera so simply constructed and staged that it could be put on in a drawing room, with — as usual — an orchestra limited to pianoforte. John Oxenford carpentered a four-character, two-act libretto out of *L'Elisir d'Amore*, and G. A. Macfarren composed new music. Scribe's plot was decidedly altered: his heroine was anglicized to "Jessy Lea" and Dr. Dulcamara feminized to a young gipsy girl. The Reeds themselves did not play in this opera, nor did the novices they engaged for it become regular members of their company.

Four years later Reed leased St. George's Hall, engaged a large chorus and an orchestra "carefully selected from the Royal Italian Opera and Her Majesty's Theatre," and undertook a season of English Opera: Sullivan and Burnand's *The Contrabandista, The Beggar's Opera, Ching-Chow-Hi,* and Reece and Reed's adaptation of Scribe's *L'Ambassdrice,* music by Auber. In the sixties, English opera, like English drama, was more than a little French. The season was not a financial success, but Burnand and Sullivan who created *The Contrabandista* supplied the Gallery of Illustration with its second greatest hit and the only German Reed piece still in a living repertory.[49]

This was *Cox and Box,* first produced by the German Reeds in 1869.

---

[48] Book of the words, printed by J. Mallett (n.d.), pp. 17; 14. "Booriboo goo" has affinities with Dickens' Borrioboola-Gha and Gilbert's Borria Bungalee Boo. The second line's "goori" is rather strong for a Reed audience. Even Gilbert at the Savoy was unable years later to name an opera "Ruddy-gore."

[49] The D'Oyly Carte Opera Company still performs *Cox and Box* as a curtain raiser.

Burnand and Sullivan had originally written *Cox and Box* for amateur performance, and it was privately staged on April 26, 1867, at an evening party. George du Maurier played Box. In May, there were charity performances in Manchester and London, where German Reed immediately recognized its suitability, acquired it, and gave it three hundred performances.

Burnand took the plot of his "triumveretta," its basic comedy, and most of its dialogue (to say nothing of an inverted title) from an 1847 farce, *Box and Cox*, by John Maddison Morton.[50] Morton's "Romance of Real Life," as its subtitle described it, is an almost perfect example of that form of Victorian farce which consists of placing a pair of characters with antithetical interests, habits, or occupations, in an eccentric situation which demands ingenuity, often of a wildly inventive kind, and which is frequently resolved arbitrarily — the forced ending being part of the fun.

In Morton's play, James Cox, a journeyman hatter who works by day, and John Box, a journeyman printer who works by night, occupy the same room, rented twice over by Mrs. Bouncer, the lodging-house keeper. Since each supposes the room is exclusively his, Mrs. Bouncer has a good deal of farfetched explanation for placating each when he is suspicious.[51] Cox is given an unexpected holiday; he meets Box in "his" room; they quarrel, and discover that both have been engaged to the same bathing-machine proprietress, Penelope Ann Wiggins. Cox still is, but Box has escaped by "drowning" himself: that is, he has left a farewell note and his clothes at the edge of a cliff. Cox insists that Box return to life and marry Penelope Ann. They gamble with loaded dice and double-headed coins to see who will have to have her. Mrs. Bouncer brings in a letter in which Cox is apprised that Penelope Ann herself has drowned, leaving her entire estate to "my intended husband." Each of the men immediately reverses himself and insists that the inheritance is his. After another argument they decide to divide it equally, just as a further letter announces that Penelope Ann was saved and is on her way to London. Box and Cox again try to give her up to each other. She arrives but does not enter; instead Mrs. Bouncer brings

---

[50] Morton, in turn, had adapted his play from two French farces: *Une Chambre aux Deux Lits* and *Frisette*.

[51] Perhaps Mrs. Bouncer's playing off one lodger against the other suggested Brough's Pamela Dibbs. Every comic writer in the second half of the century seems to have had *Box and Cox* by heart.

Miss Priscilla Horton as she appeared in the 1830's.
From David Williamson, *The German Reeds and
Corney Grain* (London, 1895).

THE YOUNG MAN FROM THE COUNTRY.

SUNG BY
MRS GERMAN REED,
IN THE CHARACTER OF
SALLY SKEGGS.

Mrs. Reed "in character" as a stupid servant during the early days of the Entertainment (1857).

I NEVER DOES NOTHING AT ALL.

SUNG BY
MRS GERMAN REED,
IN THE CHARACTER OF
PAMELA DIBBS.

A roguish Priscilla Reed plays a clever servant in *An Illustration in Discords*, music by her husband, words by William Brough (1861). Both photographs by courtesy of the Victoria & Albert Museum, Enthoven Collection.

German Reed in a stance appropriate to a public benefactor who provided "a special form of refined amusement," as the *Illustrated London News* called him (April 7, 1888). Photograph by courtesy of the Victoria & Albert Museum, Enthoven Collection.

German Reed in costume: "that wrinkle of the nose, that trick of the eye, and — oh! — that paralytic attitude" (*Fun*, August 26, 1871). From David Williamson, *The German Reeds and Corney Grain* (London, 1895).

Decorous transvestism at the Gallery of Illustration: German Reed, Mrs. Reed, and John Parry. Photograph by courtesy of the Victoria & Albert Museum, Enthoven Collection.

John Parry in retirement (1877). From David Williamson, *The German Reeds and Corney Grain* (London, 1895).

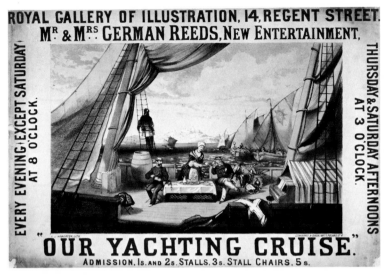

This 1866 Entertainment was written for the Reeds and Parry by F. C. Burnand; in those days "Whatever piece was written for them, allowance had to be made for the piano on the stage." (Burnand, *Records and Reminiscences*, II, 334.)

Mrs. Reed, a disguised countess, mistakes Mr. Reed, a traveling Englishman, for a fellow spy. John Parry lurks under a tree, and the piano lurks under an arbor in *A Peculiar Family* by Brough and Reed (1865). Both photographs by courtesy of the Victoria & Albert Museum, Enthoven Collection.

Arthur Cecil "in character" as Herbert, a Sunday school teacher driven to fury at the prospect of marrying a virtuous governess. Courtesy of The Reginald Allen Collection, The Pierpont Morgan Library.

Arthur Cecil (Blunt) as his gentlemanly self. David Williamson, *The German Reeds and Corney Grain* (London, 1895).

An ancestral portrait comes to life in the dream scene of Tom Taylor's *Our Family Legend*, produced at the Gallery of Illustration in 1862. Seven years later, Gilbert animated five ancestral portraits in *Ages Ago*. Within two decades he had animated a whole portrait gallery in *Ruddigore*. Photograph by courtesy of the Victoria & Albert Museum, Enthoven Collection.

Mrs. Howard Paul in a rival Entertainment, which *The Times* (April 2, 1858) found "full of interest and dashing gaiety." Nearly twenty years later she created the first Gilbert and Sullivan contralto role, Lady Sangazure in *The Sorcerer* (1877).

W. S. Gilbert in an early *carte de visite* photograph. Courtesy of Mr.
Barry Duncan.

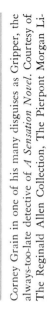

Corney Grain in one of his many disguises as Gripper, the always-too-late detective of *A Sensation Novel*. Courtesy of The Reginald Allen Collection, The Pierpont Morgan Library.

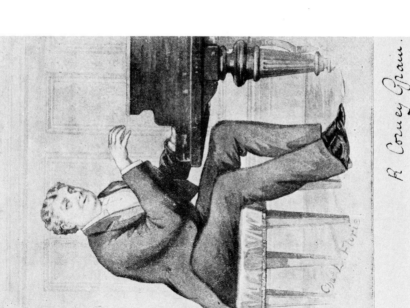

Corney Grain characteristically delivering a comic monologue, sketched in action at St. George's Hall. The *Athenaeum* (December 30, 1871) called Corney "the greatest drawing-room actor and buffo singer of the day." From

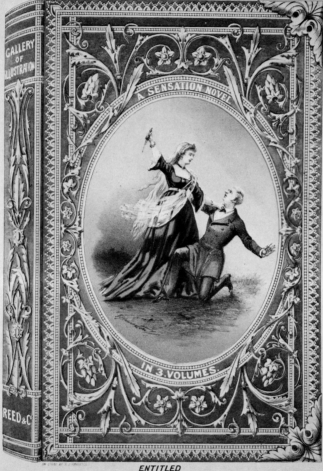

ROYAL GALLERY OF ILLUSTRATION, 14, REGENT Sᵀ.
Mᴿ & Mᴿˢ GERMAN REED'S
NEW ENTERTAINMENT,

EVERY EVENING EXCEPT SATURDAY AT 8.

THURSDAY & SATURDAY AFTERNOON AT 3.

ENTITLED
A SENSATION NOVEL,
BY
W. S. GILBERT.
ADMISSION 1/- & 2/- STALLS, 3/- STALL SPRING CHAIRS, 5/-

Mrs. Reed (Rockalda) prepares to stab Arthur Cecil (Herbert). "Unfortunately I am a Sunday school teacher or I would resist." Photograph by courtesy of the Victoria & Albert Museum, Enthoven Collection.

Fanny Holland and Mrs. Reed in a melodramatic moment from *A Sensation Novel*. Courtesy of The Reginald Allen Collection, The Pierpont Morgan Library.

Gilbert's sketch of Alfred Reed as Uncle Cassandre in *Eyes and No Eyes.* The drawing was made on a blank leaf of manuscript during rehearsal. Courtesy of The Reginald Allen Collection, The Pierport Morgan Library.

Alfred German Reed, the Colin of *Happy Arcadia.* This photograph was taken after the retirement of his parents when Alfred Reed and Corney Grain were managing the Gallery of Illustration. From David Williamson, *The German Reeds and Corney Grain* (London, 1895).

Rutland Barrington as Strephon in an 1895 revival of *Happy Arcadia*. After creating leading roles in the Savoy Operas, Barrington tried to revive the German Reed Entertainment, but "the glamour of it . . . departed with Reed and Grain, never to return" (*Rutland Barrington by Himself*, p. 104). From *Rutland Barrington by Himself* (London, 1908).

Frederic Clay, who collaborated with Gilbert on *Ages Ago, Happy Arcadia*, and other pieces. Clay introduced Gilbert to Sullivan at the Gallery of Illustration. From the *Illustrated London News*. Photograph by courtesy of The Newberry Library.

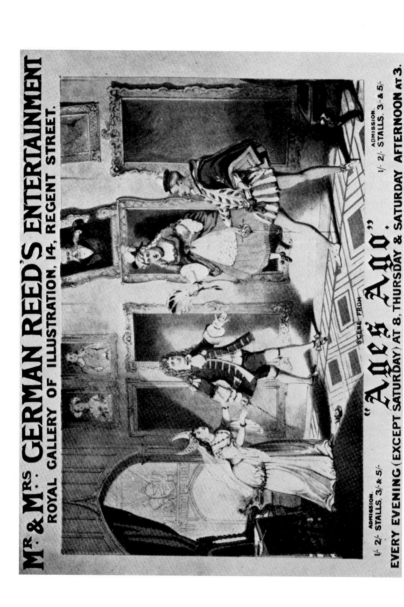

The poster for the Gallery of Illustration's greatest hit, Gilbert and Clay's *Ages Ago*, "one of those rare works that contain an idea" (*Illustrated London News* [January 15, 1870]). Here Fanny Holland (Lady Maud) tries to prevent violence between German Reed (Lord Carnaby) and Arthur Cecil (Sir Cecil Blount) while Mrs. Reed (Dame Cherry) steps from her frame. Photograph by courtesy of the Victoria & Albert Museum, Enthoven Collection.

in still another message by which Cox is informed that Penelope Ann is going to marry — Mr. Knox! Box and Cox, dancing with joy, decide to inhabit their room jointly. As they are about to embrace, Box exclaims, "You'll excuse the apparent insanity of the remark, but the more I gaze on your features, the more I'm convinced that you're my long-lost brother."

Cox. The very observation I was going to make to you!

Box. Ah — tell me — in mercy tell me — have you such a thing as a strawberry mark on your left arm?

Cox. No!

Box. Then it is he! (*They rush into each other's arms.*)[52]

This non-sequitur was famous in the Victorian theatre. Comic writers did their best to emulate or surpass it. In numerical extension and complication of absurd logic, Gilbert succeeded; but even his version lacks the neatness of the original. In his *La Vivandière* (1868), the supposed Lord Margate is asked:

> Say, are you covered, pardon the allusion,
> With strawberry marks in prodigal profusion?
> Two on each shoulder, on your bosom four;
> Twelve on your back, on each arm seven more;
> Three on your left foot, nine upon each knee;
> Five on your calves, upon each elbow three,
> Just sixty six in all.

"Exactly so," replies the Earl counting rapidly. "Then you are *not* the Earl of Margate!" for he had no strawberry marks. A nearby peasant says suddenly, "*I* have no strawberry marks," and is hailed as the rightful Lord Margate.

Burnand in turning Morton's farce into a libretto transposed Mrs. Bouncer into Sgt. Bouncer, an old soldier now landlord, who silences his lodgers' objections by singing, "Rataplan, rataplan, I'm a military man. . . ." Motivation for this change was completely non-literary. The "Moray Minstrels," as he and his friends called themselves, were exclusively masculine; Burnand had an amateur basso and wanted a martial tune. But in altering the character he unwittingly deprived Mrs. Reed of what would have been her role.

In order to make room for musical numbers, Burnand omitted some of Morton's verbal parallelism and mirror image dialogue, although he

---

[52] John Maddison Morton, *Box and Cox; A Romance of Real Life* (London: Samuel French, n.d.), p. 32.

did retain and versify longer passages such as that in which Cox anticipates his holiday. Morton's character explains:

Well, wonders will never cease! Conscious of being eleven minutes and a half behind time, I was sneaking into the shop, in a state of considerable excitement, when my venerable employer, with a smile of extreme benevolence on his aged countenance, said to me — "Cox, I shan't want you to-day — you can have a holiday." Thoughts of "Gravesend and back — fare One Shilling," instantly suggested themselves, intermingled with visions of "Greenwich for Fourpence!" Then came the Twopenny Omnibusses and the Penny Boats — in short, I'm quite bewildered. However, I must have my breakfast first — that'll give me time to reflect.

Burnand follows this speech closely in headlong rhymes:

My master is punctual always in *business,*
Unpunctuality, even slight, *is in his*
Eyes such a crime that on shewing my *phiz in his*
Shop, I thought there'd be the devil to pay.

My aged employer, with his physiognomy
Shining from soap like a star in astronomy,
Said, "Mister Cox, you'll oblige me and honour me
If you will take this as your holiday."

Visions of Brighton and back and of *Rosherville,*
Cheap fare excusions, already the *squash I feel,*
Fearing the rain, put on my macin*tosh I vill,*
Now for my breakfast, my light *dejeunay.*[53]

Elsewhere, Burnand developed Morton's situations into pretexts for musical treatment: the confrontation of Cox and Box, for instance, or Box and Cox's interchange of bacon and mutton chop, which led to a ludicrous lullaby, "Hush-a-bye, bacon, on the coal top. . . ." This song, its absurdity enhanced by Sullivan's treating it like a serious *berceuse,* was probably the most popular single number in *Cox and Box.*

Contemporary reviewers immediately recognized the comic utility of "linking exquisite melodies to idiotic words," forcing the hearer "to laugh and admire at the same moment," as the *Daily Telegraph* put it. In other songs, Sullivan's pseudo-operatic style sharpened the parodistic

---

[53] *Cox and Box; or the Long-lost Brothers,* vocal score (London: Boosey & Co. [n.d.]). I have regularized punctuation.

"bite" of Morton and Burnand's mock melodrama. In short, the composer had already begun to develop that musical wit which his collaboration with Gilbert would perfect. In 1867 he could intensify absurdity by setting it elegantly, but he did not yet sparkle through an entire score.[54] He required a librettist with more metrical ingenuity, intellectual stamina, and control of form than Burnand had. For, while it may be true, as is often asserted, that Burnand, with Sullivan, laid the foundations of Victorian comic opera, his sense of architecture was too deficient to let him build further. In his hands the Savoy libretti would have been an eruption of cupolas. Burnand had a great sense of fun but not of proportion. He could elaborate, but not construct.

The unusual unity and economy of *Cox and Box* is more the work of Morton than of Burnand, whose one universally acknowledged excellence lay in inventing comic stage business. "I do not think the dramatic faculty belongs to Mr. Burnand," said the Theatrical Lounger judiciously.[55] Content to repeat himself discursively, he rarely experimented and seldom listened to reviewers begging him to take pains. When Gilbert eliminated "breakdowns" from his burlesque of *The Princess*, Burnand's *St. George and a Dragon* kept up those "indispensible shuffling dances, alloted in due turn to nearly every one of the performers . . . more vigorous[ly] than ever," to the *Graphic*'s irritation.[56] *The White Cat* brought objections to "puns of that willfully absurd character which has now become a mere mechanical trick" and the reviewer's hope that this Burnand extravaganza will be the last

---

[54] The *Tomahawk* said that *Cox and Box* tended toward monotony, and it is significant to note that the libretto in which Gilbert was most like Burnand, that is *The Sorcerer*, has a score, the characteristics of which have more in common with *Cox and Box* than with *Trial by Jury*.

Gilbert himself, reviewing *Cox and Box* on June 1, 1867, wrote: "Mr. Sullivan's music is, in many places, of too high a class for the grotesquely absurd plot to which it is wedded."

[55] *Illustrated Times*, XVIII (February 11, 1871), 87.

The Burnand burlesque which his contemporary critics found most workmanlike was *Ixion; or, The Man at the Wheel* (1863), "a clever bit of satire," as Clement Scott described it in *Dramatic Table Talk* (London: The Railway and General Automatic Library, Limited [n.d.]; bound with *Thirty Years at the Play*). Almost immediately, however, Scott also describes it as "a regular beauty show" (p. 96). Burnand's best prose comedy was undoubtedly *The Colonel*, a broad satire on aestheticism, which appeared a short time before Gilbert and Sullivan's *Patience*.

[56] *Graphic*, I (April 9, 1870), 451.

of its sort tolerated on the English stage.[57] Thomas Purnell, "Q" of the *Athenaeum*, pepperiest of critics, pronounced a blanket indictment: "Burlesque owes its degradation to delinquencies of burlesque-writers themselves. Of these Mr. F. C. Burnand is perhaps the most prominent offender." [58]

Given the discipline of the German Reed format, where absurdity maintained a certain dignity and there was not time for pointless foolery, Burnand did well. But with his diffuse "jokeiness" and dependence on sources outside himself for form, he could not stimulate or sustain Sullivan in longer works. Unfortunately, for the rest of his life he resented the success of "Gilbert and Sullivan," which he erroneously supposed might as easily have been "Burnand and Sullivan." [59]

Gilbert and Sullivan never collaborated at the Gallery of Illustration, although they first met there, and German Reed in 1870 invited Sullivan to compose the music for a new entertainment by Gilbert — probably *A Sensation Novel*. At this time, the great success of *Ages Ago* had made Gilbert the Reeds' most important dramatist; but Sullivan was not interested. He was at work on an overture for the Birmingham Festival.

Gilbert's connection with the German Reeds had begun in 1869 with the production of *No Cards* (March 29), written to the Reed pattern of multiple "assumptions." Three of its four characters appear in one or more disguises during the simple plot, which is conventionally based on a love-money intrigue. Miss Annabella Penrose, an heiress living with her strong-minded aunt, Mrs. Pennythorne, is courted by Mr. Ellis Dee, a wealthy old bachelor, and Mr. Churchmouse, a poor young one. By one of those legal complications Gilbert liked so much, Miss Penrose's choice must be approved by her long-absent guardian, Mr. Coodle. Coodle, husband of Mrs. Pennythorne, ran away with his wife's money three weeks after marriage, leaving her, like Betsey Trotwood, to resume her maiden name, while he disappeared into the wilds of Australia. Dee

---

[57] *Graphic*, III (January 7, 1871), 15.

[58] "Q" (Thomas Purnell), *Dramatists of the Present Day. Reprinted from "The Athenaeum"* (London: Chapman and Hall, 1871), p. 46.

[59] R.G.G. Price says Burnand was jealous of Gilbert (*A History of Punch* [London: Collins, 1957], p. 86). Certainly *Punch*'s hostility toward Gilbert during the days when Burnand was its theatrical reviewer and later its editor bears this out, even though Burnand and Gilbert were friendly in private life. Perhaps Burnand's resentment began when *Ages Ago* eclipsed *Cox and Box*, as the treatment of *Ages Ago* in *Punch* seems to indicate.

and Churchmouse separately undertake a series of impersonations by which two bogus Coodles appear simultaneously. Mrs. Pennythorne then disguises herself as Aunt Salamanca Trombone, the source of Annabella's wealth, and announces that her niece is penniless. This reversal frightens off Ellis Dee, whose name indicates his love of pounds, shillings, and pence,[60] and leaves the disinterested Churchmouse in possession of the girl and her fortune. The stipulation of Coodle's approval is conveniently disregarded.

Several stock comic devices appear in *No Cards*. Dee's alternate insistence that he is Coodle when he stands to gain and that Churchmouse is Coodle when Salamanca wants to horsewhip Coodle is reminiscent of the *volte face* of *Box and Cox*. The uneasy conversation at cross-purposes between Churchmouse and Dee as each tries to live up to his disguise is a more ludicrous extension of that in *La Vie Parisienne*. Dee's real self is conventionally abused to his disguised self's face. Churchmouse, inanely shy unless acting a role in amateur theatricals, is a humour character out of Goldsmith's Young Marlow, and an antecedent for Robin Oakapple in *Ruddigore*. The denouement, also, depends on conventional comic — and melodramatic — values: Churchmouse's worthiness is shown in his willingness to marry a poor girl, a sacrifice immediately and rewardingly negated.

But within this framework, Gilbert's own characteristic comedy is clearly operative. The Pavlovian conditioning by which servant girls are to be taught never to marry, the charitable enterprise in which a half-crown can be "equally distributed among the eight hundred and sixty-seven charities of Great Britain and Ireland"; the elderly baby in a song which is also a Bab Ballad [61] — these have the Gilbertian hallmark of mad system and organized inversion. His familiar satiric theme of Topsyturvydom appears in this early work in Mrs. Pennythorne's song about Babbetyboobledore, that remarkably backward nation in which "They've little regard for money or birth — / Unless it's allied to genuine worth. . . ." Here *Utopia Limited* comes faintly into view down time's long perspective. More immediately, Gilbert utilized German Reed's

---

[60] £/s/d.

[61] The baby "born at an advanced age" is also the subject of Gilbert's two-page spread of comic drawings in *Warne's Christmas Annual* for 1866. Here the old infant grows younger as he grows up, a reversal worked out in Gilbert's farce *Topsy-turvydom* (1874), in which a grandmother appears as an attractive young girl. Gilbert's interest in people who are born old and grow younger as they "age" is a kind of comic redaction of Plato's *Statesman*, in which the dead arise and live their lives backward.

setting of "Babbetyboobledore"[62] for a song about the Druidesses' Family Fancy Fair in *The Pretty Druidess* (1869),[63] his burlesque of Norma.

Among the other self-parallels and prototypes in *No Cards* are the competitive examination for hereditary rank, as in *Iolanthe*, and the having to discover one's own identity by looking at one's visiting card, repeated in *The Pretty Druidess*. Mrs. Pennythorne's "When people ridicule the idea of marriage they forget how much they owe to that institution" was used again cynically in the prologue to *The Wicked World* ("But, let me ask you, had the world ne'er known / Such Love . . . / Pray where would you, or I, or he, have been?") and as a resolution in *The Princess* and *Princess Ida* ("If you enlist all women in your cause, / And make them all abjure tyrannic Man, / The obvious question then arises, 'How/Is this Posterity to be provided'"). Two songs in *No Cards* suggest later Savoy lyrics. Mr. Dee's solo verse "Take a manner brisker . . ." occupies a middle ground between the satirical prose recipes of *Punch* and *Fun* and Gilbert's more intricately concocted "receipts" in

---

[62] Gilbert's acknowledgement of permission gives Reed as the composer, as do both a playbill in the Enthoven Theatre Collection and an undated leaflet-handbill quoting reviews of *No Cards* in The Reginald Allen Collection. The later Joseph Williams version of the libretto credits the score to L. Elliott, identified as Lionel Elliot on a program for St. George's Hall, March 29 [1873?]. It is faintly possible that this person was really J. W. Elliott, who did arrangements for the Gallery of Illustration, including that for Planché's *King Christmas*. J. W. Elliott was also pianist and chorus master for German Reed's English opera venture at St. George's Hall. It seems likely that L. Elliott's score is a new setting for a revival. Clearly, Reed had composed his wife's numbers, whoever put together the rest of the original score. See Appendix A for a discussion of the music of *No Cards*.

[63] This burlesque, produced at the Strand, thus contained a Gallery of Illustration private joke. Corney Grain had a musical monologue called "The Fancy Fair."

In Gilbert's burlesque, Norma sings:
> In yonder domain we'll hold our tryst —
> Our Family Fancy Fair —
> A liberal gentleman can't resist
> A Family Fancy Fair.
> To flatter and wheedle, and dazzle and coax,
> These racketty, rollicking Roman folks,
> We're carefully planning that splendid hoax,
> A Family Fancy Fair!

Her druid priestesses chorus:
> A Family Fancy — Family Fancy —
> Family Fancy Fair;
> A Family Fancy — Family Fancy —
> Family Fancy Fair!

Colonel Calverley's Heavy Dragoon song and Marco's "Take a pair of sparkling eyes." Mrs. Pennythorne's "A timid, and a bashful, and a shy young man. . . . [and] over-dressed, opinionated, vain young men" is the verbal germ of Bunthorne and Grosvenor's duet in *Patience* with its "crotchety, cracked young man" and "matter-of-fact young man." [64] In these latter rhymes, Gilbert intensified the contrast by physically embodying the two types on stage and letting each describe himself.

The cast for *No Cards* included Rosa D'Erina, the Rose of Erin, whose "piquant" accent could hardly have been right for Miss Penrose; perhaps for that reason the soprano role in this work is overwhelmed by the contralto. Mrs. Reed, of course, played Mrs. Pennythorne and the pretended Salamanca Trombone, with the latter's brisk entrance line: "You must find room for the elephant in the stables." The role of Churchmouse fell to Arthur Cecil, who had just made his debut as Box in the still running "triumveretta." It is owing to Cecil's talent, as well as his author's anti-romanticism, that the tenor in Gilbert's German Reed pieces is an important comedian rather than a mere first singing gentleman. A good voice and gentlemanliness, however, were part of Arthur Cecil's equipment, and valuable traits for the Gallery of Illustration. His opening notices were excellent. *Punch* purred, ". . . it is a treat to hear a gentleman, who is really a gentleman. . . ." [65] More important to Gilbert, Cecil proved a stylish, versatile actor, who became "notorious for his attention to detail in the parts he played." [66] His Churchmouse's

---

[64] This last parallel has been noted, *inter alia*, by J. K. Clayton in "Gilbert's 'German Reed' Period," *Gilbert and Sullivan Journal* (Emergency issues, No. 11 [October, 1942], p. 240, and No. 12 [February, 1943], pp. 249–50), and by Isaac Goldberg in *The Story of Gilbert and Sullivan; or The 'Compleat' Savoyard* (New York: Simon and Schuster, 1928). Terence Rees also points out some of Gilbert's self-borrowings, especially those from his first collaboration with Sullivan; see *Thespis: A Gilbert & Sullivan Enigma* (London: Dillon's University Bookshop, 1964).

In discussing Gilbert's indebtedness to his German Reed pieces, I have not attempted to be exhaustive, but have selected representative borrowings. Gilbert's kind of creative process, in which lines, jokes, verses, characters, situations, and concepts were reworked and slowly perfected through play after play, makes every line of his the clue into a tangle of analogues.

[65] "A Capital Investment," LVI (April 10, 1869), 143.

[66] *Rutland Barrington by Himself* (London: Grant Richards, 1908), p. 80. After five years with the Reeds, Arthur Cecil made his debut on the regular stage in Gilbert's *Committed for Trial* (January, 1874). He had a reputation as a "mugger," but "in all other respects he was a genuine artist" (obituary in *The Theatre*, XXVII [May 1, 1896], 309).

impersonation of the Universal Agent for All the Charities in Great Britain and Ireland was particularly noticed by the *Morning Post.*

No Cards as a whole was well received; *The Times* commended its neatness and point, and the *Morning Post* described it as "an exceedingly agreeable little sketch. . . ." But, played on the same bill as *Cox and Box*, it was definitely the subordinate work. With Gilbert's second German Reed piece these positions were reversed. *Ages Ago: A Musical Legend*, produced on November 22, 1869, was rapidly pronounced "the best we can recollect at the popular little Gallery" by the *Daily Telegraph.* Even *Punch* found it "an amusing notion amusingly worked out," [67] and it proved to be Gilbert's most popular work for the Reeds, achieving more than three hundred and fifty performances.

The double plot of *Ages Ago* already shows a marked advance over the simple situation of *No Cards.* In a framing modern story, Sir Ebenezer Tare, tallow chandler risen to alderman, has just taken possession of a castle which Mrs. MacMotherly, his housekeeper endowed with a broad Scots accent and second sight, declares to be haunted. By a singularly complicated pact between its fourteenth-century owner and a con-

---

Cecil in his post-Gallery career, notably with the Bancrofts, sometimes essayed the pathetic, although with limited success. "The portrayal of manners upon the stage and the acting of emotion are two very distinct and different qualities," wrote Squire Bancroft of Cecil's Triplet in *Masks and Faces,* adding that Cecil was too well fed for the starving artist-of-all-trades he was intended to portray (*The Bancrofts: Recollections of Sixty Years* [London: John Murray, 1909], p. 157). Nor was he completely at home in melodramatic roles. His forte was comedy. He was adept in make-up, especially for elderly faces. He was an excellent Touchstone, and played a Dr. Caius "of singular animation and humour" in the 1874 *Merry Wives of Windsor* for which Sullivan wrote incidental music. Cecil himself wrote a curtain raiser, set to music by Alfred Cellier, which was played with *The Sorcerer.* In the eighties, Cecil and John Clayton managed the Court Theatre and Cecil acted in Pinero's early farces, including *Dandy Dick* and *The Magistrate.* He died of pneumonia on April 16, 1896, at the age of fifty-two.

Arthur Cecil seems to have been one of the most pleasant of comedians off stage as well as on. As described by the Bancrofts he resembles one of the amusing eccentrics he often played — a humour character in real life. Pursued by what Squire Bancroft called "his second self, the Demon of Indecision," Cecil once appeared at a dress rehearsal with a completely different make-up for each act (*The Bancrofts,* p. 221).

[67] A second *Punch* review, written in doggerel, very likely by Burnand, when *Ages Ago* had been running two months, makes no mention of Gilbert, calls the piece "rather funny" and "rather witty," and says that the device of pictures leaving their frames is "A notion old, but nicely *réchauffé'd.*" The rhymes end by asserting that *Cox and Box,* the afterpiece, sends audiences away holding their sides with laughter.

venient fiend, the castle's title deed can be found only at hundred-year intervals, the last of which is just ending. Next morning, the deed appears and identifies Columbus Hebblethwaite, an impoverished admirer of Sir Ebenezer's niece Rosa, as the rightful heir to Glen-Cockaleekie Castle. In order to retain the castle, Sir Ebenezer reluctantly consents to their marriage. Here we have most of the essential elements of *No Cards*: an impecunious suitor; a young person who puts love before wealth (Churchmouse in the first play, Rosa in the second); a parentless heroine with an aunt to help or an uncle to hinder her; and a legal document, which in *No Cards* provides the complication, but in *Ages Ago* the resolution.

The second but more important plot of *Ages Ago*, however, is the supernatural one which gave the cast its necessary "doubling." While the humans of the framing episode sleep, portraits of the castle's former owners come to life and engage in romantic complications themselves, also resolved by a legal expedient. Their problems are twofold: fifteenth-century Lady Maud, painted at seventeen, and sixteenth-century Sir Cecil Blount,[68] painted at twenty, are simultaneously older and younger than their descendants, Lord Carnaby Poppytop, painted in 1713 at the age of sixty-five, and Dame Cherry Maybud, painted in 1785 at the age of fifty-five. Lord Carnaby tries to take Lady Maud away from Sir Cecil on the grounds that both pictures once belonged to him and "a man may do what he likes with his own." He is thwarted by Dame Cherry, who announces that all three belong to her, bestows Maud on Cecil, and indulges successfully in a middle-aged flirtation with Lord Carnaby. A "necessary blessing" is given to both couples by Brown, a fifth portrait, the just-painted spurious maternal grandfather of Sir Ebenezer. As day breaks all resume their frames, and the two plots are tied together by Dame Cherry's leaving behind an abstract proving Hebblethwaite's title to the castle.

The conception of the animated portraits as persons in their own right, separate from the humans of the framing plot, is a decided improvement over the impersonations which were Gilbert's expedient for multiple roles in his first German Reed work. For the same reason the fantasy of *Ages Ago* is superior to that of Tom Taylor's earlier entertainment, in which a picture animates only in a dream. Gilbert had very

---

[68] See Appendix A for variations in the name of this character. In calling the tenor Sir Cecil Blount, Gilbert was again making a private joke, for Arthur Cecil's full name was Arthur Cecil Blunt. Blount, of course, is very appropriately Elizabethan.

early adopted a policy of not explaining away his ghosts or fairies, but of treating the supernatural with scrupulous realism on its own grounds. This literality not only gave "artistic verisimilitude," but deepened the comedy arising from a juxtaposition or integration of magic and logic.

In regard to the supernatural, the most obvious Savoy descendant of *Ages Ago* is, of course, *Ruddigore*. In it we find again the controlling ghostly legend retold by an old woman; a portrait gallery of ancestors who come to life and determine the fate of their descendant; the time conceit in which day is night, midnight high noon to ghosts; a withdrawing song as the pictures retire to their frames; a middle-aged romance; even a name in common, shared by Dame Cherry Maybud and Rose Maybud.[69] Yet the effect of *Ages Ago* is not so much that of *Ruddigore* as of *Iolanthe*, with its complication of a mother seemingly younger than her son. When Lord Carnaby is attracted to Lady Maud, we are told:

> So strange a meeting ne'er was seen
> For sure as I'm alive,
> His grandmama is seventeen,
> And he is sixty-five.

This young-old motif is allied to that of the elderly baby and was repeated by Gilbert in "The Fairy Curate," *Creatures of Impulse*, and *Topsy-turvydom*, all written in the same five years.

Ages Ago also anticipates *Iolanthe* in its use of what might be called Gilbert's divided-man motif: Brown's portrait cannot leave its frame because it has been painted half-length, just as Strephon's mortal legs must stay behind although his fairy upper-half can creep through a keyhole. Lady Maud's frank self-admiration displays the same charming vanity that Gilbert gave to Phyllis and hardened in Yum-Yum. In Maud's equally outspoken delight at Sir Cecil's portrait, we see an early instance of satire directed against the pretexts by which human nature evades the decorum it simultaneously upholds.

> You are very handsome — very, very handsome. I'm glad you're only a picture. If you were a real living man, I should be obliged to be rather particular, but as it is I may say what I like to you.

Satire in *Ages Ago* is generally milder but better unified with its context than in *No Cards*, where it had existed chiefly and unmistakably

---

[69] Lord Carnaby Poppytop's surname was also used by Gilbert for the market gardner in one of his adaptations of Labiche and Marc-Michel's *Un Chapeau de paille d'Italie*.

in "Babbetyboobledore." The character of Sir Ebenezer Tare is a means of showing up bourgeois pretensions to aristocracy, particularly the supposition that externals such as family portraits confer the prestige of rank. This foreshadows Major-General Stanley's ancestors-by-purchase and stuccoed baronial hall in *The Pirates of Penzance*. The portraits' discussion of their respective artists contains "Some smart hits at the R[oyal] Academy," as Shirley Brooks noted in his diary after seeing the play; [70] the ineptitude of "restoring" Old Masters was particularly made fun of.

Metrically and verbally, *Ages Ago* is discernably more varied and more complexly "Gilbertian" than was its predecessor. There is a patter song, described as "clever" by the *Athenaeum*, in which virtuoso rhymes ("Come to my thatchery, semi-detachery. . . .") join tongue-twisting reductions to inanity ("Where the violet sighs to the evening skies,/And the skies of eve receive the sigh of the violet"). Gilbert's later talent for Elizabethan conceits is foreshadowed in the duet:

> SIR C.   In pity tell, oh lady mine!
> The fate that waits me, my life is thine!
> 'Tis thine to spare, 'tis thine to kill,
> 'Tis thine to fashion to thy fair will.
> LADY M.   If this is so, what can I do?
> The word that kills thee would kill me too!
> My hand and heart to thee I give,
> The word that saves thee, now bids me live.

The immediate cause of this enlarged scope and range was Gilbert's new collaborator — Frederic Clay,[71] a thoroughly competent musician

---

[70] George Soames Layard, *Shirley Brooks of Punch: His Life, Letters, and Diaries* (New York: Henry Holt and Co., 1907), p. 378.

[71] Frederic Clay was born in Paris on August 3, 1838. Almost all his music was written for drawing room or stage. At twenty-four he had composed the music for Taylor's libretto, *Court and Cottage*, produced at Covent Garden. His most popular ballad, "I'll Sing Thee Songs of Araby," first was heard as part of his cantata *Lalla Rookh* (1877), a great success of that year's Brighton Festival. Among his scores were those for *The Black Crook*, *Catarina*, and *Don Quixote*, and he composed incidental music for *Twelfth Night*. For the last six years of his life Clay was paralyzed; he died on November 24, 1889.

Clay was described by Emily Soldene as "a most charming person, . . . [who] wore very fetching open-work shirt-fronts, with coloured silk beneath, one night pink, another night blue." (*My Theatrical and Musical Recollections*, p. 191.) Sullivan, who wrote the original entry for Clay in *Grove's Dictionary of Music and Musicians*, praised him for "a natural gift of graceful melody and a feeling for

of some note who introduced Gilbert to Sullivan. Clay's strong point was pretty melody; as the *Illustrated Times* pointed out: "A dainty minor sweetness runs all through the entertainment." The *Athenaeum* found the songs "thoughtful and elegant, the concerted pieces well-written and effective." Curiously enough, its reviewer raised the same objection to Clay's score that Gilbert made to Sullivan's in *Ruddigore*; that is, that the musical treatment tended to be too serious. But the most frequent description of Clay's music here and elsewhere was "charming." Clay and Gilbert worked together successfully on other musical comedies, notably *The Gentleman in Black*, *Princess Toto*, and *Happy Arcadia*; but the ultimate collaboration could not have been "Gilbert and Clay" any more than it could have been "Burnand and Sullivan." In 1869 Clay could support Gilbert's most complex libretto to date and give charm to its charm; but he had a crucial defect which several reviewers immediately recognized. He lacked Sullivan's sense of fun. All Gilbert's sly invitations could not really persuade Clay to gambol on the harmonium. And, as the vocal score of *Ages Ago* shows, he broke up Gilbert's lines with incessant undramatic repetitions of words to suit his own melodic phrases, whereas Sullivan, even in *Cox and Box*, was willing to maintain the integrity of his librettist's syntax. Nevertheless, at this stage of the dramatist's career, Clay's solid musicianship was a liberation.

A second advantage was the presence of Miss Fanny Holland, an amateur who had just joined the German Reed company. She combined "a ringing and joyous voice" with "marvellous verve and point" [72] and a laugh which was a work of art. [73] Replacing Rosa D'Erina, who seems to have been more suited to minor Offenbach or brogue ballads than to English comedy, Miss Holland played at the Gallery for years and married Arthur Law, the author of nineteen German Reed pieces. For this sprightly soprano, Gilbert wrote roles which were essentially comic beneath their superficially romantic function, just as he made the tenor into a comedian for Arthur Cecil. With Fanny Holland, Cecil, and the Reeds, Gilbert now had an almost ideally balanced company, whose talents he carefully exploited in *Our Island Home*, first

---

rich harmonic colouring." Clay's talent was perhaps more accurately described by a contemporary reviewer in the *Athenaeum*, who alluded to his "facile, elegant melodies." Nevertheless, *Ages Ago* was the only one of Gilbert's German Reed pieces the full score of which was published during its first production. Clay dedicated it to Sullivan.

[72] *Illustrated Times*, XV (November 27, 1869), 343.

[73] Williamson, *The German Reeds and Corney Grain*, p. 63.

performed on June 20, 1870, and for some time played on a double bill
with *Ages Ago.*

In *Our Island Home* there is no multiplication of roles as such, except
for a brief passage of undeveloped pluralism when German Reed suc-
cessively imitates a butcher, a milkman, and a grocer, while still clearly
remaining German Reed. Instead, a subtler sort of impersonation per-
vades this work. Members of the cast play themselves, but with altered
personalities. That is, the actors are called by their real names, and certain
elements of their real lives are retained: notably their profession, the success of *Ages Ago,* Arthur Cecil's pleasure in food, and the fact that the
German Reeds have a grown son. But each player's nature or disposition
is greatly modified or reversed, with the possible exception of Fanny
Holland's, which is only given a touch of acerbity. Mrs. Reed, whose
company affectionately called her "Mama" off stage, is depicted as a
strong-willed shrew who insists on having her own way, and when it
invariably leads to trouble, reproaches her husband for not restraining
a poor, weak woman. With this fictitious Mrs. Reed, Gilbert moves from
the situation comedy of a character not knowing his own identity to the
satire of a character not knowing his own nature. The ambivalence of
the masculine, managing woman who sees herself as a timid child-wife
is eventually incorporated in the more complex Katisha.

Mr. Reed, as the henpecked husband of this termagant, is merely rue-
fully long-suffering; but his son Alfred German Reed, who had just
joined the Gallery,[74] is assigned a wholly fictional adolescence and
occupation. Like the later Frederick, the stage Alfred has been mis-
takenly apprenticed to a pirate. He is now Captain Bang, the Pirate
Chief; and innocuous Arthur Cecil has become a black-hearted melodramatic villain. With the help of a mesmeric eye like that of Belvawney
in *Engaged,*[75] he forces his fellow castaways to act as his servants. Sadis-
tically, he plies them with oysters, which they all dislike.

Other dramatists have, in the past, put actors on stage to play them-

---

[74] Alfred Reed, born in 1847, was originally apprenticed to an engineering firm.
He acquired there some of the material for his later stage impersonations of
workmen. "Few actors could so truthfully copy the action of a knife-grinder as
Alfred German Reed. . . ." (*Ibid.,* p. 41.) He began his stage career in Manchester
and joined the Gallery when he was needed to fill in for his temporarily incapaci-
tated father. Upon the retirement of the elder Reeds, Alfred and Corney Grain
kept the Galley of Illustration going until 1895 when both they and Mrs. Reed
died within the same eight days.

[75] Protection against this Gothic orb is the same in both plays: green spectacles.

selves in an imaginary situation, but Gilbert's combination of real identity with radically altered persona is unique. In his rearrangement of reality, the audience, from its own knowledge of the Reeds, had to supply the necessary implicit contrast to what was explicit on stage. Thus Gilbert had begun to refine and intellectualize the parodistic technique of playing off a distortion against the standard or reality already present in the viewer's mind. At the Savoy, this principle was continued, but the two standards were usually reversed: society's real motives were displayed on stage against the conventional evasions which the audience was supposedly familiar with or even subscribed to.

Perhaps because of its psychological advance, *Our Island Home* returns to an ostensibly simple plot. For the first time Gilbert omits a romantic interest. He was hardly prepared to plight Fanny Holland to Arthur Cecil or Alfred German Reed for a conventional curtain line. Nor, perhaps, was the Gallery ready for a burlesque of melodramatic sexual dangers (although Gilbert managed to imply them in his next German Reed piece). The only passion, therefore, is Cecil's grotesque adoration of anchovy sauce.

The scene is "the shore of an Island in the Indian Ocean" where Mrs. and Mr. Reed, Miss Holland, and Arthur Cecil have been marooned during an Asiatic tour of *Ages Ago*.[76] Mrs. Reed has arbitrarily divided the island into four parts, of which only Cecil's is fertile,[77] another reason for his successful tyranny. When he is finally persuaded to exchange territories, he discovers gold in the barren rocks he now owns, whereupon the other three try to retrieve the shares they so willingly gave up. Here we have a kind of *Box and Cox* reversal put more in terms of the mid-century well-made play with its struggle for some physical object (a letter, a fan) alternately possessed by opposing characters. In *Our Island Home* there are three such objects: the fertile quarter of the island; the remaining rocky, gold-bearing three-quarters; and the cask of anchovy desired by Cecil.

At this point the action seems to be prematurely wound up, but Gilbert — perhaps suddenly realizing that his plot was escaping him — recaptured it by discarding the first line of development and to some

---

[76] Their ship is "the Hot Cross Bun," carried over from *The Bab Ballads* in which it is the name of Lieutenant Belaye's gunboat ("The Bumboat Woman's Story").

[77] This sort of division and subsequent discomfort formed the basis of "Etiquette," a Bab Ballad published in the *Graphic*, December 25, 1869, just six months before the opening of *Our Island Home*.

degree the fictitious personalities of the Reeds and Cecil. A more pronounced manipulation of reality now appears, and what is really a second miniscule plot begins. The castaways are joined by Captain Bang, whom the Reeds discover to be their long-absent son. In compliance with his articles of piratical apprenticeship, he intends to slaughter the entire company. But Arthur Cecil, in an inspired technicality, points out that Reed/Bang has just come of age and is consequently a free agent. All five happily prepare to return to civilization.

The relationship of *Our Island Home* to *The Pirates of Penzance* is obvious. There is even a stupid nursery maid, off stage, to confuse "pilot" and "pirate." The quibble over the apprentice's twenty-first birthday which complicates *The Pirates* provided for the earlier work a final *deus ex leges*, already a pattern of Gilbert's German Reed denouements. The Victorians' favourite virtue, that duty to which Frederic is a slave, is satirized in Captain Bang's willingness to sacrifice his parents to his articles of apprenticeship, as well as in their acquiescence to his topsy-turvy morality. Conversely, Bang, too tenderhearted to be a happy pirate, heads a long Gilbertian line of inadequately ruthless characters: the sentimental pirates of Penzance, Ko-Ko, Sir Ruthven Murgatroyd, even the Fairy Queen who cannot bring herself to enforce the stern letter of fairy law.

The dialogue of this third German Reed work is more ebullient and stylish than that of *Ages Ago*, especially in its burlesque of melodramatic asides and exclamations, its revelatory outbursts, and in the ingenious arrangement by which Arthur Cecil compels Mr. Reed to speak in rhyme, Mrs. Reed in blank verse, and Miss Holland in recitative.[78] This gave Gilbert greater opportunities for parodying styles of stage rhetoric, as well as for using absurd verbal expedients and seemingly impromptu comic inspiration. He extended the latter further in his characters' fantastic adductions of possibility, such as German Reed's explanation of a missing drumstick and Arthur Cecil's plans for his anchovy sauce.

Not all the lyrics of *Our Island Home* have been preserved,[79] but judging from those which remain, Gilbert made no metrical advance over *Ages Ago*, nor are the concerted works so intricate. Except for a

---

[78] In a MS note for *The Fairy's Dilemma*, written in 1904 almost at the end of Gilbert's career, this arbitrary arrangement recurs: "Sir Trevor conducts his share of the dialogue in highly strung blank verse. Demon carries on his in cockney rhyme." (Gilbert Papers.) This intention was not fully carried out in the finished play.

[79] See note on texts in Appendix A.

rudimentary autobiographical song, "Oh tremble, I'm the Pirate Chief!," the prose dialogue is more interesting than the verses, set by German Reed himself in lieu of Frederic Clay. Nevertheless, the music was highly praised by several reviewers as Reed's most ambitious to date, the Theatrical Lounger describing it as "occasionally extremely clever."[80] Gilbert was congratulated for departing from the beaten track of farce and thanked for preferring wit to broad effects. In one specific comparison of *Our Island Home* with *Cox and Box*, Gilbert's work was pronounced the more original and therefore better.[81]

The first night of *Our Island Home* put a sudden strain on the ingenuity of the Reeds:

> For some reason or another their costumes had failed to arrive. With only an hour to spare before the rise of the curtain, Mrs. Reed bethought her of the garden nets! Mr. Gilbert volunteered to fetch them from Tooting, and Mrs. Reed, who was a genius at improvising, deftly draped them with such success that she and her husband continued to wear them throughout the run of the piece. Mr. Reed got Mr. O'Connor, the scene-painter, to add some leaves to his costume, which were sewn on by his daughter, and he went on to the stage while the paint was still wet![82]

These impromptu costumes were not put to the test of a long run. In spite of good reviews, *Our Island Home* fell far short of the record set by *Ages Ago* — perhaps because it had been produced at a "dead" season, perhaps because it lacked the "daintiness" of its predecessor. In six months it was replaced by Gilbert's fourth work for the German Reeds, *A Sensation Novel in Three Volumes*, first performed on January 30, 1871, a week after *Ages Ago* finally left the playbill.

To keep up the conceit of its title, each act of this new entertainment was called a "volume"; its scenery, the "frontispiece"; performances, "vignettes"; and German Reed's score, "musical notes." Reed and Corney Grain, who now enters a Gilbert cast for the first time, had to double their roles, but nothing was made of this. Instead, Gilbert continued to experiment with a more intellectualized kind of double identity. The result anticipated Pirandello's *Six Characters in Search of an Author* and the fate of Don Juan in Rostand's *La Dernière Nuit de Don Juan*.

The first "volume" of *A Sensation Novel* opens with an Author, whom

---

[80] *Illustrated Times*, XVI (June 25, 1870), 411.

[81] This was the reviewer for the *Illustrated Times*, which Gilbert wrote for. Perhaps it was intended to redress the balance of *Punch* a little.

[82] This anecdote was told to Williamson by Mr. Reed. (Williamson, *The German Reeds and Corney Grain*, p. 13.)

the Demon of Romance enables to turn out fifty books a year. The Demon supplies him with stereotyped characters: former human beings now expiating trivial faults by impersonating "those stock characters of the sensation novelist which are most opposed to their individual tastes and inclinations." At the end of each "volume" they are permitted to step out of their roles temporarily and to discuss or try to alter the plot whose unwilling subjects they are.

There is, therefore, scarcely any physical action in the body of the play. The events of the novel presumably transpire during intermissions, and stage time is devoted to the stereotypic dramatis personae's recapitulation of what has happened and anticipation of what they fear is to come. Finally, at the end of volume three, the characters force their Sensation Author to rearrange his plot to suit their private ends, thus achieving a conclusion simultaneously more original and more outrageously improbable than the intended cliché closing.

The audiences for this play had to keep at least three frames of reference in mind: first, the literary conventions parodied throughout; second, each character's nature and position when he is "inside" the plot of the novel; and finally, his nature and preferences "outside" the novel. Furthermore, in this complex welter of relationships, not only is each character the opposite of what he supposedly was like "in life," but he or she is also revealed as someone other than he seemed to be when the fictional plot began.

For example, Rockalda, "the lovely fiend of fiction, / With the yellow, yellow hair," was, when alive, an indulgent, middle-aged mother. In the novel she is a villainess who plans to murder Herbert, a virtuous Sunday School teacher, whom she adores "outside" the novel. During the plot, Rockalda is exposed as having been exchanged with the infant daughter of the Duke of Ben-Nevis, himself now in disguise as a stationmaster. Each of the other characters has a comparable set of ambivalences, those of Gripper, the Sensation Detective, including a series of blatant costume disguises. Gilbert retained something of *Our Island Home*'s trick of setting role against actor in giving the "assumption" of Rockalda to Mrs. Reed, and by exploiting Corney Grain's massive physique and bass voice for Gripper, the always-too-late detective, whose features the Author describes as "delicately chiselled," whose figure is "slight, indeed, almost girlish," and whose voice is touchingly feminine.

The demonic compulsion which forces these characters into unwilling alliances and antagonisms is a more intricately worked-out version of Arthur Cecil's mesmeric eye. Arbitrary reversals of personality or identity seem almost to have obsessed Gilbert in the early 1870's. He

35

used this device not only for three German Reed pieces but also in *The Palace of Truth* (which makes its inhabitants speak inconvenient veracities); *The Gentleman in Black* (who changes souls from one body to another in a way strongly reminiscent of Lord Byron's *Deformed Transformed*); *Creatures of Impulse* (moved irresistibly to behave contrary to their intentions and interests); and *The Wicked World* (from whence human love enters and corrupts Fairyland).[83]

All these plays — and more — are variations of what Sullivan called Gilbert's "lozenge plot": that is, a plot in which some supernatural agent or device changes persons into their opposites or forces them to become in actuality what or whom they have insincerely or dishonestly pretended to be. Sullivan disliked the "lozenges"; so, after *The Sorcerer*, Gilbert generally kept them psychological or legalistic, and tacit. For example, a "morbid love of admiration" makes Bunthorne affect the aestheticism he dislikes; meek Ko-Ko becomes Lord High Executioner through his townsfellows' sophistry; and even when a supernatural influence impels Sir Ruthven Murgatroyd to crime, it cannot operate until he is invested with his title. Nevertheless, these subtler manifestations still satirize the arbitrary and artificial manipulations of life, characteristic of Victorian melodrama in whatever genre.

In *A Sensation Novel* Gilbert has made his borrowings from melodrama parody themselves by pushing over the edge the coincidences, unlikelihoods, and impossibilities, which, in circulating libraries and popular drama, stood already at the brink of absurdity. For the unlikely natural, he substituted the artificial accepted as natural: instead of possessing a birthmark, the long-lost daughter has the identifying family trait of back hair growing in the shape of a ducal coronet. No one is incredulous when an adult passes herself off as an infant twenty-five years younger, a burlesque of baby-switching which foreshadows the Captain Corcoran / Ralph Rackstraw equation of *Pinafore*.[84] This exchanged-child motif, with its obvious links to the comic lozenge plot,

---

[83] The plot of *The Palace of Truth* was derived from a story by Madame de Genlis; the plots of *Creatures of Impulse* and *The Wicked World* came from Gilbert's own short stories. *Randall's Thumb* might also be included here, except that its hero's altered behavior is caused by blackmail, not by black magic.

[84] Plot parallels, verbal resemblances, and characterizations shared by *A Sensation Novel* and the Savoy Operas, to say nothing of Gilbert's non-Sullivan work, are too frequent and too interwoven for a prolonged discussion here. In addition to those which should by now be obvious, there are others such as the joke about the girl of a thousand (*Pirates*), self-decapitation (*Mikado*), Seven Dials versus Belgrave Square (*Iolanthe*), and so on and on.

was perhaps the favourite device of "serious" melodrama in all its forms. To cite only a few representative examples: Tennyson's Lady Clare was a lowly-born babe, substituted for a dead infant aristocrat by her real mother, "Alice the nurse"; Verdi's Manrico is really Count di Luna's brother, not Azucena's son; and in the same year as *A Sensation Novel*, W. G. Wills's romantic play *Hinko* asked audiences to seriously believe that a burgomaster's child had been exchanged with the rightful son of the King of Bohemia. M. E. Braddon's novels luxuriated in impostures,[85] and from her *Lady Audley's Secret* Gilbert drew his "yellow-haired panther," whose name could have been taken from Fitzball or Monk Lewis. The sensation detective in disguise obviously parodies Hawkshaw in Tom Taylor's *Ticket-of-Leave Man*, perennially revived on the London stage.[86] Gilbert satirized this strictly melodramatic type by making him expose his literary function, which is just the opposite of what a real detective's should be: if Gripper ever arrived on time the plot would come to an end; ergo, his duty is to *not* catch the miscreant. His outlandish costumes, the only arresting thing about him, completely defeat any rational intention of concealment. This character is also a medium for the social satire directed against contemporary treatment of criminals that Gilbert had already touched on in *No Cards* and in several Bab Ballads.

In *A Sensation Novel*, Gilbert's most daring confrontation of cliché with reality lies in his treatment of love, on which theme he was acquiring a cynic's reputation. In melodrama, the threat of sexual violence was almost always present but never carried out.[87] The romantically pure clove to the purely romantic, and neither rape nor marriage was understood to be consummated, exchanged infants to the contrary notwithstanding. Thus the maximum excitement could be united with the minimum consequences. As the *Mask* admiringly pointed out, Miss Braddon's "sensational effects are never used for the glorification of immorality as in the works of [George Sand]. . . ."[88]

In Gilbert's play, Alice, the virtuous governess, and Herbert, the pure curate, explicitly defy this moral code. By tradition and the Author

---

[85] In the late sixties and early seventies, *Fun* was filled with burlesques of *Lady Audley's Secret* and *Aurora Floyd*.

[86] The complete libretto of *A Sensation Novel*, published in 1897 makes Gripper turn out to be Sherlock Holmes in disguise, but this is clearly a later substitution.

[87] "Well, hardly ever!"

[88] *Mask*, I (June, 1868), 138.

they are destined for each other. "Outside" the novel they are united only by mutual distaste. Herbert's preference for Rockalda is a lapse sometimes temporarily permissible even for a hero of "serious" melodrama; but he adds to it "Marry and live happily ever after! And this is a novel that pretends to give a picture of life as it is." Alice's language and choice of lover are likewise unthinkable conventionally. Rebelling against the Author and despising Herbert's milk-and-water, she longs for the more intoxicating passion of wicked Sir Ruthven Glenaloon. She demolishes the expected maidenly reticence by her open invitation to her villain to "follow me, worry me, harry me. . . ." even though she does rhyme *harry me* with *marry me.* Perhaps this more realistic motivation accounts for some reviewers finding *A Sensation Novel* indelicate — even indecent!

Most critics, on the other hand, shared E. L. Blanchard's privately noted opinion: "very good and well acted"; [89] one even went so far as to call the work the best entertainment ever produced by the Gallery of Illustration. Some, like the *Graphic*, wondered if perhaps the humor was "a little too ingenious and subtle for general audiences," but usually agreed "it is the triumph of Mr. Gilbert's art . . . that while it furnishes plenty of significance only to be enjoyed by the few, it has abundance of fun which all can appreciate." The *Graphic*'s reviewer unconsciously removed himself from the discerning few by supposing that most of the play might be taken as the Author's dream.

Little mention is made of German Reed's music,[90] although Gilbert had given him his most dextrous set of lyrics to date, including an autobiographical, an occupational, and a "torments" song, to say nothing of a preliminary version of the Grand Inquisitor's "I stole the Prince." The parodistic prose dialogue is scarcely distinguishable in quality from that of the Savoy libretti. Its deliberately stylized formality is interrupted by

---

[89] Diary entry for January 30, 1870, in *The Life and Reminiscences of E. L. Blanchard, with Notes from the Diary of Wm. Blanchard,* ed. Clement Scott and Cecil Howard (London: Hutchinson and Co., 1891), II, 393.

Contrariwise, *Fun*'s reviewer, while praising Gilbert's work, denigrated his cast. Admitting that Mrs. Reed played her part "capitally," *Fun* dismissed her husband as "exhibit[ing] his usual fund of gymnastic comicality" and remarked acidly that "in a company which devotes itself entirely to singing as an attraction, and which presents to the beholder but faint and amateurish specimens of acting, the most brilliant writer is apt to run a little slow." (July 8, 1871.) But even this reviewer was forced to admit that *A Sensation Novel* contained "some of the author's best specimens." Perhaps the fact that he saw a matinee accounts for some of the deficiencies.

[90] *A Sensation Novel* was later reset by "Florian Pascal."

the irrepressible songs or is elaborated into prose cadenzas of mad syllogisms. This is also true of *Happy Arcadia*, Gilbert's next German Reed work, and, with *A Sensation Novel*, the high point of his Gallery of Illustration career.

Happy Arcadia was not produced until October 28, 1872. In the meantime Gilbert had collaborated with Sullivan on *Thespis*, staged as the Gaiety Christmas attraction of 1871. John Toole, the leading comedian, gagged Gilbert's lines into inanity; but even so *Thespis* was an artistic regression for Gilbert rather than a step forward. Its mythological travesty had already been amply exploited in the works of Planché and of Meilhac and Halévy. The topsy-turvy plot of Olympian gods and goddesses being replaced by a theatrical troupe was stated but scarcely developed. Apart from the technical perfection of his metrics, Gilbert had presented Sullivan with the sort of burlesque which Burnand might have risen to. Judging from some of the reviewers' comments on his music, Sullivan must not have exceeded the level of *Cox and Box* — excellent, though limited in effects.[91]

Happy Arcadia, on the other hand, sparkled; in reviewing it, the *Athenaeum* compared the Gallery of Illustration to the *Bouffes Parisiens*, without, of course, the *Bouffes'* "coarseness." *Happy Arcadia* is a lozenge plot, and Gilbert's manipulation of identity in it is a more sophisticated and extended treatment of the compulsion motif as it appeared in *Creatures of Impulse* (then being revived at the Court Theatre) and of the body-soul exchange in *The Gentleman in Black*.[92] The plot is reminiscent of the folk tale "The Three Wishes"; and the satire is very clearly directed against human nature itself.

In an idyllic landscape we are introduced to the usual German Reed quartet: Daphne, a middle-aged Arcadian; Colin, her husband; Chloe, their daughter; Strephon, her suitor. All four loathe the tiresomely happy life they cannot choose but lead in Arcadia, yet when Lycidas, the hand-

---

[91] The score was never published, but Sullivan re-used it in later operas. Only one number, however, can be identified: "Climbing over rocky mountain," the words and music of which were incorporated into *The Pirates of Penzance*. One reviewer of *Thespis* accused Sullivan of merely adapting tunes from French light opera.

[92] Gilbert's work for *Fun* was full of changed identities or alteration of persona. "The Phantom Head," a Bab Ballad published in the issue of December 19, 1868, tells how a clergyman, his clerk, and a doctor exchanged their own noble countenances for the heads of three brothers "beheaded, through / The wicked Second James." The result is that parishoners and patients shun them. This set of verses is only one of many which made their grotesque family way through the periodical.

somest man in the world, comes to court Chloe, they insincerely praise its delights. A departing "blighted bogy" leaves magic articles (cap, cloak, box, ring), each of which will grant its owner one wish. With these objects in their possession the Arcadians find themselves suddenly exchanging identities because of unguardedly or unintentionally expressed desires. Daphne becomes Strephon; Strephon becomes Chloe; Chloe becomes Colin; and Colin becomes Daphne. Each member of the company thus had to play two roles, a duality shown only in lines, mannerisms, and props, not in person or costume; in fact the comedy arose from the simultaneous duality of a personality at odds with its body. Mrs. Reed, for example, as Colin-turned-Daphne was called on to stride about brusquely and to smoke a pipe, while as Strephon-turned-Chloe, Fanny Holland entered shadow-boxing, and so on, with perhaps the widest dichotomy that between the grizzled appearance of Colin and the girlish behavior of Chloe inhabiting his body. Here is a kind of psychological transvestism instead of the physical transvestism still dominating the mid-Victorian musical stage.[93]

The comedy of scrambled persons had appeared more rudimentarily in *Creatures of Impulse*, where the circumstances of the initiating device are the same: a supernatural being lodging with, but not paying, one of the characters. In the earlier play this is an old lady, really a Perrault kind of fairy; in *Happy Arcadia* it is Astrologos, the bogy.[94] The five characters of *Creatures of Impulse* try to force the old tenant to leave her room: the landlady by pushing; her super-shy niece by kissing and coaxing; a miser by bribery; the niece's cowardly suitor by bluster. The fifth, a brave soldier, ducks to avoid a blow of the old lady's crutch. The fairy compels each to repeat his or her atypical behavior to everyone; and each is miserable, ashamed, indignant, or terrified at acting so contrariwise. Perhaps the funniest is the miser in agonies of outraged penuriousness pressing gold pieces on everyone. Here Gilbert used only simple rever-

---

[93] Even in *Thespis*, Mercury was played by Nellie Farren, a "quicksilver" soubrette in tights. Hans in *The Gentleman in Black* was also a woman's role, but Gilbert did not capitalize on its possibilities for comedy.

[94] An exploding bogy with a lozenge appears twenty years later in *The Mountebanks*, on which Gilbert collaborated with Cellier. Here it is an old Alchemist who habitually blows "himself up with dynamite in his researches after the Philosopher's Stone." When the Alchemist finally explodes, he leaves behind a bottle of medicine which *"has the effect of making every one who drinks it exactly what he pretends to be."* This magic liquid is infused into the wine drunk by all the dramatis personae, as the love philtre is in the communal teapot of *The Sorcerer*.

sal, whereas in *Happy Arcadia* identities as well as ruling passions were shuffled.

In the dichotomy of body and soul — or personality, for Gilbert does not speak of the soul in *Happy Arcadia* — the German Reed play owes something to *The Gentleman in Black*, with its diabolic agent who orders:

> Otto's body, grim and droll,
> Shrine young Hans's simple soul;
> Otto's soul, of moral shoddy,
> Occupy young Hans's body!

That Baron Otto is ugly, wicked, and middle-aged, and Hans young, good-natured, and virtuous, presented the actors with some exercise in differentiation; but the exchange is most worked out in terms of who will partner the formidable Baronness and who the pretty sweetheart of Hans. *Happy Arcadia,* by comparison, is almost entirely free of love intrigues. There is a nominal romantic triangle of Strephon, Chloe, and Lycidas, but the latter is off stage while the other two change identities. The comedy which might have arisen from Corney Grain hugging Alfred Reed *in loco Fanny Holland* was not really Gilbert's sort — nor the Gallery's either, even though the feminine principal boys of pantomime and extravaganza embraced unreprovedly their feminine principal girls.[95] Lycidas is not so much amorous as functional: his advent makes Strephon see Chloe as desirable, and his departure is a convenient means of sending away the magic articles.

To bring about the necessary reversion to *status quo ante* in this group of plays, Gilbert used a range of devices. *Creatures of Impulse* ends with a simple physical expedient which might have occurred at any time during its loosely plotted but repetitive action. All five characters converge simultaneously on the old fairy. Unable to cope with them all at once, she disenchants them. In *The Gentleman in Black*, Gilbert again circumvents one of his letter-of-the-contract agreements, this time by an acceleration of date achieved through the adoption of the Gregorian calendar, a time juggle analogous to those of *Our Island Home* and *The Pirates of Penzance*. The solution of *Happy Arcadia* is simple but legalistic. The four characters interchange the four magic objects, consequently acquiring a new wish apiece with which to free themselves. This pattern recalls but shortens that of "The Three Wishes" and related

---

[95] Gilbert did admit transvestism in several of his own burlesques and early comedies; but at the Savoy he was loudly and notoriously against it.

folktales: that is, an old couple having been granted three wishes, the wife thoughtlessly uses the first for sausages; her exasperated husband wishes they were on the end of her nose; then he has to use the third wish to get them off again.

In *Happy Arcadia* a further exchange of articles might give the characters another opportunity for wishing more wisely, but Gilbert does not raise this possibility. Human beings, as he depicts them here — and as farce must have them — are scarcely capable of making right choices. Other satiric themes developed in this work are by now familiar. The young lovers are almost as loudly dissatisfied with each other as were Herbert and Alice in *A Sensation Novel*. Chloe is a typically Gilbertian girl with an eye to the main chance. Indeed, all the Arcadians desire money ardently even while admitting its uselessness. Colin's desire to become a woman in order to conduct a life of unpunished crime juxtaposes the realistic picture of practical, selfish woman with the sentimental stereotype of innocent weak femininity, a contradiction already explored in Mrs. Reed's role in *Our Island Home*.

The most thoroughgoing satire in *Happy Arcadia*, however, is directed against man's fallacious definition of the good life, in which he praises innocuity while prefering excitement, and exalts simple rustic delights while enjoying artificial city pleasures — a kind of universal sentimental hypocrisy. In fact, happy Arcadia is Gilbert's equivalent of Dr. Johnson's Happy Valley or Voltaire's Eldorado.

This satiric point of view was strongly criticized. Admitting that "There is a good deal of smart writing in the piece," the *Graphic*'s reviewer found it excessively cynical and consequently painful; ". . . for surely the conclusion, that most men find pure and innocent pleasures insipid is not calculated to produce cheerfulness." The *Graphic* preferred "fun of a heartier, wholesomer quality, the humour of which is not invariably steeped in gallic acid." [96] Its critic apparently recognized the resemblance to Offenbach's *Orphée aux Enfers* with its gods who, rebelling against nectar, ambrosia, and heavenly decorum, go to hell for a good time.

Gilbert's depiction of the monotony of simple pleasure which so discomfitted the *Graphic* reappeared in *The Wicked World*, which reviewers also found "cynical"; in *The Happy Land*, Gilbert's own travesty of *The Wicked World*; and in *Patience*, where the Duke of

---

[96] *Graphic*, VI (November 2, 1872), 409. Less touchy reviewers found *Happy Arcadia* pleasant and Gilbert's "usual happy satirical hits, as subtle as they are refined." (Unidentified clipping in the Enthoven Theatre Collection.)

Dunstable compares his weariness of adulation to the nausea of eating toffee incessantly. The fickle Defendant of *Trial by Jury* appeals to natural principles ("The moon in her phases is found") and to inherent human variability ("You cannot eat breakfast all day"). Putting this into general terms — that change is the condition of human life — we arrive at a proto-Bergsonian outlook which led Gilbert to conclusions almost diametrically opposed to those of George Bernard Shaw. Shaw, pursuing Bergson's Life Force, was a revolutionary satirist, welcoming the bombs of *Heartbreak House* so that a new and better society might arise. Gilbert, on the other hand, depicting imperfection, dissatisfaction, and inconsistency as inherent in human nature, saw no persuasive reason for any radical alteration of society, since any social framework must be filled by absurd mankind. At times in his serious plays and in moments of his comedies, Gilbert made a Dickensian protest against contemporary inhumanities, and one of his favourite targets was certainly bourgeois materialism, which he did not see limited to the bourgeoisie. But more fundamentally he satirized man's lack of self-knowledge. Hence, while Shaw prefers to attack human institutions, Gilbert more often exposes human nature. In Gilbert's most Shavian play, *Utopia Limited*, the insufficiency of Elysium mooted in *Happy Arcadia* and its cluster of early plays becomes crucial. Anglicized Utopia, "swamped by dull Prosperity," has to be saved from its success by introducing the incompetence and dishonesty of the two-party political system as practiced in England.

Besides these important thematic parallels, *Happy Arcadia* made even more suggestions for the Savoy than had any of its four predecessors: the Watteau-ism of *Iolanthe*; the infant betrothal of *Princess Ida*; and the cosmetically camouflaged contralto of *Patience*. There are passing verbal likenesses to *Ruddigore*, *Pinafore*, *The Mikado*, and *The Gondoliers*, while the first line of Lycidas' solo "Far away from care and strife" is an echo of "Far away from toil and care" from *Thespis*, later transferred to Kate in *The Pirates of Penzance*. The situations in which all three are sung are roughly comparable. Another *Thespis* lyric, Mercury's "Celestial Drudge" solo, seems to have suggested Colin's "Only a Woman," with its double standard of responsibility.

More important than these is the "Identity Quartette" which is a link between "You're Diana, I'm Apollo" (*Thespis*) and "Here is a case unprecedented" and "In a contemplative fashion" (*The Gondoliers*), to say nothing of "If Saphir I choose to marry" (*Patience*). In this group of songs Gilbert postulates, elaborates, and works through the logical alternatives of an emotional situation to which one would suppose logic inapplicable or inappropriate. What might be called the comedy of thoroughness[97] also appears in Lycidas' running request for all necessities of the immediate situation. For example:

> I will be a simple shepherd and come and
> live with you. Oblige me with the address
> of a house agent, a field, a fold, a flock of
> sheep and a list of local charities.
>
> . . . .
>
> Then I have a rival! His name and those
> of his physician, family undertaker and
> monumental mason!

No doubt Corney Grain's gentle, deliberate demeanor contrasted amusingly with the verbal verve of these demands.

The music for *Happy Arcadia* was composed by Frederic Clay in his last collaboration with Gilbert. Reviewers called his tunes pleasant, but did not repeat the enthusiastic praise given to *Ages Ago*. The cast was notable for the absence of German Reed, just retired and permanently replaced by his son. Gilbert therefore lost some of the comic advantage of having Colin and Daphne played by husband and wife. To compensate, Alfred Reed was a much better comedian than his father, although German Reed, "who never was, never is, and never will be, like anybody but Mr. German Reed,"[98] must have given authenticity to his role in *Our Island Home* and piquancy to *A Sensation Novel*. Some years later when Alfred Reed and Corney Grain were managing the Gallery of Illustration in partnership, they revived both *Happy Arcadia* and *A Sensation Novel*. After their deaths in 1895 Rutland Barrington played Strephon in an unsuccessful attempt to keep the Gallery going.

Not for three years after *Happy Arcadia* did Gilbert write again for the German Reeds, and then *Eyes and No Eyes*, which opened on July 5, 1875, was his last work for them. The Entertainment itself was in a state of transition, having moved from Regent Street to St. George's Hall. The elder Reeds were increasingly inactive, although Mr. Reed

---

[97] See also Gilbert's short story, "The Burglar's Story," with its rundown of the burglar's training for his career, amusingly couched in the commonplace terms of any preparation for a "City" career. Colin resembles the burglar in his systematic presentation of having been "taught from my infancy to look upon fraud and dishonesty as the legitimate means of earning a dishonorable competency!"

[98] A review of Arthur Sketchley's *Near Relations*, in *Fun*, XIV (August 26, 1871), 85. *Fun*'s reviewer was probably too hard on Mr. Reed; others found him competent, some fairly good, and the *Tomahawk*, excellent.

arranged the music for Gilbert's last work as he had done for his first.[99]
Mrs. Reed was approaching retirement; Arthur Cecil had left for a
wider stage; but Leonora Braham, who later created Patience and Yum-
Yum, had joined the company. Gilbert still had the imposing comic
talents of Alfred Reed and Corney Grain to write for, but they did not
stimulate him to logical lunacy in 1875. *Eyes and No Eyes; or, The Art
of Seeing* is vivacious but somewhat mechanical: the work of a dramatist refining his achievement rather than extending his range.

Avowedly based on Hans Christian Andersen's tale of "The Emperor's
New Clothes," this was Gilbert's only German Reed piece without some
sort of impersonation. There is no lozenge, but there is pretense and
pretension, and consequently a satiric view of human nature. The
dramatis personae include names drawn from *commedia dell'arte* and
its English descendant, Christmas pantomime, but without the typical
characteristics or relationships of either. Pierrot and Arlequin, twin
brothers, love Clochette and Columbine, whose uncle Cassandre loves
Nicolette, an elderly coquette.[100] The plot is merely a twofold elaboration of a practical joke in which the girls pretend they have a cloak
visible only to true lovers (or false lovers depending on the circumstances). The action is simpler than any since *No Cards*. There is
scarcely any parody of melodrama except for Nicolette's *scena*: "Yes,
yes, I am that miserable Beauty, / Whose lot it is to wither hearts and
homes," reminiscent of Rockalda's "fiend" song in *A Sensation Novel*.
Nicolette's appearance, like Katisha's, is the occasion for a great deal of
double-meaning dialogue.[101] Consequently, *Eyes and No Eyes* has more
repartee and pertness than its predecessors. The dialogue is sharper, less
extravagant, and less given to long speeches, except for an occasional
prose "aria" such as Cassandre's explanation of how he taught himself
to love Nicolette. His comic process (first isolating each of Nicolette's
traits and then working on loving each, *seriatim*) recalls Churchmouse's
project for conditioning servants and looks forward to Katisha and to
Ko-Ko's plan of learning execution by degrees.

The device is additionally amusing because it makes presumably spon-

---

[99] This was later reset by "Florian Pascal."

[100] The names of all of Gilbert's characters except Clochette had appeared in
Planché's *Love and Fortune* (1859), a "Watteau colour" which combines elements
of *Le Bourgeois Gentilhomme* and *La Ceinture de Vénus*. There is no other
resemblance to Gilbert's work except that Cassandre is also a middle-aged lover.

[101] Like Katisha, too, Nicolette is an "acquired taste"; and she suggests wearing
a false nose to disguise her beauty as Josephine was to do years later in Gilbert's
retelling of the story of *H.M.S. Pinafore* for children.

taneous emotion into a calculated procedure. In this reversal of normal reaction, it resembles the group of analytic songs discussed in connection with *Happy Arcadia*. Arlequin and Pierrot, too, are cool where they should be warm, disclaiming any preference as to brides, "Only — we should like one apiece." They resemble Marco and Giuseppe Palmieri who "really do not care / A preference to declare." Both pairs of brothers are further alike in their linked-arm stance, copied from an earlier Gilbert drawing;[102] their sometimes simultaneous speech; and their questions of identity, necessary to the plot of *Gondoliers*, but artificially spun out for a trio in *Eyes and No Eyes*. The emphasis on physical connectedness suggests that Arlequin and Pierrot may be travestying the Corsican Brothers' mystic sympathy.[103]

Arlequin and Pierrot's reformation (they give up flirting) is carried over from the original short-story version of *The Wicked World*, in which Prince Snob stands in a corner for fifteen minutes and reforms himself. The brothers take half an hour. The absurdity of a quarter-hour reformation is a reversal of the comic spun-out process, for here we have an instantaneous change which would ordinarily take long and subtle psychological modifications: a credulity of melodrama but not used melodramatically in this work.

Nicolette's propriety prepares us for Lady Sophy's in *Utopia Limited* and fits into Gilbert's recurrent satire of decorum and false delicacy. For the most part, *Eyes and No Eyes*, like Andersen's tale, takes hypocrisy for its target, but here it is the mild hypocrisy of flirtatious sweethearts wanting to seem true. In fact, the theme is handled more gently in this play than in Andersen or in the fairy comedies which Gilbert had been staging at the Haymarket.

The lyrics of *Eyes and No Eyes* include workmanlike versions of several typical Gilbert songs: the autobiographical; the self-revelatory; and the identity song developed through questions or logical propositions. More important, Gilbert used a serious song for the first time in his German Reed work. ". . . I am, at my life's beginning, / A thread in the hands of Fate." This rather subdued note of Clochette's spinning song opens the performance, as Phoebe's pensive "heigho" to her wheel begins *The Yeomen of the Guard*. Clochette's song initiates the series

---

[102] For *An Algerian Monkey versus British Apes. A Satirical, Political, Poetical Squib.* By "*The Spectre*" (London: Chapman and Hall, 1864).

[103] Cf. Gilbert's "A. and B.; or, The Sensation Twins," a Bab Ballad published in *Fun*, November 2, 1867. The telepathic communication between the twin heroes of Boucicault's sensation drama, *The Corsican Brothers*, was frequently burlesqued on the mid-Victorian stage.

of solos and concerted numbers which, in the Savoy operas, speculate more wistfully than logically; among them, "Comes a train of little ladies" (*Mikado*) and "Try we lifelong" (*Gondoliers*).

Eyes and No Eyes, opening in the dead of summer, seems to have attracted little press notice. The *Graphic* for July 10, 1875, found it "eminently amusing"; but the *Athenaeum* of the same date grumbled because the play was not a fairy spectacle, and said, with some justice, that the plot was not treated in Gilbert's happiest vein. That happiest vein was flowing elsewhere. Four months before *Eyes and No Eyes* was produced at St. George's Hall, *Trial by Jury* reached the stage of the Opera Comique. The German Reed renaissance was over; the era of Gilbert and Sullivan had begun.

One cannot say that the German Reeds were essential to the form and success of the Savoy Operas, for at the turn of the seventies Gilbert's other work was already giving him the reputation of an innovator and reformer. But the Gallery of Illustration provided an ideal laboratory for his experiments by approximating most closely the future conditions of the Savoy. In other works written concurrently with those for the Gallery, he had also begun to develop elements of that particular style of intellectual comedy we call Gilbertian, but with the Reeds he could concentrate on wholes. When he left them he took with him both the Lozenge Plot and a dramatic conception of psychological Topsyturvydom, two of the three leading structural elements in his form of comic opera. The third, whose development comes from the early Gilbert burlesques, from *Thespis*, and more subtly from the fairy comedies, may be called the Invasion Plot. Here alternate and opposing groups penetrate each other's territory, the antagonism or juxtaposition serving both to organize the plot and to enhance the comedy. In *Thespis*, actors "invade" the realm of the Olympian gods, who, in turn, descend to the world of mortals; in *Iolanthe*, first the Peers penetrate a fairy glade and then the Fairies "invade" Westminster; in *The Pirates of Penzance* the girls enter the "pirates' lair" and the Pirates in turn come to burglarize the young ladies' pseudo-ancestral mansion. Clearly, a chorus is almost the *sine qua non* of an Invasion Plot, and at the Gallery of Illustration Gilbert did not have a chorus. At this stage of his career, the deficiency was all to the good.

The absence of chorus and therefore of spectacle; the smallness of cast, limitation of scenes, and shortness of playing time made him emphasize tight plotting and made his comic devices more compact and more dramatic. Early reviewers of Gilbert's non-musical plays sometimes complained that an amusing two-act comedy was let sag into three. Writing for the Reeds made his naturally strong feeling for form more conscious and sharpened it, even though he still might be tempted to overwork a joke. He also learned how to make musical numbers an integral part of a swift farce rather than an interruptive embellishment. Lacking a chorus, Gilbert's German Reed pieces escape the padding which a number of unemployed villagers generally gave most light operas. His burlesques of the late sixties had used their choruses efficiently but conventionally; his musical plays of the early seventies advanced metrically but not in construction. To these the chorus-less German Reed pieces were a strong counterbalance. When Gilbert returned to a chorus with Sullivan, he used it Aristophanically as a composite character, not as musical filler.

The Reeds' tight-knit repertory company was a prototype of that which Gilbert and Sullivan later selected and trained. Once again, the limitations in size of cast tightened form, while the marked and equally pre-eminent personalities of the small troupe gave the dramatist experience in the later crosscurrents and interplay of adjusting Rutland Barrington's talents to those of George Grossmith or Jessie Bond. The Reeds' habits of impersonation were especially congenial to Gilbert's kind of mind. They led him to subtler versions of the Lozenge Plot and of the transformation scenes of conventional pantomime as well as to the plurality of Pooh-Bah. The mental demands which the multiple identities of *Our Island Home, A Sensation Novel*, and *Happy Arcadia* made on audiences exceed those of any other early Gilbert works, not excluding the fairy plays. In fact, it would not be too much to say that *A Sensation Novel* is a more complex work in its treatment of levels of reality than anything at the Savoy.

But the Gallery's most important contribution to individual character drawing was Mrs. Reed's. She set the pattern for Gilbert and Sullivan contraltos far more than did Mrs. Howard Paul, who actually created the first of them in *The Sorcerer*. Middle-aged women on the Victorian light musical stage were usually ludicrous harridans impersonated by male low-comedians, a tradition which still survives in the pantomime "dame." The parts Gilbert wrote for Mrs. German Reed bear some resemblance to these dames, but their comedy never descends to pointless slapstick and derisive insult. If her "assumptions" were sometimes marked by shrewishness, groundless vanity, a heavy use of cosmetics, they also had independence, forcefulness, ingenuity, and even a frosty attractiveness. They were, in short, star roles for a middle-aged soubrette.[104] Mrs. Reed is thus the ancestress of the indomitable Savoy contraltos; and with her Gilbert first worked out one of the principles for the creation of Katisha, his greatest comic female figure. To see what such roles might have been without Priscilla Reed's influence, we need only look at the cold, uninteresting Lady Blanche in *Princess Ida*, drawn from Gilbert's earlier burlesque of Tennyson and completely undistinguished.

The respectability of the Gallery encouraged Gilbert in his protest against what *Punch* called "leg-itimate successes." In the final lines of *The Pretty Druidess* he had asked his audience to overlook stale jokes and puns, scanty apparel and meaningless dances, all of which were *de rigueur* in burlesque; but he did not have to apologize at the Gallery of Illustration. Instead, he could concentrate on "those whimsical conceits and ingenious paradoxes which characterize Mr. Gilbert's entertainments."[105]

Isaac Goldberg describes Gilbert among the Reeds as a dramatist walking gingerly upon eggs while he adapts his burlesques to the special requirements of a new public.[106] But there is no reason to suppose that Gilbert was repressing his own sense of comedy. His "entertainments" display not caution, but agility. Much more than such burlesques as *The Merry Zingara* and *La Vivandière*, the German Reed pieces fit their author's later assertion that "all humour, properly so called, is based upon a grave and quasi-respectful treatment of the ridiculous and absurd."[107] This is the style, certainly, of *Happy Arcadia* and *Iolanthe*, but it is exactly opposite that of mid-century burlesque, which was a ridiculous treatment of the grave and respectful.

It is true, nevertheless, that any Victorian dramatist, no matter what theatre he wrote for, was hampered by the concept of comedy held by most reviewers and presumably by most audiences: "in the true spirit

---

[104] It is not my purpose here to discuss the widely held but mistaken view that Gilbert was unusually — even abnormally — cruel in depicting middle-aged women. A look at his contemporaries will show that he was atypical in his treatment of this sort of stock character only by being more witty and less grotesque.

[105] *Graphic*, IV (August 19, 1871), 179. This statement occurs in a review of Arthur Sketchley's *Near Relations*, which the *Graphic* found decidedly inferior to Gilbert's works.

[106] Goldberg, *The Story of Gilbert and Sullivan*, p. 109. Goldberg points out the advantage Gilbert had in not being tied to precomposed tunes and extant plots and that he now had to fit manner and matter to specific actors.

[107] Quoted in Percy Fitzgerald, *The Savoy Opera and the Savoyards* (London: Chatto and Windus, 1894), p. 14 n.

of comedy . . . sarcasm and humour are perfectly harmless." [108] Gilbert, whose sarcasm was intended to be nocuous, early recognized the necessity of gilding the philosophic pill; and in his German Reed pieces and "cynical" fairy comedies he was discovering how he could make light opera a criticism of life. This was at its best when the *données* of his work were essentially English, as at the Reeds, even though the scene might be an Indian Isle, Arcadia, Japan, or Barataria. After the great days of Gilbert and Sullivan, Rutland Barrington suggested that the Savoy Operas' decline was in part owing to their ceasing to be "English." Chauvinism aside, it is quite true that when Gilbert went to those European hinterlands so common in light opera, he was not at home as he was at Portsmouth or in anglicized Titipus and Fairylands.

Finally, the Reeds gave Gilbert another stage in the long series of varied embodiments through which he passed details of his work. He was pre-eminently a polisher, a perfector. From first to last, through forty years of creative life, his satiric vision scarcely altered; but he had endless patience and ingenuity in combining, reworking, and improving his statements of what he saw. Plots, characters, situations, denouements, songs, paradoxes, repartee, phrases even, are carried over from Bab Ballad or short story to German Reed Entertainment to fairy comedy to prose comedy to Savoy libretto, where they finally appear with what seems to be spontaneous inevitability. This long evolution helps to account both for the high quality of Gilbert's best work and for his relatively small output compared to the prodigiously prolific Burnand, Byron, and Blanchard, who often repeated themselves but rarely listened critically to what they had said.

For some elements in his Entertainments, Gilbert was indebted to mid-Victorian stage conditions generally rather than to the peculiar nature of the Gallery itself: the prevailing emphasis on parody, word play, and melodrama; the time-honored combining of music and magic; the official censorship often extended idiosyncratically beyond the social censorship exerted by the public. But in his German Reed Entertainments, Gilbert practiced transcending and circumventing these. In a company which had no villain [109] he could satirize the principles of melodrama as well as parody its behavior. His word play could be more inventive when prose dialogue removed the need for puns to force a

---

[108] "The Theatre," *Dark Blue*, IV (December, 1872), 508. The statement appears in a commendatory review of H. J. Byron's current burlesque.

[109] Arthur Cecil stops being a villain when Captain Bang appears, and the whole point of the "villain" in *A Sensation Novel* is that he isn't one.

couplet rhyme. On a stage *sans* trapdoors and pantomime machinery, his magic depended on sparkling wit rather than on the sudden proliferation of gold leaf.

To sum up their contribution to Gilbertianism, the German Reeds made it profitable — aesthetically and financially — for Gilbert to take the high road of comedy down which he preferred to go; and his works for them showed him a bright image of what he was to find there.

The Plays

No Cards

A MUSICAL PIECE IN ONE ACT

for four characters

Characters

MISS ANNABELLA PENROSE————*An heiress, Niece of* MRS. PENNYTHORNE.

MRS. PENNYTHORNE ——————*A lady of considerable matrimonial experiences, with strong opinions and convictions on "Woman's Rights."*

MR. ELLIS DEE ——————————*A wealthy old bachelor.*

MR. CHURCHMOUSE ——————*A poor young bachelor.*

SCENE: *Interior of* MRS. PENNYTHORNE's *boudoir.*
MRS. PENNYTHORNE *discovered at table, working.* MISS ANNA-
BELLA *at piano.*

MRS. P. My dear Annabella, I've lived much longer in the world than you have. I've seen a great deal more of it. And believe an experienced old woman when she says, that for one unhappy marriage there are at least a hundred happy ones. It's the fast fashion of the day, my dear, to sneer at married life; and fast fashions are always wrong in principle. When people ridicule the idea of marriage they forget how much they owe to that institution. No girl who places any value upon her existence should turn up her nose at the institution to which she is indebted for it.

MISS P. No, Aunt, I don't sneer at marriage in the abstract. I sneer at marriage with an old bachelor like Mr. Ellis Dee.

MRS. P. Bachelor! Why, what in the world does a girl want to marry but a bachelor?

MISS P. I said an *old* bachelor, Aunt.

MRS. P. Old? A boy! Fifty at the very outside. But rich as he is, I don't press Mr. Ellis Dee upon you. Marry whomsoever you like (so that you do like him), but for goodness sake marry someone. That's my advice to everybody — marry someone.

MISS P. Do you know, Aunt, I often wonder how it is that you, whose personal experiences of married life have certainly not been fortunate, should nevertheless be so enthusiastic a matchmaker. You say that ninety-nine marriages out of a hundred turn out happily, but certainly in your case —

MRS. P. My dear, mine was the hundredth. Somebody's marriage must be the hundredth. Bless me, if I'm run over by a Pickford's van in Fleet Street, is that any reason why you should never go east of Charing Cross? Nonsense. My marriage was a miserable one — well, my misfortunes have made me more keenly alive to the happiness I should have enjoyed if I'd married anybody else. Mr. Coodle was a bad man — a thorough scamp, my dear. He ran away with all my money three weeks after we were married, and for twenty years I have neither seen nor heard anything of him, so I resumed my maiden name and washed my hands of him for ever.

Miss P. It was too bad of Aunt Salamanca to make such a man my guardian. I can't marry without his consent, and as he hasn't called for twenty years, I suppose I shall have to remain single all my life.

Mrs. P. Single? With £25,000? Nonsense. Why all we have to do is to tell the Lord Chancellor that Mr. Coodle, your guardian, is a bad character who has run away, and his Lordship will adopt you on the spot. That what he's paid for. But why do you object to Mr. Dee? He's a very wealthy man.

Miss P. But he is so old and so dreadfully rich, and such a terrible story-teller. It's impossible to believe a word he says. I don't pretend to be a Scotland Yard detective, but then, on the other hand, I'm not the Royal Regiment of Marines.

Mrs. P. Well, there's Mr. Churchmouse. He doesn't tell stories, and he is poor enough in all conscience.

Miss P. But he is so dreadfully shy, Aunt. He couldn't be more nervous in speaking to me if I were both Houses of Parliament rolled into one. I have my faults, but I'm not the House of Commons!

Mrs. P. But that will all wear off. Look at him when he plays in amateur performances — he's as self-possessed as possible then.

Miss P. Yes — it's very curious — I don't know how it is, but whenever he is dressed for a part, his shyness seems to vanish immediately.

Mrs. P. My dear, all that is attributable to an unnecessarily keen sense of his own personal defects. Mr. Churchmouse is so ashamed of Mr. Churchmouse, that he is delighted to appear as anybody else. It's a very good sign in a young man, my dear, and I only wish it were more common.

No. 1. — SONG. — Mrs. Pennythorne.

I

A great deal of experience in life I've had,
Remember, when you come across a bashful lad,
He's a rarity, so cultivate him, if you can,
I've a very high opinion of a shy young man:
A timid, and a bashful, and a shy young man —
A nervous, and an awkward, and a shy young man,
In lacking all precocity, a moral curiosity,
I'm very much in favour of a shy young man.

II

The regulation gentry at a croquet-crush
Are people who have never yet been known to blush,
I'll undertake to wager you that nine in ten
Are over-dressed, opinionated, vain young men —
Such very, very, very, very vain young men,
Such singularly silly and inane young men,
And, spite of all their vanity and simpering inanity,
Such very, very, very, very plain young men!

III

But beauty doesn't matter in a man — that's true —
When an eligible gentleman addresses you,
His type of physiognomy you need not scan,
Should he chance to be a modest and urbane young man,
A gentlemanly, sensible, urbane young man,
A quick and unquestionably sane young man —
No matter an economy of pretty physiognomy.
But marry that particularly plain young man!

(*After Song, exit* Mrs. P.)

(*Enter* Mr. Ellis Dee.)

(*He believes that* Annabella *has been singing.*)

Dee. Bravo! Bravo! Very charming indeed! Miss Penrose, your fresh young voice is in splendid condition to-day, isn't it, Mrs. Pennythorne? Come, encore! No? Well, well, perhaps not. It don't do to over exert the voice, Miss Penrose. Talking of encores, I remember hearing the famous Russian singer, Mdlle. Shrieka, at the Scala many years ago. Enormous sensation she made. Encored in "Robert toi que j'aime" fifty-seven times in one performance. It lasted two days and three nights. The band were carried out, one by one, as they dropped from their stools, until no one was left but the triangle, who held out like a man. She married him, ma'am. He founded the celebrated Euclid concerts.

Miss P. Euclid concerts?

Dee. Yes — nothing but triangles. Very popular in the provinces, especially with three-cornered constituencies. (*Looking off.*) Hullo! Who's this?

Miss P. Oh — that's Mr. Churchmouse.

DEE. Confound Mr. Churchmouse. He's always here.

MISS P. Yes. We are getting up some private theatricals, and Mr. Churchmouse is assisting us.

DEE. What! Churchmouse an actor! Ho! ho! ho!

MISS P. Oh, you may laugh, but I assure you that with all his timidity and nervousness he's a very capital actor. Here he is.

(*Enter* MR. CHURCHMOUSE.)

CH. Good morning, Miss Penrose. How-de-do to-day? Quite well? Thank you, yes, I'm quite well, I'm much obliged to you. Yes, I'm wonderfully well for me, Miss Penrose. How-de-do, Mr. Dee?

DEE. I hope you're well, Sir — I hope you're well.

CH. Well, no. I am so plagued with this terrible tooth of mine. I haven't had a wink of sleep this week. Oh, Miss Penrose, I have such a toothache!

MISS P. A toothache, Mr. Churchmouse? Why you said you were so well!

CH. Quite well, thank you, Miss Penrose. It's a chilly day, isn't it?

DEE. Chilly, Sir? No, Sir, I call it warm — decidedly warm.

CH. Well, it is warm — in the shade. Dreadfully warm. Gardening, Miss Penrose?

MISS P. Yes, Mr. Churchmouse, I'm planting double stocks.

DEE. Ah, Miss Penrose, I often wish I was a double stock.

MISS P. Indeed! Why?

DEE. (*tenderly*). To be born double instead of having to achieve doubleness — especially if one might choose one's partner beforehand.

CH. Like the Siamese twins?

DEE. (*angrily*). No, Sir! — not at all like the Siamese twins. I am referring, Sir, to marriage. I wish I was born married, that's what I mean.

CH. So do I, Sir. Don't you, Miss Penrose?

MISS P. Don't I what?

CH.   Don't you wish Mr. Dee had been born married?

DEE.   Sir!

CH.   Such an economy, Miss Penrose. One breakfast for the marriage and the christening — one announcement in the *Times* for both events. Something like this: "On the 1st of April, 1780, Mrs. Dee" — that's your mamma, you know — "of a son; at St. Pancras Church, to Julia, only daughter of Theophilus Brown, of Nova Scotia. No cards."

MISS P.   There would be one advantage attached to being born married, there would be no occasion for any guardians. Now I have a guardian who hasn't been heard of for twenty years, and I can't possibly marry without his consent.

DEE.   And is it possible, Miss Penrose, that the disposal of such a prize is in the hands of a man who hasn't been heard of for twenty years? His name, ma'am, his name?

MISS P.   Oh, he is Mrs. Pennythorne's husband.

DEE.   Mrs. Pennythorne's husband? I pledge myself to discover Pennythorne within the next two hours.

MISS P.   Oh, but his name isn't Pennythorne — it's Coodle.

CH.   Then, if you will allow me, I think I should like to undertake the discovery of Coodle.

DEE.   Nonsense, Sir — I have already undertaken —

CH.   To discover Pennythorne. You shall find Pennythorne — I will find Coodle.

MISS P.   And if a portrait of the gentleman will assist you to discover him, I think I can find you one.

(*Looks in work-basket.*)

BOTH.   A portrait! The very thing.

MISS P.   It's considered a wonderful likeness. Here it is.

(*Produces black profile.*)

CH.   Hum — ha! A negro gentleman, I presume?

MISS P.   No — only a very black character.

DEE.   But not as black as he's painted, we'll hope. Well, Miss Penrose, don't allow the matter to worry you any further. In half-an-hour Coodle —

CH. Pennythorne—

DEE. Coodle, Sir — Coodle. In half-an-hour Coodle shall be here. If I don't produce him, call me a blatant imposter.

CH. I will — I will — with pleasure.

No. 2. — TRIO. —MR. ELLIS DEE, MR. CHURCHMOUSE, MISS PENROSE.

DEE.
From this pretty bower hence
   I depart instanter.
If I don't, an hour hence,
   Beat him in a canter,
Rose, devoid of any thorn,
   Christen me a noodle.

CH.
You discover Pennythorne,
   I'll discover Coodle!

DEE.
Pooh! pooh! Pennythorne!

CH.
Coodle-oodle-oodle!

MISS P.
There's no Mr. Pennythorne,
   It's Coodle-oodle-oodle!

Ensemble (Yödel). Coodle-oodle-oodle!

SOLO. — MISS PENROSE.

How they stand asunder,
Looking black as thunder,
'Pon my word I wonder
   What their plan will be.
If you want to wive it,
Carefully contrive it,
Or you won't survive it,
   Mr. Ellis Dee.

SOLO. — MR. DEE (aside).

Listen — this is my receipt —
   Take a manner brisker,

62

Take a suit of clothes complete,
Take a wig and whisker:
Take a comic voice; of course,
Heralding a noodle,
Dish it up with any sauce,
And call it Mr. Coodle!

Ensemble.   Coodle-oodle-oodle, &c.

SOLO. — Mr. Churchmouse (*aside*).

Annabella is the goal
I would fain arrive at,
But I dare not tell a soul
(This is strictly private!).
If my artful plans succeed
Then the girl I've wooed'll
Soon be mine, and mine indeed,
Given me by Coodle.

Ensemble.   Coodle-oodle-oodle, &c.

(*At end of Trio, exit* Mr. Dee.)

Ch. Charming man, Mr. Dee.

Miss P. Do you think so? He bores me terribly.

Ch. Well, yes; he is tiresome — sometimes.

Miss P. He has a certain amount of intelligence —

Ch. Oh, he's decidedly intelligent. With all his faults, he's a very well-informed man. I should call Mr. Dee clever — decidedly clever.

Miss P. Oh, come, Mr. Churchmouse; with all your good-nature, you must admit that his conversation is terribly vapid.

Ch. Well, do you know, it is — it really is. Almost idiotic, at times.

Miss P. For a man of his age, he is not at all bad looking.

Ch. Oh, he wears well. I call Dee a handsome man — a really handsome man.

Miss P. But his unfortunate nose.

Ch. Well, his nose is ugly, and an ugly nose is fatal to a face.

Miss P. (*aside*). He don't know his own mind for a minute together.

Ch. (*overhearing and thinking she refers to* Mr. Dee). You're quite right — quite. I don't think I ever knew such a vacillating person.

(*A pause. He looks aside at piece of paper.*)

Miss P. What are you looking at, Mr. Churchmouse?

Ch. Oh, it's only my list.

Miss P. Your list?

Ch. Yes — my programme.

Miss P. Your programme?

Ch. Yes. Whenever I am going to make calls, I always prepare a list of subjects of conversation. You see, by that means I am never at a loss.

Miss P. May I look?

Ch. Oh, certainly (*hands it to her*).

Miss P. (*reads*). The return of the Jews to Palestine — Doctrines of Confucius — Manhood Suffrage — New rule for finding the parallax of fixed stars — The Talmud — Good cure for corns.

Ch. Yes, they are all subjects on which I feel very strongly — very strongly indeed. (*Confidentially.*) This, Miss Penrose, between ourselves, is the secret of my reputation as an agreeable rattle. They are the only subjects on which I may be said thoroughly to have made up my mind.

Ch. Well, good-bye, Miss Penrose, I must be off now. I wanted to see Mrs. Pennythorne about those theatricals of ours.

Miss P. Oh, Aunt will be here directly.

Ch. Ah, but I can't wait — I ought to be at the Poppletopper's, half-a-mile away by this time, and I haven't a moment to lose. Good morning, Miss Penrose.

(*Exit R.*)

(*Enter* Mrs. Pennythorne, *followed by servant.*)

Mrs. P. A strange gentleman to see me, who refuses to send in his card? How very mysterious! Wants to see me alone, too! Well, let him come —

(*Exit servant.*)

Miss P. My dear Aunt, you'll surely never admit a stranger who refuses to give any account of himself.

Mrs. P. My dear Anna, I've been married to the very worst man on the face of the earth, and after that I'm not easily terrified. I'm a poor weak defenceless woman, by law, but I'm quite equal to any man I ever met. Besides, perhaps his name's a comic name and he's ashamed of it. I'm sure, when I was Mrs. Coodle I never gave my name, except on compulsion. Ah! here he comes. A bad face, my dear. But, never mind; go away. I'm quite equal to the emergency.

(Exit Miss P.)

(Enter Mr. Dee, *disguised.)*

Mrs. P. Well, Sir; who are you, and what do you want?

Dee. (*melodramatically*). Then it is as I said, and you *don't* know me! I go!

(Going.)

Mrs. P. Bless the man, what's the matter? Know you — how should I know you?

Dee. True! How should you? Ah, ma'am. Many changes have taken place since we met!

Mrs. P. (*aside*). One change, at least!

Dee. I, ma'am, have altered a great deal for the better — you have altered a great deal for the worse. I am comparatively younger than I was — you are positively older than you were. I have risen in the world — you have not. I have grown a beard — you have not —

Mrs. P. Bless the man, be more explicit, do. Who in the world are you?

Dee. Who am I? Pardon this tear — it's a passing weakness. Who am I? To explain that I must ask you to carry your memory back nearly a quarter of a century.

Mrs. P. A quarter of a century!

Dee. Yes, ma'am. Do you think you can charge your memory with events that took place so long ago?

Mrs. P. Well, really, my memory is a very good one, but a quarter of a century is a very long while.

Dee. True. So it is, that never occurred to me. It is a long while —

you must have forgotten the circumstance to which I was going to allude. Forgive me, ma'am. I go — *(Going.)*

MRS. P. Stop, pray. What circumstance do you allude to?

DEE. A mere trifle, ma'am. Do you happen to remember a very cold January morning, nearly a quarter of a century ago, at a quarter past eleven o'clock, at St. George's, Hanover Square — you — but no — impossible. It must have escaped you. I go —

MRS. P. Now do stop — go on —

DEE. If I stop I can't go on — If I go on I can't stop. Well, ma'am, do you happen to remember that on a cold January morning, at a quarter past eleven o'clock, you were married to a gentleman named — but no! you must have forgotten it.

MRS. P. To a person named Coodle? Perfectly!

DEE. You do? Is it possible! Wonderful old lady! I was Mr. Coodle's best man!

MRS. P. Mr. Coodle was a very disgraceful character, who left me three weeks after my marriage and has been living in Australia ever since.

DEE. He was a boy, ma'am — a mere boy — don't be too hard on the imprudence of early youth.

MRS. P. He ran away from me with all my money —

DEE. He was such a creature of impulse —

MRS. P. And although he made a large fortune at the diggings he never refunded one penny of my property!

DEE. Boys will be boys. Come, come — don't be too hard upon him. He intends to make you ample compensation.

MRS. P. Intends, Sir! Why, what in the world do you know about him?

DEE. Ma'am — prepare yourself for a surprise. I bring a message from him. He and I landed at Southampton last night and he has sent me on to say that in the course of a day or two at farthest he will be with you.

MRS. P. *(aside)*. Oh indeed, Mr. Dee! *(Aloud.)* Well, if he evinces any signs of sincere sorrow I may, perhaps, be induced to forgive him. But what is his special object in returning?

DEE. Ma'am, I won't deceive you.

MRS. P. You can't, Sir.

DEE. I wouldn't if I could, and that is saying a great deal. His special object in returning to you is to confer the hand of his niece and ward, Miss Annabella Penrose, on a highly eligible young gentleman of property living in this neighbourhood, a Mr. Bee or Cee, or —

MRS. P. Dee?

DEE. Dee — that was the name. A Mr. Dee. Do you happen to know him?

MRS. P. Perfectly. A very undesirable acquaintance for any young lady.

DEE. Eh?

MRS. P. One of the very worst characters in the county, Sir — a person we certainly tolerate, because I knew his poor father, and besides, we are very good-natured people, and don't like to hurt anybody's feelings, but I never knew a man so universally disliked.

DEE. Oh, ah! And does Annabella dislike him?

MRS. P. Dislike him? She detests him.

DEE. But he's very rich —

MRS. P. Rich? Ha! ha! ha! My dear sir, he hasn't a brass farthing he can call his own.

DEE. What do you mean, ma'am?

MRS. P. You know the Royal Indelible Bank that holds securities and deposits of his to the value of £32,000?

DEE. Yes — yes — that is, I've heard of it —

MRS. P. I've just heard that it has stopped payment, and not only that, but the Atmospheric Castle Building Company, Limited, in which he had invested all his spare capital, is on the eve of winding-up! I just sent round to him to tell him so, but he wasn't at home.

DEE. (*Aside*). Good gracious! Is it possible! I must see about this! (*Aloud.*) But your niece, ma'am, has money.

Mrs. P. £25,000.

Dee. Just so — Well, remember, Mr. Coodle has sent me to say that she is to marry Mr. Dee under any circumstances — rich or poor — rich or poor. Mind, ma'am, it's Coodle's order — I'm going to see Mr. Dee, ma'am, and tell him the happiness in store for him, good morning, ma'am! (*Aside.*) The Indelible gone and the Atmospherics blown up! Oh dear, oh dear, oh dear, what shall I do!

(*Exit.*)

Mrs. P. Ha! ha! Well, Mr. Dee, I think I've taught you a lesson, but I haven't done with you yet. Hey? Why, what's this?

(*Enter* Servant.)

Servant. Another gentleman to see you and he, also, declines to send in his card.

Mrs. P. Another? Refuses his card, too, does he? The fashion of "No Cards" has extended from weddings to morning calls, it seems. Well, send him here. (*Exit* Servant.) Some nonsense of Mr. Churchmouse's this time, I'll be bound. Oh, here comes the mysterious gentleman, and as I live it *is* Mr. Churchmouse.

(*Enter* Churchmouse *as* Coodle, *a begging-letter impostor.*)

Ch. Good morning, madam. I come on a sweet errand of mercy. Madam, you are rich, others are poor; you are in possession of your senses, others are not. You have the full enjoyment of a valuable set of limbs; others, unfortunately, are short of the proper complement. Madam, in me you behold the channel of communication — the conduit-pipe, if I may so express myself — between the wealthy, and the wise, and the well made, on the one hand — the destitute, the delirious, and the disjointed, on the other.

Mrs. P. You represent some charity, I presume?

Ch. Madam, I represent no individual charity. I am not of those who make invidious distinctions. I am the Universal Agent for All the Charities in Great Britain and Ireland. I deal rather with the broad principle of charity, than with its details.

Mrs. P. I see. You look upon it in the abstract.

Ch. Very much so indeed, ma'am. At the same time you are quite at liberty to say whether you wish your half-crown to be devoted to any special institution, or whether you prefer that it should be equally distributed among the eight hundred and sixty-seven charities of Great Britain and Ireland. The truly charitable usually prefer the latter course, for their names being printed 867 times, they have the advantage of setting 867 good examples at a very moderate outlay. I am an eleemosynary pillar post. Post four half-crowns in this waistcoat pocket and don't trouble yourself any further about it. Dismiss it, ma'am, from your mind altogether. You will never hear of it again.

Mrs. P.   I really haven't my purse with me — you can ask the servant for half-a-crown — the housemaid I mean — not the man.

Ch.   Your housemaid? You have a housemaid, then?

Mrs. P.   Certainly.

Ch.   Oh, allow me — the Humble Housemaid's Happy Home (*giving prospectus*). An admirable charity, ma'am, where humble housemaids are taught that postmen are pitfalls and bakers a snareful abomination.

Mrs. P.   A curious charity.

Ch.   But a highly valuable one. A young woman — a housemaid — comes to our home and confesses that she would like to marry a baker. Do we dismiss her on that account? Oh, no! We are all love. We read her "Lives of Bakers who have been Convicted." We throw her into the society of butchers. We draw comparisons between butchers and bakers to the manifest disadvantage of the latter. We lend her little tracts, "Butchers as they are and Bakers as they might be," "I'll have your Alum and Potatoes!" We sing her little songs in praise of a butcher's life, "Chump-chop Charley is my name," or "Come, and we'll dismember Little Frolicking Lambs!" until her soul is absolutely impregnated with the poetry of a butcher's life.

Mrs. P.   And she marries a butcher?

Ch.   Oh, de-ar no! We then proceed to disgust her with butchers as we disgusted her with bakers, flooding her, so to speak, with postmen, reminding her that postmen alone knock double knocks and all tradespeople single knocks, and we draw a moral from this that the character of their knock is an emblem of the state of life for which they are most fitted. When her mind is charged with postmen, we turn on a supply of grocer's young men, then policemen, then milkmen, and so on, showing the hollowness of each class of suitor in turn, the whole course of instruction tending to point the stock moral of our establishment, that "all men are vanity." Your name, madam, that I may emblazon it on the 867 scrolls of the 867 charities I have the honour to represent.

Mrs. P. My name is Pennythorne — but you need not trouble your-self to print it.

Ch. Pennythorne? Is it possible? No — no —

Mrs. P. That, Sir, is my name.

Ch. Then it is — it must be —

Mrs. P. Sir?

Ch. But no — impossible —

Mrs. P. What's impossible?

Ch. You cannot be the Frederika Pennythorne (now Coodle) whom I married thirty years ago —

Mrs. P. Twenty.

Ch. True — twenty — at St. James's Church, Piccadilly —

Mrs. P. St. George's, Hanover Square.

Ch. True — St. George's, Hanover Square — one lovely July day —

Mrs. P. January.

Ch. True — January — it's the same thing. No, no — I won't believe it. Your theory is ingenious but it won't do.

Mrs. P. What does the man mean?

Ch. Mean, ma'am? Why that you are *not* the Frederika Penny-thorne, now Coodle, whom I have been sighing for during the last twenty years in the backwoods of North America —

Mrs. P. West Australia.

Ch. True — it was West Australia. Frederika, it is impossible to resist the persuasive eloquence of the facts you adduce to identify me. You have conquered, and the prize is yours!

Mrs. P. Oh, you are Mr. Coodle, are you? You have arrived rather earlier than you intended. Your friend said you would not be here till to-morrow or the next day.

CH. (*taken aback*). Oh, my friend said that, did he?

MRS. P. Of course he did. He brought your message.

CH. Oh, he brought my message.

MRS. P. Certainly. He has only just left. He will be back directly.

CH. (*aside*). This is extremely awkward. I wonder what on earth she means —

(*Enter* MR. DEE, *still disguised.*)

MRS. P. Oh, your message was hardly necessary, for Mr. Coodle has arrived.

DEE. Oh, Coodle has arrived, has he?

MRS. P. Yes, here he is. I'll go and fetch Annabella, and Mr. Coodle and she can fight it out together. (*Exit* MRS. P.)

DEE. How d'ye do, Coodle?

CH. How de do? You — you — gave my message?

DEE. Oh, yes. I gave your message.

CH. I hope you gave it word for word. It was of very particular importance that it should be given word for word.

DEE. Oh, yes. Word for word.

CH. That's right. (*Aside.*) It might help me a little if I knew what the message was. (*Awkward pause.*)

DEE. Sir, this is not a time for ceremony. Are you, or are you not, Mr. Coodle?

CH. (*aside*). Must brazen it out! (*Aloud.*) Oh, yes, I'm Mr. Coodle.

DEE. Are you sure you are Mr. Coodle?

CH. Sure? Well one can never be sure of anything, but I have an impression —

DEE. An impression, Sir, is not enough. (*Aside.*) This man is an impostor. (*Aloud.*) What should you say, Sir, if it turned out that I was Mr. Coodle?

CH. I should say it would be a remarkable instance of mistaken identity on my part.

DEE. (*aside*). He is an impostor, I knew he was. (*Aloud.*) Well Sir, I am Mr. Coodle.

CH. You are?

DEE. I am.

CH. Then, Sir, I frankly admit I was mistaken. I was misled, Sir, by an accidental resemblance. We are wonderfully alike, Sir. (*Aside.*) This is getting very awkward.

DEE. But what could have been your object in assuming my name, Sir?

CH. I will be candid with you. It was simply to spare you the trouble of giving your consent to the marriage of a dear young friend of mine — one Churchmouse — with your ward Annabella Penrose.

DEE. Churchmouse, Sir? Nothing of the kind, Sir! I had intended her from her earliest childhood for my worthy old friend Mr. Dee.

CH. Oh — well. But, between ourselves, Mr. Dee is not exactly — you know — the sort of man for an accomplished young lady — He's a decent fellow — poor chap — but he's not — you understand. (*Tapping his forehead.*)

DEE. Oh, Dee isn't quite right there, isn't he?

CH. Right? He's as mad as a hatter. Dangerous. Rabid. He's been three times in a lunatic asylum.

DEE. You astonish me — He seems quite quiet.

CH. Yes; that's his cunning. He's all right till after sunset — then his paroxysms begin and last till daylight! Awful, isn't it?

DEE. Humph — I've known that young man since he was so long, Sir, and I never had the slightest idea of this.

CH. Young man? He's fifty.

DEE. Nonsense, Sir, thirty-five.

CH. You know what the song says about elderly gentlemen who propose to marry?

DEE. No, I don't, Sir.

CH. I'll tell you.

No. 3. — SONG. — Mr. Churchmouse.

An elderly person, a prophet by trade,
  With quips and tips on withered old lips,
He married a young and a beautiful maid.
    This shocking old blade,
    Though rather decayed,
Married a young and a beautiful maid.
Of all his acquaintances, bidden, or bad,
  With loud high jinks, and underbred winks,
None thought they'd a family have — but they had —
    A singular lad,
    Who drove 'em half mad,
For he turned out a horribly fast little cad.
For when he was born he astonished all by,
  (With their "Law! Dear me! Did ever you see?")
He'd a weed in his mouth, and a glass in his eye,
    His hat all awry,
    An octagon tie,
And a miniature, miniature glass in his eye.
He grumbled at wearing a frock and a cap,
  With his "Oh, dear oh!" and his "Hang it, you know!"
And turned up his nose at his excellent pap.
    "My friends, it's a tap,
    Dat am not worth a rap —"
Now this was remarkably excellent pap.
His father, a pleasant old gentleman, he
  With nursery rhyme, and "Once on a time,"
Would tell him the story of "Little Bo P."
    "So pretty was she,
    So pretty and wee,
As pretty, as pretty, as pretty can be!"
But the babe, with a dig that would startle an ox,
  With his "C'ch! oh my! Go along wis 'oo! Fie!"
Would exclaim, "I'm affaid 'oo a socking old fox!"
    Now a father it shocks,
    And it whitens his locks,
When his little babe calls him a shocking old fox!
The name of his father he'd couple and pair,
  With ill-bred laugh and insolent chaff,
With those of the nursery heroines rare:

73

Virginia the Fair,
And good Goldenhair,
Till the nuisance was more than a prophet could bear.
"Dere's Jill and White Cat" (said the bold little brat,
With his loud "Ha, ha! 'oo sly ickle Pa!").
"Wiz 'oo Beauty, Bo-Peep, and 'oo Mrs. Jack Sprat.
    I've notice you pat
    My pretty White Cat;
I sink dear mama ought to know about dat!"
He early determined to marry and wive,
    For better or worse, with his elderly nurse;
Which the poor little boy didn't live to contrive.
    His health didn't thrive;
    No longer alive,
He died — an enfeebled old dotard — at five.

MORAL.

Now, elderly men of the bachelor crew,
    With wrinkled hose,
    And spectacled nose,
Don't marry at all. You may take it as true,
    If ever you do
    The step you will rue,
For your babes will be elderly, elderly too.

(*Enter* MRS. P. *as* SALAMANCA TROMBONE.)

MRS. P. (*speaking off*). You must find room for the elephant in the stables. Keep the panther and leopard apart because they fight. A couple of dog kennels will do for the tigers, and look here, you can hang up the boa constrictors on the umbrella stand in the hall. (*To* CH. *and* DEE) How de do?

BOTH. (*aghast*). How de do?

MRS. P. Don't know me? Ha! Of course not. How should you? Take off your hat.

DEE. But really, ma'am —

MRS. P. Take off your hat — you are in the presence of royalty!

DEE. Of Royalty?

Mrs. P.   Yes. I am the Queen of Babbetyboobledore.

Dee.   Oh! my geography is rather shaky.

Mrs. P.   You never heard of the place? Benighted ignorance! It's an island in the Indian Archipelago.

Dee.   I hope you found the climate agreeable, ma'am.

Mrs. P.   Very.

Dee.   Then why leave it?

Mrs. P.   I am here to cultivate amicable relations with Great Britain, and as a first step I've called upon my old friends Mr. and Mrs. Coodle.

Ch.   But they are not amicable relations. They haven't spoken for twenty years.

Mrs. P.   No matter. My people, Sir, are in a very unhappy condition.

Ch.   I can quite believe it, ma'am.

Mrs. P.   The dawn of civilization has not yet broken upon them, but I have undertaken to tame them.

Dee.   They couldn't be in better hands. But may I ask, are you a native?

Mrs. P.   No. I am a native of Great Britain, I am ashamed to say.

Dee.   The feeling is mutual, ma'am, I'm sure.

Mrs. P.   Twenty years ago I was wrecked on the island. Their queen had just died, and the selection of a successor was being carried on by competitive examination. It was a question of physical strength. I won.

Ch.   (*warmly shaking her hand*).   My dear madam, I congratulate you I'm sure —

Mrs. P.   Go away and don't be ridiculous. They elected me their queen —

Dee.   Benighted beings! Some people never know when they are well off.

Mrs. P.   Benighted? You're right there. You can form no idea of the depths of ignorance into which this unhappy people is plunged, they have positively no sense of propriety. Listen! I'll tell you all about them.

75

No. 4. — SONG. — Mrs. Pennythorne.

You ask me what species of people I met
    In Babbetyboobledore?
They're a very remarkably backward set
    In Babbetyboobledore.
They live in a foolishly simple way,
And whatever they happen to think, they say —
Oh pity the ignorant darkies, pray,
    Of Babbetyboobledore!

Barbarity rampant seems to thrive
    In Babbetyboobledore!
The ignorant savages rise at five
    In Babbetyboobledore.
They breakfast at seven — at two they dine,
The gentlemen never sit over their wine,
So everybody's in bed by nine
    In Babbetyboobledore!

The girls of the island are pretty and fair
    In Babbetyboobledore!
But they never attempt to colour their hair
    In Babbetyboobledore!
They're horribly wanting in matters of taste,
They haven't a notion of jewels or paste,
And as for their figures, there isn't a waist
    In Babbetyboobledore!

They are strict in their method of dealing with thieves
    In Babbetyboobledore!
But they come down as well on the man who receives
    In Babbetyboobledore!
If they know that a thief in that singular clime
Is planning a robbery, coming in time,
They take him before — and not after — the crime
    In Babbetyboobledore.

Civilization takes no stride
    In Babbetyboobledore.
There's nothing like self-respect or pride
    In Babbetyboobledore.

They've little regard for money or birth —
Unless it's allied to genuine worth.
There isn't another domain on earth
         Like Babbetyboobledore!

Mrs. P. (*speaking*). Now, then, to business: which of you two is Coodle?

Dee. I am Coodle.

Mrs. P. Sure of that?

Dee. (*Looking at cardcase.*) Quite sure.

Mrs. P. Ha! Because I've come to shoot Coodle.

                              (*Producing revolver.*)
Dee. To shoot Coodle?

Mrs. P. To shoot Coodle.

Dee. (*going to* Churchmouse). My dear Coodle, I'm sorry — I'm very very sorry for you.

               (Churchmouse *has his face buried
               in his hands, in apparent grief.*)

Mrs. P. That Coodle? I thought you said you were Coodle.

Dee. Did I say so? that's so like me! absence of mind, my dear madam. Yes, this is Coodle! Poor, poor Coodle!

               (Churchmouse *removes his hands,
               and discovers his natural face.*)

Mrs. P. Nonsense, Sir, Mr. Coodle is more than two and twenty.

Dee. More than two and twenty? More than two and fifty. (*Sees* Churchmouse.) Hullo, Churchmouse!

Ch. Hullo, Coodle!

Dee. Coodle, Sir, nonsense. But why do you want to shoot him?

Mrs. P. Because he forged a certificate of my burial — also my will.

Dee. Then you are —

Mrs. P. Miss Salamanca Trombone.

Dee. Oh, go along — you're dead.

77

Mrs. P. Am I? (*Squeezes his arm.*)

Dee. No — I apologize. Then Annabella Penrose hasn't £25,000.

Mrs. P. Not 25,000 pence.

(*Enter* Miss Penrose.)

Dee. Poor little thing! How young she looks! And I — how old I look! It would be too bad, after all, to graft such a tender rosebud on such a tough old oak as I. No — I'll be magnanimous, Miss Penrose, you have had a narrow escape. You love me, but I will not take advantage of your youth and inexperience. I resign you — you are too young for me!

Miss P. Too young for what, uncle?

Dee. Uncle? Oh, of course. I forgot; yes, Uncle, to be sure.

(*He fidgets with his beard; it comes off in his hand.*)

All. Mr. Ellis Dee!

Dee. Yes. Odd, isn't it! Yes, Miss Penrose, I am sorry for you, but you are too young for me.

Ch. But not too young for me?

Miss P. Nor too poor?

Ch. Nor too poor!

Mrs. P. (*discovering her identity.*) Nor too poor, I am sure — unless £25,000 is insufficient.

All. Mrs. Pennythorne!

Mrs. P. Yes, Mr. Churchmouse, I have much pleasure in handing you this little autograph of mine, in the hope and belief that you will want it before very long. (*Hands slip of paper.*)

Dee. (*reads*). At St. Stickleback's, Clifferton-by-the-Sea. By the Revd. Chasuble Highfly —

Mrs. P. Peter, only son of the late Solomon Churchmouse, to Annabella, only daughter of the late Sir Peter Penrose, of the Penrosery, Penrith. No cards!

No. 5. — FINALE.

Ch. Believe me, as far as with me it remains,
　　　　　You'll never see Coodle more!

DEE. I vow — under penalty, penance, and pains —
      You'll never see Coodle more!

MRS. P. Ah, Coodle and I, we could never agree,
   Let that be a lesson to each of the three.
   Take warning, my dear Annabella, from me.
      I'll never see Coodle more!

ALL. Coodle-oodle-oodle! &c.

ALL. Ah! Coodle and $\left\{ \begin{array}{l} \text{I, we} \\ \text{she, they} \end{array} \right\}$ could never agree,
  Let that be a lesson to each of the three.

MRS. P. $\left\{ \begin{array}{l} \text{Take warning, my dear Annabella, from me.} \\ \text{Her terrible fate is a warning to me.} \end{array} \right.$
THE OTHERS.

MRS. P. $\left\{ \begin{array}{l} \text{I'll} \\ \text{She'll} \end{array} \right\}$ never see Coodle more!
THE OTHERS.

CURTAIN

Ages Ago

Characters

SIR EBENEZER TARE ———— *of the firm of Tare and Tret, Alderman and*
Tallow Chandler, later LORD CARNABY POPPY-
TOP.
ROSA ————————————— *(his niece), later* LADY MAUD.
MRS. MAC MOTHERLY ——— *later* DAME CHERRY MAYBUD.
MR. COLUMBUS HEBBLETHWAITE
later SIR CECIL BLOUNT.
STEWARD ————————— *later* BROWN.

LADY MAUD DE BOHUN ——was born ———————————— 1455
came into possession ———— 1469 Edward IV.
painted by Leonardo da
Vinci 1472 Aged 17.
died ———————————— 1473 Louis XI.

SIR CECIL BLOUNT ————was born ———————————— 1540 Elizabeth.
painted by Michael Angelo 1560 Aged 20.
Henry II to IV.
came into possession ———— 1569
died ———————————— 1579

LORD CARNABY POPPYTOP..was born ———————— 1648
came into possession ———— 1669 Queen Anne.
was painted by Godfrey
Kneller 1713 Aged 65.
died ———————————— 1720

DAME CHERRY MAYBUD ——was born ———————— 1730
came into possession ———— 1769 George III.
was painted by Sir Joshua
Reynolds 1785 Aged 55.

ROSA ————————————Picture Costume tenth year of Edward IV.
SIR CECIL ———————— Picture Costume second year of Elizabeth.
LORD CARNABY ———————Last year of Queen Anne's reign.
DAME CHERRY ——————— Twenty-fifth year of George III.
BROWN ——————————— Modern Cockney Dress.

SCENE: *Picture Gallery in Glen-Cockaleekie Castle.*

SCENE: *A Picture Gallery. Oriel window R. The walls are covered with pictures, but five full-length portraits are veiled.* MRS. MAC MOTHERLY (*an old housekeeper*) *and* ROSA, MR. ALDERMAN TARE'S *pretty niece, discovered.*

ROSA. Mrs. Mac Motherly, I'm a dreadful little goose, I know, but it's a great many years since I believed a ghost story — Haunted! Why, if the place had the ghost of a ghost in it, Uncle Tare would have ferretted it out long ago. He has already been three weeks in uninterrupted possession, and I should like to see the ghost that would escape Uncle Tare's vigilance for that space of time.

MRS. MAC. Eh weel — it may be sae, I hae naething to say anent it — either the tae way or the tother. But this I ken weel. Your true hieland ghostie is just a pairfect gentleman, and wadna dream of intrudin' himself upon ye until ye'd settled down comfortably in your new habitation.

ROSA. But why should these goblins choose our castle of all others?

MRS. MAC. Yours? Why it's nae more yours than ilka ither body's, the auld castle has been uninhabited for the last four score and seven years (save by ghosties and sic like) since the death of Dame Cherry Maybud, whose portrait hangs there.

ROSA. I know — the last on the left.

MRS. MAC. Like ilka ither possessor of the auld castle, when she died there was ne'er a will or a title deed to be found, and the ghosties stepped in and folk wadna hae anything to do wi' sic an uncanny place. So it remained uninhabited until your Uncle, Sir Ebenezer Tare, of the firm of Tare and Tret, Alderman and tallow-chandler, tuk it into his head to try the value of the auld maxim that possession is nine points of the law, and walked in one braw morning three weeks since, wi' ne'er a "wi' yer leave," or "by yer leave," wi' nae mair right to the place than the Sultan o' Morocco himself.

ROSA. But nobody is likely to disturb him.

MRS. MAC. Eh! but I'm nae sa sure about that, if there's any truth in the auld legend about the wicked Sir Roger Bohun, how he sold himself to an awful uncanny apparition on the 13th day of July, 1369, for right and title to the castle for a hundred years. Sir Roger de Bohun was a prodigal knight who had just a life interest in this castle, and nae mair than a life interest. Being sairly pressed for siller and wishing to mortgage the castle, he entered into a compact with the fiend on the 13th July, 1369, that on Sir Roger's death nae heir should be found to the auld castle until a century had slippet by. Well, Sir Roger mortgaged the castle and spent the siller like a graceless loon as he was, and then he died and left ne'er an heir or a title deed, and ne'er a title deed was found, and the castle remained empty until the 13th July, 1469, when the Lady Maud de Bohun, whose portrait hangs there, found them quite unexpectedly in the drawer of her work-table. Well, she took possession, died and left ne'er an heir or a title deed, and ne'er a title deed was found till Sir Cecil Blount — who hangs there — a collateral descendant of the auld Barons, found them in a disused portmanteau on the 13th of July, 1569. Well, he died and left ne'er an heir or a title deed, and ne'er a title deed was found till Lord Carnaby Poppytop — there he hangs — hit upon them, wrapped up in an old disused periwig, on the 13th July, 1669. Well, he died and left ne'er an heir or a title deed, and ne'er a title deed was found until Dame Cherry Maybud came upon them in the stuffing of an auld farthingale on the 13th July, 1769. Well, she died in 1782, and from that moment till three weeks sin, the castle has just been handed over to the machinations of the de'il and his evil hobgoblins.

Rosa. Then the next century will expire to-morrow!

Mrs. Mac. If there's any truth in legends, the weird maun be fulfilled, and the legal descendant of Dame Cherry Maybud will come to-morrow morn at cockcrae wi' the title deeds in his grif, and just turn ye a' out bag and baggage, neck and crop. I've just a notion that I can speer some awfu' misfortune hanging over the House o' Tare, and I've nae manner o' doubt but that it's associated wi' the dreadful legend of the wicked Sir Roger de Bohun.

Enter Sir Ebenezer Tare.

Tare. I am only acquainted with one misfortune with which the House of Tare is threatened — the probable loss of its housekeeper, Mistress Mac Motherly, if she continues to fill my niece's ears with her abominable superstitions. It's a misfortune, ma'am, which the House of Tare will bear with Christian fortitude. Now, go — I mean, "gang awa' wi' ye."

Mrs. Mac. Eh, Sir! but ye ken weel I'm just telling her naught but what ye ken yoursel' to be true. Wha was it prophesied ye'd lose twa braw ships by fire and tempest this year? Why, Mistress Mac Motherly!

Wha was it prophesied ye'd be down wi' the measles last fall? Why, Mistress Mac Motherly! Wha was it prophesied that a bonny young callant wad come a-courting Miss Rosa this week? Why, Mistress Mac Motherly! And, mark me! Sir Ebenezer; if I'm to be burnt alive for a warlock, I'll say it: there's just an unco' bad misfortune hangin' over ye; and it's no associated wi' the dismissal of your auld housekeeper, Maggie Mac Motherly. (*Exit.*)

TARE. My dear Rosa, if ever you go into housekeeping —

ROSA. If!

TARE. Well, *when* you go into housekeeping, take care to ascertain that none of your domestics are gifted with the curse of second sight. That woman has been in my service for thirty years, and she has done nothing but prophesy misfortune from the day she entered it until now. And what is worse, her predictions all come true. What was that she said about "a bonnie young callant coming a-courting Miss Rosa"?

ROSA. (*frightened*). Oh, I can't imagine what she could have referred to.

TARE. No one has been here except Mr. Columbus Hebblethwaite. (ROSA *starts*.) Eh? It's my belief, Miss, she referred to him.

ROSA. I'm sure I don't know why, Uncle. He's always very agreeable, but nothing more.

TARE. Now, Rosa, it's as well we should have a distinct understanding on this point — I've noticed that that impoverished young man is unpleasantly marked in his attentions to you, and I've noticed that, far from discouraging his penniless addresses, you have afforded him fifty means of prosecuting them during his week's residence with us in this castle. He quartered himself upon us without invitation — but, thank goodness, I've got rid of him at last.

ROSA. Uncle, how can you be so unkind!

TARE. Cry away, my dear, it's satisfaction enough to know that at this moment he's careering away at the rate of 60 miles an hour on his road to his native London. Let's see, the express started at 10.15, and it's now half past eleven, so he's exactly 75 miles away from his beloved Rosa. And by a remarkable coincidence his beloved Rosa is precisely the same distance from him. Ha! ha! ha!

(*Loud knocking at outer gate.*)

No. 1. — RECIT.

TARE.	Ha! what was that? It shook me to the core! What was it, Rosa? tell me I implore!
ROSA.	I rather think, but mind I won't be sure, I think it's someone knocking at the door.

ARIA.

(*aside*)	Columbus dear, thy knock I hear with mingled hopes and fears. Its murmur laves with eddying waves the portals of my ears.
TARE.	You tremble so, I am sure you know Who's knocking at my gate.
MRS. MAC.	(*entering*). 'Tis Mister Hebblethwaite!
ALL.	'Tis Mister Hebblethwaite!

Enter MR. HEBBLETHWAITE *with carpet bag, etc.* [*and* STEWARD]

HEBBLE.	Permit me a short explanation,
	I left you to go to the station,
	   And thought not to see you again;
	The time was so short that I hurried,
	I really felt terribly flurried
	   At the notion of missing my train.

ALL.	He really felt terribly flurried At the idea of missing his train.

HEBBLE.	This modern edition of coaching,
	I heard like a rocket approaching,
	   I had not a moment to look;
	So forward in agony springing,
	   I ran to the place where they book.

ALL.	So forward in terrible agony springing, He ran to the place where they book!

HEBBLE.	I eagerly ran to the small office door,
	I well knew the way, for I'd been there before;
	   I tapped at the wicket,
	   I asked for a ticket,
	And laid down the price of the journey, and more,

	"Give me," quoth I, "to my home I fly,

"Give me," quoth I, "to my home I fly,
Where the violet sighs to the evening skies,
And the skies of eve receive the sigh of the violet."

ALL.   Where the violet sighs to the evening skies,
And the skies of eve receive the sigh of the violet.

HEBBLE.   Come with me, clerk (if excuse you can trump any),
Bother the station and bother the company.
Come to my thatchery, semi-detachery,
    Roses and posies shall flower the way.
My ticket I seized, I rushed to the station,
The clerk had refused my polite invitation,
Oh, horror! oh, horror! I fell to the earth;
    For I noticed the train, it was only too plain,
It was moving off to the land of my birth!

ALL.   Oh, horror! he fell to the earth,
    Seeing the train, only too plain,
'Twas moving off to the land of his birth!

ROSA.   We'll do our best to make your rest as pleasant as can be,
    Sir.

STEW.   Your cheery face, in such a place, we're very glad to see,
    Sir.

TARE.   But stop, I say, you went away, and spoke not of returning.

MRS. MAC.   It's very clear, he's come back here, for Mistress Rosa
    burning.

No. 2.—COUPLETS AND QUINTETT.

HEBBLE.   It does perplex, annoy and vex, forgive the observation,
When just too late, in breathless state, you see with
    irritation,
The starting train, while you remain in dreadful
    perturbation,
To spend the night, till morning light, at some unheard
    of station.

ROSA.   Your room is old, and damp and cold, unworthy
    habitation,
The spider crawls about the walls and fills you with
    vexation,

Had I but known you would have flown, you'll judge by
this narration,
To make it good, this morning would have been my
occupation.

(TARE *is standing apart in a great rage.*)

ROSA. (*aside to* TARE). Uncle, you must say something to him, poor
fellow.

TARE. Say? Why, what can I say?

ROSA. Oh, a few words of course — that you are glad to see him back
again and so on.

TARE. But I'm not.

ROSA. Never mind, pretend you are — leave it to me. (*Goes up to*
HEBBLETHWAITE.) Mr. Hebblethwaite, Uncle tells me to say that he is
delighted at the fortunate accident that has procured him the pleasure
of seeing you again.

HEBBLE. My dear Sir (*shaking hands with* TARE).

ROSA. That he hopes you will consider his house your home until
to-morrow evening.

HEBBLE. Until to-morrow? until to-morrow week if you like!

TARE. But I say, Rosa —

ROSA. He also wishes me to say that he would have told you this
himself, but he thought it would come more prettily from my mouth.

HEBBLE. It does, it does. My dear Sir Ebenezer, the warmth of this
welcome overpowers me.

TARE. But, Sir, I say — (*sharply to* ROSA) Rosa, go to bed!

ROSA. But, Uncle —

TARE. Go to bed, Miss. (*aside to* ROSA) I'll talk to you about this to-
morrow. (*Exit* ROSA.)

TARE. Well, Sir, as it seems my niece has given you to understand
that I'm extremely glad to see you back again. . .

HEBBLE. Thank you, thank you, I know you are.

TARE. I said nothing of the kind, Sir; I say, as my niece has expressed
as much, I am put to the disagreeable necessity of echoing her opinion.

So, Sir, if you will take your candlestick, Mistress Mac Motherly shall show you to your room. The room is in the roof, Mistress Mac Motherly, where the rats are. Good-night, Sir, and pleasant dreams to you.

(*Ensemble* TARE, HEBBLETHWAITE, [STEWARD] and MRS. MAC MOTHERLY).

No. 3.—QUARTETT.

MRS. MAC.	⎞	We fly to fields of fancy,
HEBBLE.	⎟	Achieve our mystic flight,
TARE.	⎨	By Nature's necromancy,
STEW.	⎠	Good night, by gentle Luna's light.

MRS.	No passing breath of sorrow
HEBBLE.	Shall cloud our visions bright;
ALL FOUR.	We meet again to-morrow.
	Good-night! good night.

(*Exeunt.*)

(*The stage is darkened; moonlight streams through oriel window. The clock strikes twelve, and the veil before* LADY MAUD's *picture is withdrawn.* LADY MAUD *is discovered full length in the frame. She sings the following recitative.*)

No. 4.—RECIT.

LADY MAUD. I breathe! I live! Since last I saw the day
Five tardy centuries have passed away.
No longer o'er my grave let chaplets wreathe,
My bosom throbs with life! I live! I breathe!

(LADY MAUD *descends from the frame.*)

No. 5.—SONG.

LADY MAUD. Moments so fleeting stern spirits give,
My heart is beating, I breathe! I live!
For three short hours, while darkness lowers,
By mystic powers I breathe! I live!

Night's sombre awning has set me free;
The daylight's dawning brings night to me.
My heart is aching, the daylight's breaking,
All others waking, brings night to me.

89

LADY MAUD. Am I in the world? And if so, where in the world am I? (*Looking round.*) A picture gallery! oh, of course, *our* picture gallery. But the pictures. I don't know them. What extraordinary costumes. They are all strangers to me. They were not there when I died. Died? Then I'm dead! I'm sure I died. But here I am walking about in my own picture gallery. Then I suppose I'm a ghost! My own ghost! I wonder if I ought to be frightened? But who has the castle now? The title deeds disappeared the day before I died in accordance with the wicked compact by which Sir Roger de Bohun obtained possession of this castle a hundred and fifty years ago, and by the terms of the compact it would remain unoccupied for about eighty years after my death. But evidently it *is* occupied. Then at least eighty years have elapsed. I wonder how my portrait has kept? It was painted many years before I died by Leonardo da Vinci. A rather clever young artist. He sent it to the Royal Academy, but he didn't know anybody on the Hanging Committee, so he didn't get it in. Let me see, where did it hang? (*Walks up to frame.*) Why the picture's gone. Faded away. Nothing left but the background. Oh, it's too bad. I paid I don't know how much for it. These modern painters seem quite to have lost the art of mixing colours. Now a Cimabue or a Giotto would be as fresh as if it had been painted yesterday. Oh, it's too bad! (*Looks at her dress.*) Why this is the very dress I was painted in! and all my jewels exactly as I wore them. What an extraordinary coincidence! (*She has a rose in her hand.*) And here is the very rose that Messer Leonardo made me carry because he wanted a bit of colour down here. But I came from there just now! I remember distinctly coming from that frame. Then I'm only a picture. Well, I'm glad I'm not a ghost. Then I've done Messer Leonardo da Vinci a very serious injustice. (*Takes up a hand mirror.*) Oh, there's another picture of me here and it moves. Stop — I remember — it's a mirror. I saw one when I was quite a little girl. It was sent over from Venice and cost a mint of money. How exceedingly foolish to leave a valuable object like this about. Now I suppose this is worth about four or five hundred pounds (*looking at herself in it*). Yes, I'm looking very well — I'm very like — quite a speaking likeness. I wonder whose portraits these are. (*Reads tablets on frames.*) Dame Cherry Maybud. Lord Poppytop. (*Then seeing* SIR CECIL.) Oh, how perfectly charming! What a noble face! What magnificent colour! There's a flesh tint! and then such dignity! such expression! I wonder who painted it! (*Reads.*) Michael Angelo — I never heard of the gentleman. Quite an unknown man. After all, on looking at it again it's very tricky, quite a fourth or fifth-rate production. Date 1602 — Oh, some mistake. They must mean 1502. I died in

1500. I should really like to know whose portrait it is, for with all its faults, there is really a manly dignity about it which must have been strongly impressed on the original. (*Apostrophising picture.*) You are very handsome — very, very handsome. I'm glad you're only a picture. If you were a real living man, I should be obliged to be rather particular, but as it is I may say what I like to you.

No. 6. — SONG. — Lady Maud.

So please you, Sir, to hear my story while I tell
The happiness awaiting you: a maiden loves you well.
She dares not to declare the love that makes her sigh,
And would you know that maiden, so please you, Sir, 'tis I.

She would a saint beguile, her hair is soft and bright,
A happy laugh, a pleasant smile, and eyes that dance with light,
A dimple here and there, a pretty, touching sigh,
And would you know that maiden, so please you, Sir, 'tis I.

Sir C.   A sweeter fate I never heard, my gratitude you've earned.

Lady M. (*aside*). (My goodness me, he's talking!)

Sir C.   The compliment, upon my word, was very neatly turned.

Lady M. (My goodness me, he's walking!)

Sir C.   Her goodness she, I'm walking!

Lady M. To laugh it off I can't contrive, with fright I'm nearly fainting,
     I never thought you were alive, I thought you were a painting!

Lady M.⎫
Sir C. ⎬ To laugh it off $\left\{ \begin{array}{c} I \\ she \end{array} \right\}$ can't contrive, with fright $\left\{ \begin{array}{c} I'm \\ she's \end{array} \right\}$ nearly fainting.
     ⎪ I never thought $\left\{ \begin{array}{c} you\ were \\ I\ was \end{array} \right\}$ alive, I thought $\left\{ \begin{array}{c} you \\ I \end{array} \right\}$ $\left\{ \begin{array}{c} were \\ was \end{array} \right\}$ a painting.

Sir C.   I am indeed, so are you.

Lady M. How do you know that?

SIR C. How do I know it? Why, didn't you hang up there during the ten years I occupied this castle?

LADY M. Did you occupy this castle for ten years?

SIR C. I did indeed.

LADY M. But how do you know that I'm not the original of whom that picture is a portrait.

SIR C. Because there's a limit to the beauties of Nature, there's no limit to the beauties of Art. In other words, you're a great deal too good to be true. Angels are not half as bright as they are painted, and the famous Leonardo da Vinci was a terrible flatterer.

LADY M. Famous! Why he was a mere nobody who painted me for a few pounds.

SIR C. Ah! but after your melancholy decease, pardon my alluding to that distressing topic, he grew in fame and fortune, and before he died, Europe rang with his fame. Now (*looking at* LADY M. *critically*), I should say you are worth at least £2,000.

LADY M. Is it possible? And you?

SIR C. I'm a Michael Angelo. A very fine example, painted by him five years before I came, quite unexpectedly, into possession of this castle, and six years before his death. I'm worth at least as much as you. Indeed, I'm a much finer picture.

LADY M. Sir!

SIR C. I am indeed — look here (*showing legs*). Here's drawing! You are the work of an artist — I am the work of an accomplished anatomist.

LADY M. How can you say so? Look at that hand; look at its colour; look at its drawing!

(*One of* SIR CECIL's *hands is painted a queer flesh colour.*)

SIR C. Yes — ah — that's rather a sore point with me, but it's susceptible of explanation. The fact is that this hand of mine has been re-cently restored by a Royal Academician. In point of fact I've only one hand — this is not mine.

LADY M. (*with great tenderness*). Oh, Sir Cecil, forgive my thoughtless remark. Indeed I had no intention of paining you. Believe me that I sympathise deeply with your terrible misfortune.

Sir C. That sympathy more than reconciles me to it. Besides, although it's certainly deformed, after all I can use it freely enough. It was awkward at first, but I've become quite used to it.

Lady M. So I've spent years in this castle with Sir Cecil Blount without knowing it.

Sir C. Yes, that soft melting gaze of yours has been continually turned on me for ten delicious years.

Lady M. (*aside*). I wonder if he's married! (*Aloud*.) I'm surprised that Lady Blount allowed it. If I had been Lady Blount —

Sir C. Lady Blount? My mother?

Lady M. No, your wife.

Sir C. Oh, I never had a wife.

Lady M. (*aside*). I thought not.

Sir C. Shall I tell you a secret? I never married because I had fallen desperately in love with you.

Lady M. With me? oh, nonsense!

Sir C. I'm perfectly serious. I used to sit opposite to you all day long smoking and vowing to myself that I would never take a wife until I found your counterpart. "Maud," I used to say, "my own Maud." (Lady Maud *looks indignant*.) You were mine you know together with everything else in the Castle. "My own Maud" (*takes* Lady Maud's *hand*) with all my heart and soul I love you. I love you with the devotion of a lover who knows his happiness is on the eve of being crowned and with the desperation of a lover who feels that there is not the remotest chance of anything of the kind.

Lady M. Sir, you are too bold.   (*Struggling to free herself*.)

Sir C. Oh, one may say what one likes to a picture, you know. I gazed all day at those eyes, those cheeks, those lips, and dreamt about them all night.

Lady M. (*looking in mirror*). I was just remarking before you — revived that my lips seem to have lost their colour. Indeed, I almost fancy I can see the canvas through them.

Sir C. Ah, that's not Leonardo da Vinci's fault, it's mine. For ten years, night and morning, I was in the habit of covering them with kisses.

Lady M. Sir!

(*Indignantly.*)

Sir C. One may do what one likes to a picture, you know, but if I had had the least idea that we should ever meet under these peculiar circumstances, I need hardly say that I should not have ventured on such a liberty.

Lady M. Well, I suppose I must pocket my indignation.

Sir C. Besides, remember after all, the offender was not I, but my prototype.

Lady M. That's true, you can't be responsible for everything that he did, so say no more about it. Let us shake hands.

Sir C. With pleasure. (*Offers* Lady Maud *the restored hand.*)

Lady M. No, the other.

Sir C. I beg your pardon. (*Takes* Lady Maud's *hand and kisses it, and retains it in his.*) So I am quite forgiven?

Lady M. Quite. A portrait after all is not like its original.

Sir C. Very often it is not.

Lady M. One may say what one likes to a picture.

Sir C. You allow that?

Lady M. Yes. (*Blushing.*)

No. 7. — DUET.

Sir C.   In pity tell, oh lady mine!
    The fate that waits me, my life is thine!
    'Tis thine to spare, 'tis thine to kill,
    'Tis thine to fashion to thy fair will.

Lady M.   If this is so, what can I do?
    The word that kills thee would kill me too!
    My hand and heart to thee I give,
    The word that saves thee, now bids me live.

94

SIR C.   A life of death, a life of life
With joy abounding, with sorrow rife.

LADY M.   They should be one, my life and thine,
Oh give it then, if it be mine.

SIR C.   } A term of joy, a term of grief,
LADY M. } So long without thee, with thee too brief.

                     (SIR CECIL *and* LADY MAUD *embrace.*)

(*During the Duet the veil before* LORD CARNABY POPPYTOP's *portrait has been silently drawn back. At the end of Duet* LORD CARNABY *coughs.*)

LORD C.   Ahem! (SIR C. *and* LADY MAUD *start and look round.*)
Ahem!

LADY M. (*looking into* SIR CECIL's *face*). Eh?

SIR C.   I didn't speak.

LADY M. You said "Ahem!"

LORD C. (*from picture*). *I* said "Ahem!"

LADY M. Gracious, who are you?

LORD C. I'm Lord Carnaby Poppytop. How-de-do? (*Comes down from picture and embraces* LADY MAUD.)

SIR C.   Sir! what is the meaning of this outrage?

LORD C. Outrage?

SIR C.   Yes, Sir, outrage. You kissed this lady.

LORD C. I did.

SIR C.   And by what right, Sir, did you take such a liberty?

LORD C. Liberty? Why she's my great, great, great, great, great-grandmother.

SIR C.   Nonsense, Sir, you are old enough to be her father.

LORD C. Because I was painted at the age of sixty-five; Lady Maud was painted at the age of twenty-two. I was not born until a hundred and seventy years after Lady Maud's death. And talking of liberties, may I ask by what right my Michael Angelo puts his arm round the waist of my Leonardo da Vinci?

SIR C. We are companion portraits, Sir. Besides, don't it strike you that it is hardly dutiful on your part to interfere with the proceedings of your great, great, great, great, great-grandmother?

LORD C. She's my picture, Sir, and I may do what I like with her.

SIR C. She's your great-grandmother, Sir, and she claims the respect due to her extraordinary old age. Besides, who *are* you? *I* don't know you.

LORD C. I'm Lord Carnaby Poppytop, painted by Sir Godfrey Kneller, in 1713, at the age of sixty-five, and forty-four years after coming into possession of this castle.

SIR C. Sir Godfrey Kneller! Nobody ever heard of the man!

LORD C. No one would ever have heard of you if you hadn't been painted by an old master.

LADY M. Gentlemen, pray don't quarrel on my account. (*To* LORD CARNABY, *with authority*.) My dear, your grandmama is quite old enough to take care of herself.

No. 8. — TRIO. — LADY MAUD, SIR CECIL, *and* LORD CARNABY.

LADY M.   I stand on my authority,
            And wonder what you mean.

LORD C.   You're still in your minority,
            You're hardly seventeen.

LADY M.   Lord Carnaby, in verity,
            Your rudeness pains me much.

SIR C.   You're Lady Maud's posterity,
            Behave yourself as such.

⎧ LADY M. ⎫ Your grandmama, in charity,
⎪ SIR C. ⎭   Concludes you must be mad.
⎨
⎪ LADY M. ⎫ Now be that moral rarity,
⎩ SIR C. ⎭   A good, obedient lad!

⎣ LORD C.   My grandmama, in charity,
            Concludes I must be mad!

$\left\{\begin{array}{l}\text{LADY M.} \\ \text{LORD C.}\end{array}\right\}$ I stand on my authority,
  And wonder what you mean.

SIR C. She stands on her authority,
  And wonders what you mean.

LADY M. So strange a meeting ne'er was seen,
  For sure as I'm alive,
  His grandmama is seventeen,
  And he is sixty-five.

$\left\{\begin{array}{l}\\ \\ \\ \\ \\ \end{array}\right.$

LADY M. Why, sure as I'm alive; why, sure as I'm alive,
  His grandmama is seventeen, and he is sixty-five.
  She is seventeen, and he is sixty-five.

$\left.\begin{array}{l}\text{SIR C.} \\ \\ \text{LORD C.}\end{array}\right\}$ So strange a meeting ne'er was seen,
  For she is seventeen, and $\left\{\begin{array}{l}\text{he is} \\ \text{I am}\end{array}\right\}$ sixty-five.

$\left\{\begin{array}{l}\text{LADY M.} \\ \\ \text{SIR C.} \\ \\ \text{LORD C.}\end{array}\right.$

LADY M. $\left.\begin{array}{l}\\ \end{array}\right\}$ Should he respectful homage pay:

SIR C. Should he make $\left\{\begin{array}{l}\text{me} \\ \text{her}\end{array}\right\}$ his will obey.

LORD C. Should I respectful homage pay;
  Should she make me her will obey.

(DAME CHERRY's *picture has gradually uncovered at end of Music.*)

DAME C. *(from frame).* If there's any question as to whom you all belong, I think I can set it at rest, Lord Carnaby.

LORD C. You know me then?

DAME C. Perfectly, you are Lord Carnaby Poppytop who came quite unexpectedly into possession of this castle on the 13th July, 1669; you died in 1716, and the castle remained uninhabited and unclaimed until the 13th July, 1769, when I, Dame Cherry Maybud, quite as unexpectedly found the title deeds in my possession and entered on the property accordingly. (*Comes down from picture.*) Now, allow me to settle the question that you were discussing when I interfered. You will abide by my decision?

ALL. With pleasure.

DAME C. Very well then. You, Lady Maud de Bohun are clearly the property of Sir Cecil Blount, the gentleman who succeeded to the property after your death. Have you any objection to that?

97

LADY M. None whatever. Cecil, I am yours.

DAME C. By the same rule, Sir Cecil, and you, Lady Maud, are both of you the property of Lord Carnaby Poppytop, who after Sir Cecil's death succeeded to the castle and all that it contained.

SIR C. But allow me to protest.

LORD C. It is useless, Sir, both of you are clearly my property, and a man may do what he likes with his own. Lady Maud, come here; Sir Cecil, go there. (*Separates* LADY MAUD *and* SIR CECIL, *placing himself between them. They are much annoyed and make signs to each other behind his back.*) Lady Maud, I think I shall marry you.

SIR C. You! But Lord Carnaby Poppytop —

LADY M. Oh! I protest against anything of the kind. Dame Cherry Maybud, please be careful how you make your award.

LORD C. My valued Leonardo da Vinci, expostulation is useless.

LADY M. This marriage is out of the question, Sir.

SIR C. It's out of the question, Sir.

LADY M. It's impossible, Sir.

LORD C. Why? Why?

LADY M. Because a man may not marry his grandmother.

DAME C. I think it is unnecessary to discuss that at present. Let me go on. We have decided that Lady Maud belongs to Sir Cecil; that Lady Maud and Sir Cecil belong to Lord Carnaby Poppytop. It follows, therefore, that Lady Maud, Sir Cecil and Lord Carnaby Poppytop all belong to me.

ALL. To you?

DAME C. To me. You are all mine, and as Lord Carnaby Poppytop says, I can do what I like with my own. Now I'm going to dispose of my property. Lord Carnaby, let the young people alone. Sir Cecil, take Lady Maud.

LORD C. And if I refuse?

DAME C. If you refuse, my Lord, my course is clear. I shall sell you to the Nation. You will be hung up in the National Gallery, where nobody will go to see you, and you will spend an ignominious existence in the society of sham Rubenses, fictitious Raphaels, and other imposters of every degree.

LORD C. But they won't buy me — I'm genuine.

DAME C. Won't they? Don't be too sure of that. If you don't take care I'll have you so restored that there won't be a trace of the original work left. They'll snap you up directly.

(*The veil before* BROWN's *portrait is withdrawn.*)

BROWN. You're settling all this very coolly and comfortably, but don't it occur to you that it is a matter in which *I* am entitled to be consulted?

ALL. You?

DAME C. And who in the world are you, Sir?

BROWN. I'm no other than the maternal grandfather of the present possessor of this castle, Mr. Alderman Tare.

DAME C. Who are you by?

BROWN. I don't know.

LORD C. When were you painted?

BROWN. I was finished yesterday and hung up yesterday afternoon.

DAME C. You're a dreadful daub.

BROWN. I'm afraid I am, but that's my misfortune, not my fault, you know. We don't paint ourselves.

LORD C. Are you considered like?

BROWN. Like, like whom?

LORD C. Like whom? Why like Mr. Alderman Tare's maternal grandfather, of course.

BROWN. Ho! ho! ho! ho!

DAME C. What is the man laughing at?

BROWN. Ho! ho! ho! ho! ho!

LORD C. How dare you laugh in my face, Sir! Explain yourself. I insist upon it.

BROWN. My dear fellow, don't excite yourself, but the question is really so absurd that you must excuse my merriment. Like his maternal grandfather! Ho! ho! ho! Why, my dear friend, old Tare never had a maternal grandfather.

DAME C. Never had a maternal grandfather!

BROWN. Never had a grandfather of any kind whatever. And what is more, he never *will* have.

LORD C. Oh, this is too absurd. Then who are you?

BROWN. I tell you, I'm the portrait of old Tare's maternal grandfather.

DAME C. But bless the man, you say he never had a maternal grandfather.

BROWN. Never, but what has that to do with it?

LORD C. You're an impostor, Sir!

BROWN. Not at all; or if I am we're all impostors.

LORD C. Explain yourself, Sir!

BROWN. With pleasure. Tare says I'm his maternal grandfather.

DAME C. But you know you're not?

BROWN. Of course.

LORD C. Then you're lending yourself to an imposture. A picture with any sense of decency would have rubbed himself out rather than be a party to such an imposition.

BROWN. But Tare's assurance don't stop there; he says that you're his great, great-grandmother, and you his great, great, great, great-grandfather!

LORD C. He does? Oh, it's monstrous!

DAME C. What an infamous fabrication!

LORD C. I never had any family at all.

DAME C. And I died a spinster.

BROWN. But Tare declares it's true.

DAME C. But we know that it's impossible.

BROWN. Then rub yourselves out without loss of time. A picture with any sense of decency would take any steps rather than be a party to such an imposition.

LORD C. (*in a great rage*). Come down, Sir, and I'll teach you to bandy words with me. Come down!

BROWN. I can't!

LORD C. Why not?

BROWN. Because I'm only a half-length, besides I'm not dry, and I might rub.

LORD C. Coward! But who could expect to find nobility of soul in such a misshapen frame!

BROWN. (*Looking at frame of his picture.*) Oh, my frame is very good — very good indeed. Well-made, and solid. A good piece of work.

LORD C. I'm alluding to your body, Sir, not your setting.

DAME C. There now, Lord Carnaby, let the poor man alone. He's a wretched daub, but he can't help that, you know. Besides, you mustn't quarrel in the presence of a lady — you won't, I know.

LORD C. Oh, won't I —

DAME C. No, I'm sure you won't — if I ask prettily (*making eyes at* LORD CARNABY). You won't, you won't, you won't, now will you?

LORD C. (*gradually relaxing*). No, I won't, indeed. (*To* BROWN.) Miserable signboard, your life is spared.

(*Coquets with* DAME CHERRY.)

LORD C. But, I say; where have they gone?

DAME C. Who?

LORD C. Sir Cecil and Lady Maud. This won't do, you know.

DAME C. There they are, in the next corridor.

LORD C. It's very disgusting. So young, and yet so lost to all sense of propriety. I shall go and call them back.

DAME C. Stop! — reflect one moment. They are two or three hundred years older than we are. Would it be delicate to interfere?

LORD C. It's rather a difficult point. Are we to judge of their age by their years or their personal appearance?

DAME C. Oh, my dear Lord Carnaby! If you judge a lady's age by her personal appearance, there'll be no end to the mistakes you'll make. Be content with the fact that they are our ancestors, and let well alone.

LORD C. I suppose there's no alternative. I say, he's kissing her!

DAME C. Well, let him kiss her. Young people will be young people.

LORD C. But you just said they were old!

DAME C. Well, then, there are no fools like old ones. If they are young, we've been young too; if they are old, we've no right to interfere. Anyway, it's no business of ours.

LORD C. Yes, we've been young; but we haven't been young together. If we had —

DAME C. If we had, we should have made ourselves very ridiculous, I dare say. Now, sit down, and leave them alone, do.

LORD C. Do you think we should have made ourselves *very* ridiculous? Very — *very* ridiculous?

DAME C. I don't know. I was very thoughtless, and extremely pretty.

LORD C. And I was very thoughtless and remarkably handsome.

DAME C. Ah! time works wonders! Now, there (*pointing to picture of a pretty young girl*) is myself at the age of nineteen.

LORD C. Exquisite! And there (*pointing to picture of young man*) am I at the age of twenty-three.

No. 9. — DUET.

LORD C. At twenty-three, Lord Carnaby, tho' anything but plain,
Was quite a coxcomb as you see, so empty-headed, vain!
I rather think he us'd to drink, no greater rake alive!
How different to Carnaby at sober sixty-five.
 Oh! not a bit like to Carnaby at sober sixty-five.

DAME C. }
LORD C. } Not a bit like, &c.

DAME C. Dame Cherry too, at seventeen was such a sad coquette,
She flirted here, she flirted there with ev'ry beau she met,
She sent a dart into each heart, and play'd such thoughtless tricks,

But oh, how different is she at sober fifty-six.
But not a bit like, in truth, is she at sober fifty-six.

DAME C. ⎫
LORD C. ⎭ Not a bit like, &c.

DAME C. Perfect! (*They gaze in rapture on each other's pictures.*)

LORD C. I say, I don't want to be rude, but wouldn't it have made it pleasanter for all parties if *that* portrait of Dame Cherry Maybud had come to life instead of *this* one (*indicating* HER).

DAME C. Oh, you think so? Very good. Shall I go back to my frame and send her down instead?

LORD C. Do! do! You won't be offended, I'm sure — it's still you, you know, only younger and — ahem! — prettier!

DAME C. Offended! not a bit — only —

LORD C. Yes.

DAME C. I was going to say that if Dame Cherry at the age of eighteen is to take the place of Dame Cherry at the age of fifty-six, it is only fair that Lord Carnaby at the age of twenty-one should take the place of Lord Carnaby at the age of sixty-five.

LORD C. Ah! Do you insist upon that?

DAME C. Oh yes, I insist upon that. Dame Cherry at eighteen would would nothing to say to an old gentleman like you, you know.

LORD C. Don't you think she would?

DAME C. I'm quite sure she wouldn't. She wouldn't hear of it.

LORD C. Am I to gather from that that Dame Cherry at the age of —

DAME C. Fifty-six.

LORD C. Oh, impossible — say thirty-five — that Dame Cherry, at the age of thirty-five, would hear of it?

DAME C. (*coquettishly*). Oh, Lord Carnaby.

(LORD CARNABY *places his arm around* DAME CHERRY'S *waist.*)

BROWN (*from frame*). I say, ahem! I don't want to interfere — but really you know — before a third party — you shouldn't; you shouldn't, indeed.

Lord C. Be quiet, Sir, and look the other way.

Brown. By all means. (*Turns his back to them.*) Will that do?

Lord C. Capitally. Stop like that until I tell you to turn round, or I'll rub you out. (*To* Dame Cherry.) Then there is only one thing to be done — to ask the sanction of our respected ancestors to our union. Ah! they come!

Enter Lady Maud *and* Sir Cecil.

Sir C. There is, however, one duty we owe to our venerable relatives — we must obtain their consent to our marriage. Ah! they are here!

(Sir Cecil *and* Lady Maud *kneel at the feet of the elder couple, who at the same moment kneel at the feet of* Sir Cecil *and* Lady Maud.)

Lord C. (*kneeling*). Eh! What's this?

Sir C. (*kneeling*). We were about to ask your consent —

Lord C. To what?

Sir C. To my marriage with Lady Maud.

Lord C. But why ask our consent?

Sir C. Because you are our oldest relatives.

Lord C. But we were going to ask your consent.

Sir C. To what?

Lord C. To my marriage with Dame Cherry.

Sir C. But why?

Lord C. Because you are my great, great, great, great-grandfather. You are our ancestors.

Sir C. But we are your property.

Brown. (*from picture*). Allow me to arrange this — you are all Alderman Tare's property — whose representative I am. Allow me to act for him, and bestow the necessary blessing.

All. With pleasure.

Brown. Then, bless you, my ancestors.   (*All rise.*)

Dame C. Well, that's comfortably settled. But bless me, the sun will rise in a few moments, when we shall all have to retire to our respective frames for a hundred years, and I declare we've been forgetting the very purpose for which we have been revived! The title deeds! (*Taking deeds from pocket.*)

LORD C. Of course, they must be given over to our next lineal descendant of the wicked Sir Roger de Bohun.

DAME C. I declare that lineal descendant to be Mr. Columbus Hebblethwaite, who is now stopping in this very house. We will leave the deeds on this table, where he will find them as soon as he descends to breakfast. (*Places deeds on table.*) There the spell is broken and may not be revived for a hundred years.

(*All kneel. Crash. Cock crows. Daylight dawns. The lights go out.*)

No. 10. — QUINTETT.

LADY M.	'Tis done, the spell is broken.
DAME C.	We must away!
SIR C.	The herald rays betoken
LORD C.	The coming day.
BROWN.	Once more we die,
	In slumber deep,
	We soundly sleep
	A century!

(*All retire to their pictures, the veils fall over them. Day breaks. lights up.*)

Enter STEWARD *rubbing his eyes and carrying portmanteau.*

STEW. Half past five in the morning and Mr. Hebblethwaite starts at six. It's little of Miss Rosa he'll see this morning. Why, what's this? (*Sees deeds.*) "Abstract of title of Columbus Hebblethwaite to Glen-Cockaleekie Castle." Why, what does it mean? And here are the original deeds sure enough. Mr. Columbus Hebblethwaite, the owner of Glen-Cockaleekie Castle! Why, Sir Ebenezer can't know of this, sure-lie! He ordered me last night to have everything ready for Mr. Hebblethwaite's departure by the 6.30 train, as he wouldn't have him in the house five minutes longer than it was necessary. Here! (*calling*) Sir Ebenezer! Mistress Mac Motherly! Miss Rosa! Mr. Hebblethwaite! Here's news for you!

Enter MRS. MAC MOTHERLY, ROSA, *and* MR. HEBBLETHWAITE.

Mrs. Mac. Eh, ye noisy loon, what are ye making a' that noise about, is the house a' fire, or have ye found yer senses. Which is it?

Stew. My senses! I've found something more than my senses, look here! "Abstract of title of Columbus Hebblethwaite to Glen-Cockaleekie Castle." I found it on the table just this minute.

Mrs. Mac. Eh! then the legend's come true! The hundred years expire this very day; and the auld castle passes into the hands of its legitimate owner, who turns out to be nae ither than Miss Rosa's Mr. Columbus.

Enter Tare, *who seizes the deeds.*

Tare. But I protest against this, Sir. It's absurd — it's impossible! I'll dispute it, Sir!

Hebble. Stop a bit. Don't let us go to law about it. I'll make a bargain with you. If you'll consent to my marriage with Rosa, you shall stop here as long as you like. Come, what do you say? Shall we all live together?

Tare. Well, Sir, if — mind, *if* — the deeds turn out to be authentic, and there is no doubt whatever of your title to this castle. Why, in that case — I say, in that case — I have no objection to entertain your proposal. Rosa, on that condition, he is yours.

No. 11. — FINALE.

Hebble. The subject drop, no need to stop to make a long oration, To make all sure I will endure her elderly relation.

Rosa. He goes not yet, so breakfast get, he needs no invitation, There'll be no need, to-day indeed, to hurry to the station.

Tare. The subject drop, no need to stop to make a long oration,

Mrs. Mac. There'll be no need, to-day indeed, to hurry to the station, There'll be no need,

Tare. There won't indeed.

All. There won't, there won't, there won't.

The subject drop, no need to stop to make a long oration, He'll endure (to make all sure) his elderly relation.

CURTAIN

"AGES AGO"

WORDS BY **W. S. GILBERT.**   MUSIC BY **FREDERIC CLAY.**

PRELUDE.

(N<u>o</u> 1.)

(Nº 1.)

(Nº 1.)

(Nº 1.)

" GOOD BYE, GOOD BYE,"

TRIO.

N° 2.

(N°2.)

bye, good bye, good bye, he's gone he's running a.long in the rain, he's gone, Good

sigh and cry, for why, he's gone he's running a.long in the rain, ha ha! Good

fie come dry your eye, he's gone he's running a.long in the rain, ha ha! Good

_f_

bye, good bye, good bye he's gone, he's running along in the rain.

bye, good bye, good bye he's gone, he's running along in the rain, he's off at

bye, good bye, good bye he's gone, he's running along in the rain, he's off at

last, he's off at last he won't come back, the train is fast.

last, he's off at last he won't come back, the train is fast. The night is

last, he's off at last he won't come back, the train is fast, The night is

(_No 2._)

'Tis not so

black, the night is black, he'll catch, he'll catch the train I know.

clear, dear Mrs Mac. for lis _ ten here, for lis _ ten here, the clock's put

back the clock's put back, it's half an hour too slow, it's half an hour too

(N⁰ 2.)

bye, good bye, good bye, good bye, Ah! he is gone, ____ good

bye, you sigh and cry, for why? Ah! he is gone, ____ good

bye, good bye, come dry your eye, Ah! he is gone, ____ good

bye, good bye, good bye, good bye, Ah! he is gone, good bye, ____

bye, you sigh and cry, for why? Ah! he is gone, good

bye, good bye, come dry your eye, Ah! he is gone, good

____ good bye, ____ *ff* he's gone.

bye, good bye, he's gone.

bye, good bye, he's gone.

(*N° 2.*)

"WHEN NATURE SLEEPS"

N⁰ 3.   DUET.

(N⁰ 3.)

and slumber creeps __ o'er mor _ tal eyes, then witch _ _ _ es

and slumber creeps __ o'er mor _ tal eyes, then witch _ _ _ es

leggiero.

play. An elf in ev_ry shadow hides!

play. On ev'_ry cloud a Warlock

to hold his tryst in moun _ tain mist. To hold his

rides, to hold his tryst in moun _ tain mist. To hold his

(N⁰ 3.)

tryst in moun _ tain mist.

On

tryst in moun _ tain mist. An elf in ev'ry shadow hides.

ev'ry cloud a Warlock rides The moon supplants the light of day,

To light the Warlocks

The moon supplants the light of day,

on their way.

To light the War _ _ locks on their

(N.º 3.)

The moon supplants the light of day— the light of day.

way. The moon supplants the light of day— the light of day.

When nature sleeps, and slumber creeps O'er mor_tal eyes then witch__es

When nature sleeps, and slumber creeps O'er mor_tal eyes then witch__es

play. When na_ture sleeps and slumber creeps O'er mor_tal

play. When na_ture sleeps and slumber creeps O'er mor_tal

(Nº8.)

eyes,   o'er mor – tal   eyes,   then   witch – es,   play, ____   then

eyes,   o'er mor – tal   eyes,   then   witches,   then   witches play,   then

witch – es   play,   When nature sleeps, when nature sleeps,   then witch – es   play, ____

witch – es   play,   When nature sleeps, when nature sleeps,   then witch – es   play, ____

Then witches play. ____

Then witches play. ____

(*N? 3.*)

"EH! WHAT IS THAT YE SAY"

SONG.

Più lento.

smirk and you may twirl, You're a var_ra sau_cy girl, And you'll

have to buy ex_pe_rience with sighs and tears, but there's nae excuse for you you're an

ancient bo_dy too, You've been forty_three for rather more than fif__teen years. There's

a tempo.

nae excuse for you, You're an ancient body too, Oh there's nae excuse for you, You're an

ancient bo_dy too. You may smirk you_may twirl, You're a very saucy girl, You may

(Nº4.)

smirk you may twirl, You're a verra sau-cy girl.

I'm blind enough, I know, But I wasn't al-ways so, Though you treat your puir old Mag-gie as a jest- -ing butt. Ye'd have had an ug-ly throw, Mony, mony years a-go, If she'd tot- -ter'd through her du-ty with her eye- -lids shut. You may

(*To Rosa.*)

(N? 4.)

Più lento.

smirk and you may twirl, You're a var _ ra sau _ ey girl, And you'll

have to buy ex _ pe _ rience with sighs and tears, but there's nae excuse for you you're an

ancient bo _ dy too, You've been forty _ three for rather more than fif _ _ teen years. There's

a tempo.

nae excuse for you, You're an ancient body too, Oh there's nae excuse for you, You're an

ancient bo _ dy too. You may smirk you _ may twirl, You're a very saucy girl, You may

(N⁰4.)

(Nº 4.)

(№ 5.)

_ _ lum _ _ bus dear, thy knock I hear with min _ _ gled hopes and fears, _ _

It's mur _ mur laves with edd _ ying waves, the por _ tals of my

_ ears! Co _ _ _ lum _ _ _ _ _ _ _ _ bus dear,

You tremble so, you tremble so, I'm sure you know, I'm sure you

Thy knock, thy knock I hear! Co _ _ _ lum _ _ _

know, Who's knock _ ing at my gate, I'm sure you know,

ritard:

ritard:

TARE.

a tempo.

(.Nᵒ 5.)

(.N⁰ 5.)

MODERATO.

HEB:

Per - mit me! Per - mit me! Per -

- mit me a short ex-pla-na-tion, I left you to go to the station, and

thought not to see you a - - gain, to see you a - gain, The time was so short that I

hur - - ried, the time was so short that I hur - - ried, I really felt ter-ri-bly

flur - ried at the no - - tion,——— the notion of miss - - - - - - ing my

(.v.g.s.)

(N° 5.)

HEBB:

This mo_ _ dern e_ _di_ _tion _____ of coach_ _ing,

I heard like a rock_ _et ap_proach_ing, I

had not a mo_ment to look, So for_ _ _ward_ in a_go_ny

spring_ _ing, in a_go_ny spring_ing, _____ I ran, _____ I

ran, I_ _ran, I ran, I ran to the place, to the place where_ they

(Nº 5.)

eager_ly ran to the small office door, I well knew the way, for I'd been there before!

I tapp'd at the wicket, I ask'd for a

tick _ _ et, And laid down the price of the jour_ _ ney, and more, I

ritard: laid down the price of the jour _ _ _ _ _ ney, and more.

colla voce.

Piu Lento.

Piu Lento.

"Give me" quoth I _ "to my home, to my home I fly, Where the

(.Nº 5.)

(Nº 5.)

skies of eve re_ceive__ the sigh of the vi_o_let, The sigh of the vi_o_let!

skies of eve re_ceive__ the sigh, _____ The sigh of the vi_o_let!

skies of eve re_ceive__ the sigh, _____ The sigh of the vi_o_let!

skies of eve re_ceive__ the sigh _____ of the vi_o_let!

skies of eve re_ceive__ the sigh _____ of the vi_o_let!

Piu Vivo.

Come with me, clerk (if ex_cuse you can trump a_ny), Bo_ther the sta_tion and

bo_ther the com_pa_ny. Come to my thatche_ry, Se_mi_detach_e_ry, Ro_ses and posies shall

(N.º 5.)

flow _ er the way, ro _ ses and posies shall flow'r the way, Come, come

clerk _ oh come.

Primo tempo.

My ticket I seized, I rush'd to the

sta _ _ tion, The clerk had re _ fused my po _ lite in _ vi _ ta _ _ tion,

Oh! hor _ _ ror, oh! hor _ _ ror, I

(*N⁰ 5.*)

fell, _____ I fell to the earth!

con forza.

Or this.

For I noticed the train it was on_ly too plain,
It was just moving

For I no _ _ ticed the train,
It was

off to the land of my birth, Was mo _ _ _ ving off to the land, the land of my

on _ ly too plain, Was mo _ _ ving off to the land, the land of my

ff

(N⁰ 5.)

(Nº 5.)

birth!

birth!

birth!

birth!

birth!

ALLEGRO MA NON TROPPO MOSSO.

ROSA.

We'll

do our best to make your rest as pleasant as can be, Sir.

(Nº 5.)

STEW:

Your cheery face, In such a place, We're ve_ry glad to see, We're

TARE.

ve_ry glad to see, Sir. But stop. I say, You went a_way, And

spoke not of re_turn_ing and spoke not of re_turn _ ing.

MRS MC

It's ve_ry clear

ri _ _ _ _ tar _ _ _ do.

it's ve_ry clear He's come back here for Mistress Ro_sa burn _ ing!

colla voce.

a tempo.

f

ff

(Nº 5.)

Nº 6. "IT DOES PERPLEX, ANNOY AND VEX"

COUPLETS & QUINTETT.

VOICE.

ff

1st Verse Columbus.

p

It does per_plex, An_

2nd Verse Rosa.

p

Your room is old, And

noy and vex For_give the ob_ser _ va_ _tion, When just too late, In breathless state, You

damp,and cold, Un_wor_thy hab_i _ ta_ _tion, The spi_der crawls A_bout the walls And

see with ir_ri_ ta_tion, The starting train,while you re_ main In dreadful per_tur_

fills you with vex_a_tion, Had I but known you would have flown, You'll judge by this nar_

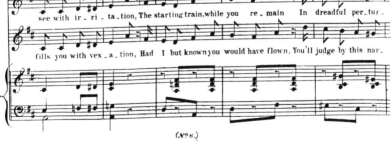

(*Nº 6.*)

_ba_tion, To spend the night, Till morning light, At some un_heard of sta_tion, To

_ra_tion, To make it good, This morning would Have been my oc _ cu _ pa _ tion, To

spend the night Till morning light, In some un_heard of sta_tion! It does perplex, An_

spend the night Till morning light, In some un_heard of sta_tion! It does perplex, An_

_noy, and vex, an _ noy, and vex! It does per_plex! An_noy, and

_noy, and vex, an _ noy, and vex! It does per_plex! An_noy, and

(№ 6.)

(№ 6.)

starting train, While you remain In dreadful per_tur _ ba _ _ tion To spend the night Till

starting train, While you remain In dreadful per_tur _ ba _ _ tion To spend the

morning light, At some unheard of sta_tion. It does perplex, An_noy and vex, For_

night At some unheard of sta_tion. It does perplex, An_noy and vex, For_

It does perplex, An_noy and vex, For_

It does perplex, An_noy and vex, For_

It does perplex, An_noy and vex, For_

(N°6.)

give the ob_ser_va_ _tion, To spend the night Till morn_ing light, At

give the ob_ser_va_ _tion, To spend the night Till morn_ing light, At

give the ob_ser_va_ _tion, To spend the night Till morn_ing light, At

give the ob_ser_va_ _tion, To spend the night Till morn_ing light, At

give the ob_ser_va_ _tion, To spend the night Till morn_ing light, At

1st time.   2nd time.

some unheard of sta_tion!   sta_ _ _ tion!

some unheard of sta_tion!   sta_ _ _ tion!

some unheard of sta_tion!   sta_ _ _ tion!

some unheard of sta_tion!   sta_ _ _ tion!

some unheard of sta_tion!   sta_ _ _ tion!

(No 8.)

"WE FLY TO FIELDS OF FANCY"

QUARTETT.

mystic flight, By Nature's ne _ cro _ man _ cy. Good night! good

mystic flight, By Nature's ne _ cro _ man cy. Good night! good

mystic flight, By Nature's ne _ cro _ man cy. Good night! good

mystic flight, By Nature's ne _ cro _ man cy. Good night! good

night! By gen _ _ tle Luna's light, by gen _ _ tle Luna's

night! By gen _ _ tle Luna's light, by gen _ _ tle Luna's

night!

night! By gen _ _ tle Luna's light, by gen _ _ tle Luna's

(Nº7.)

bright.　　We meet a-gain to-mor-row.

We meet a-gain to-mor-row. Good night! Good

Good night! Good

No pass- -ing breath of sor-row shall dim our vi-sions

No pass- -ing breath of sor-row shall dim our vi-sions

night.

night.

(№ 7.)

bright, We meet again to mor _ _ row, Good night, we meet again to mor _ _ row, Good

bright, We meet again to mor _ _ row, Good night, we meet again to mor _ _ row, Good

We meet again to mor _ _ row, Good night, we meet again to mor _ _ row, Good

We meet again to mor _ _ row, Good night, we meet again to mor _ _ row, Good

ritard.

night We meet, we meet again to mor _ _ row,

ritard.

night We meet, we meet again to mor _ _ row,

ritard.

night We meet, we meet again to mor _ _ row,

ritard.

night We meet, we meet again to mor _ _ row,

colla voce.

(№ 7.)

(№ 7.)

night   But though we wing our flight   We   meet   again to

night   But though we wing our flight   We   meet   again to

night   But though we wing our flight   We   meet   again to

night   But though we wing our flight   We   meet   again to

mor _ _ row   We   meet   a _ _ _ gain   to   mor _ row.

mor _ _ row   We   meet   a _ _ _ gain   to   mor _ row.

mor _ _ row   We   meet   a _ _ _ gain   to   mor _ row.

mor _ _ row   We   meet   a   gain   to   mor _ row.

mf

(.Nᵒ 7.)

Good night! Good night! Good night! We meet a-

Good night! Good night! Good night! We meet a-

Good night! Good night! Good night! We meet a-

Good night! Good night! Good night!

_ gain to _ mor _ _ _ row Good night! Good night!

_ gain to _ mor _ _ _ row Good night! Good night!

_ gain to _ mor _ _ row Good night! Good night!

to _ mor _ _ row Good night! Good night!

ritard. _ _ _

_ al _ fine _ _ _ _

(Nº 7.)   (The stage grows dark.)

Nº 8.   ENTR'ACTE & RECIT:

HARMONIUM.

PIANO.

ANDANTE.

ANDANTE.

tremolo.

G.J. (but pia.)

Piu vivo.

Piu vivo.

(Nº 8.)

(Harp on the Stage.)

(N.º 8.)

LADY MAUD. RECIT.

I breathe! I live! since last I saw the day, Five tar - dy

cen - tu - ries have pass'd a - - way —— No long-er o'er my

(Nº 8.)

grave let chap-lets wreathe, My bosom throbs with life— I live! I

breathe! My bo - - - som throbs with life, I breathe! I

HARP.

HARMONIUM.

live!

(*Nº 8.*)

Nº 9.

ANDANTINO. **"MOMENTS SO FLEETING"**
SONG.

PIANO

LADY MAUD.

Mo_ments so fleet_ing   Stern spirits give,   My heart is beat_ing I

breathe I breathe I live!___   For three short hours   While dark_ness lowers.

By mystic powers I   breathe___ I live!   By mys_ _tic powers I

breathe   I live!

(Nº 9)

Night's sombre awn-ing Has set me free, The daylight's dawn-ing brings

night to me. My heart is ach-ing, The daylight's breaking,

All others wa-king, Brings night. brings night to me, brings night to

me, Brings night to me, Mo-ments so fleet-ing,

stern spirits give, My heart is beat-ing, I breathe, I breathe, I live.

(Nº 9.)

For three short hours, While dark _ _ _ ness low _ ers, By mys _ _ tic pow _ ers, I

live, _____ by mystic pow'rs I live, While dark _ ness, while dark _ _ ness

sempre f.

low'rs, I breathe, I live, By mystic pow_ ers I breathe, I

live, While dark _ _ _ ness, while dark ness low'rs, I breathe, I

breathe, _____ I live!

ritard -
.(№ 9.)

"WOULD YOU KNOW THAT MAIDEN FAIR".

N° 10.   SONG.

N° 10.

hap‿pi‿ness a‿‿‿wait‿ing you a mai‿den loves you well a

mai‿‿‿den, a mai‿‿‿den, a maiden loves you well She

dares not to de‿‿‿clare the love that makes her sigh And

would you know that mai‿‿den Ah! would you know that mai‿den fair! So

please you Sir, 'tis I . . . 'tis I . . . 'tis I . . . . and would you know that

Nᵒ 10.

mai......den, Ah! would you know that mai.....den so please you Sir, 'tis

I 'tis I........ So please you Sir 'tis I

She would a Saint be

-- guile ... Her hair is soft and bright She would a saint be

Nº 10.

__guile· Her hair is soft and bright A happy laugh a

plea___sant smile, and eyes that dance with light And

eyes .... that dance .... and eyes that dance with light A

dim_ple here and there A pret_ty touching sigh And

would you know that mai___den Ah! would you know that mai_den fair, So

N?. 10.

N? 10.

ANDANTE

SIR AUBREY. *from the picture*

A sweeter fate I ne...ver heard............. My gra..ti..tude, my gra..titude you've earned

LADY MAUD (aside)

(My goodness me......... he's talk......ing)

SIR AUBREY.

The com..pli..ment upon my word............. was ve...ry neatly turned

LADY MAUD.

.....ve...ry neat..ly turned (My goodness me.... he's walk.......ing!)

Nº 10

SIR AUBREY.

Her goodness she..... I'm walk......ing!

LADY MAUD. p

ALLEGRO.

To laugh it off I can't con_trive with

fright I'm near_ly fainting- I never thought you were a..live I

thought you were a pain...ting! I never thought you were a..live I

SIR AUBREY.

thought you were a ...pain..ting! To laugh it off she can't con_trive with

Nº 10.

fear she's near...ly fainting. I ne_ver thought I was a ...live I

thought I was a 'pain..ting I ne..........ver ne.........ver

thought I was a __live I never thought I was a ...live

LADY MAUD.
To laugh it off I can't con..trive with fright I'm nearly

To laugh it off she can't con..trive with fright she's

fain..ting I never thought you were a __live! I never thought you were a_

fain_ting I never thought you were a__live!

Nº 10

"IN PITY TELL, O LADY MINE."

DUET.

In pi...ty tell, oh La...dy mine!.... the fate that waits me, my life is thine! 'Tis thine..... to spare 'tis thine to kill, 'tis thine to fashion to thy fair will...... 'tis

Nº 11.

thine   'tis   thine   'tis thine to fashion to thy..... fair

LADY MAUD

will!   If   this   is   so, what can I   do........ the word that

kills.... thee would kill   me   too .....   My   hand........... and

heart .... to   thee.......   to thee   I   give ......

the   word   that   saves   thee, now bids me live, now   bids   me

Nº 11

live! The word, the word that kills thee –

In pi_ _ty tell, Oh! La......dy! Oh! tell the fate that

that word would kill me too, my hand and heart to thee...... I.......

waits me. Oh! La...............dy

give, my hand and heart to thee I........ give, the word that

mine! Oh! La..........dy mine!

Nº 11.

saves thee, now bids........... me live................ now

Oh! La........

hids..... me live! Ah!........... me!

...dy................... mine! Ah!........... me!

They................ should..... be one my life and thine Oh!

A........................life of death, a life of life with

give it then if it be mine A term..... of joy, a

joy abounding, with sor__row rife A term..... of joy, a

term of grief So

term of grief So long..... so long with_out thee!

long..... so long with_out thee with...out thee with thee too

With thee too

ff

ff

Nᵒ 11.

brief! So long with‿out thee With thee too

brief! So long with‿out thee With thee too

brief too brief........................... with

brief too brief........................... with

thee too..... brief..................

thee too..... brief..................

Nº 11.

"I STAND ON MY AUTHORITY."

TRIO.

stand on my au..tho...ri...ty and won...der what you mean!

still in your mi....no...ri...ty you're hard_ly se..ven...teen

Car......na..by, in ve.....ri..ty your rude...ness pains me much

You're

Your

La...dy Maud's pos....te..ri...ty, be have your-self as such

Your

My.

grand ma..ma in Cha..ri..ty con.....cludes you must be mad! Now

grand ma..ma in Cha..ri..ty con....cludes you must be mad! Now

grand ma..ma in Cha..ri...ty con......cludes I must be mad! My

No 12.

sure as I'm a live, why sure as I'm a live his grandmama is

strange a meet ing ne'er was seen so strange a

strange a meet ing ne'er was seen so strange a

seven teen and he is six ty five She is sev en teen and he is

meet ing ne'er was seen For she is sev en teen and he is

meet ing ne'er was seen For she is sev en teen and he is

six ty five! Should

six ty five! Should

six ty five! Should

Nº 12.

Should he   make me his   will o__

her   pro_pri__e___tor!

her   pro_pri__e____tor!

_bey!

As........   her   pro____pri___e___tor!

As........   her   pro____pri___e____tor!

Should   he

make   me his   will   o_____bey   As.....   my   pro___pri_____e_

N.º 12.

strange a meet_ing ne'er........ was seen, for sure his

strange a meet_ing ne'er........ was seen, for sure his

strange a meet_ing ne'er........ was seen, for sure my

Grand_ma__ma is se__ven_teen and he is six__ty five

Grand_ma__ma is se__ven_teen and he is six__ty five

Grand_ma__ma is se__ven_teen and I am six__ty five

"AT TWENTY THREE LORD CARNABY."

DUET.

At twen__ty three, Lord Car_____na___by tho'
an_____y thing but plain was quite a cox___comb
as you see so emp___ty head___ed, vain! I

Nº 13.

ra.....ther think, he us'd to drink, no great...er rake a-

live..... how dif..fer..ent to Car..na..by at so....ber six...ty

Rit: *a Tempo.*

five_ Oh! Not a bit like to Car.......na....by at

molto Rit: *a Tempo.* *p*

so.......ber six.....ty five......... not a bit like to

a Tempo.

Car.......na....by at so.......ber six.......ty five.....

a Tempo.

Nº 13.

DAME CHERRY.

Not a bit like to Car---na--by at so---ber six---ty five!........ Not a bit like to Car-----na---by! at so-------ber six-------ty five!.......

DAME CHERRY.

Dame

Nº 13.

Cher-ry too at sev-_en_teen was such a sad co-----quette she

flir-__ted here, she flir-_ted there with ev'-__ry beau she met She

sent a dart in-_to each heart and play'd such thought_less tricks but

molto Rit:

Oh! how dif-__fer__ent is she at so-__ber fif-_ty six But

molto Rit:

a Tempo.

not a bit like in truth is she at so-__ber fif-_ty six-------

N° 13.

Not a bit like in truth is she Dame Cherry at fif...ty six!

Not a bit like in truth is she at so...ber fif..ty six

Not a bit like in truth is she at so...ber fif..ty six

Not a bit like in truth is she Dame Cherry at fif....ty

Not a bit like in truth is she Dame Cherry at fif....ty

six!

six!

Nº 13.

'TIS DONE THE SPELL IS BROKEN.

QUINTETT.

LADY MAUD.
DAME CHERRY
SIR AUBREY.
LORD CARNABY
BROWN.
HARP.
PIANO.

'Tis done ...... the spell is

'Tis done, 'tis

'Tis done, 'tis

'Tis done, 'tis

'Tis done, 'tis

N° 14.

N⁰ 14.

N.º 14.

No 14.

Once more

Once more

Once more we sleep a cen_tu_-ry!

Once more we sleep a cen_tu_-ry!

once more we sleep a cen.........tu_-ry we must a_

once more we sleep a cen...tu...........ry

once more we sleep a cen.........tu...........ry

once more we sleep a cen....tu...........ry

once more we sleep a cen...tu...........ry

Nº 14.

"THE SUBJECT DROP."

FINALE.

VIVACE.

COLUMBUS.

The sub_ject drop, no need to stop to make a...long o-

ROSA

....ra...tion, to maké all sure I will en_dure her el_der_ly re__la_tion. He

N.º 15.

goes not yet, so breakfast get he needs no in..vi......ta.......tion Therell

be no need, to day in_deed to hur__ry to the sta...tion The

Colla voce.

a Tempo.

sub_ject drop, no need to stop to make a long o ....ra....tion.Therell

f *a Tempo.*

he no need to.....day in deed to hur.......ry to the

sta.......tion Therell be no need There won't in_

ff

TARE.

M⸸ˢ M.

TARE

N⸰ 15.

N.º 15.

day in_deed to hur_ry to the sta___tion He goes not yet so

need __to hur__ry to the sta____tion He goes not yet so

He goes not yet so

He goes not yet .so

He goes not yet so

breakfast get he needs, he needs no in_vi___ta__tion There's no need to

breakfast get he needs, he needs no in__vi___ta__tion There's no need to

breakfast get he needs, he needs no in__vi__ta__tion There's no need to

breakfast get he needs, he needs no in__vi__ta__tion There's no need to

breakfast get he needs, he needs no in__vi__ta__tion There's no need to

Nọ 15.

-day in deed to hur..ry to the sta.........tion!

-day in deed to hur..ry to the sta.........tion!

-day in deed to hur..ry to the sta.........tion!

-day in deed to hur..ry to the sta.........tion!

-day in deed to hur..ry to the sta.........tion!

Nº 15.

Our Island Home

Characters

SCENE: *The shore of an Island in the Indian Ocean — the left of the platform is covered with luxurious tropical vegetation — the right is barren, and rocky. A portion of the rock (R.) is covered with matting.*

MRS. REED *is discovered on a rock, dressed in fantastic but picturesque clothing of leaves.*

MRS. R.   Three dreary months have passed away and yet we starve on this uncomfortable piece of rock. Three months have passed since Mr. Reed and I together with Miss Fanny Holland and that fiend incarnate, young Arthur Cecil, were by the Captain of the "Hot Cross Bun" upon this hateful isle deposited.

Oh, I have borne such wrongs since I've been here, such infamies, such cruel injustices, at Mr. Cecil's hands that I could tear his evil eyes from their abiding place — well, well — no matter — but a time *will* come. In the meantime we will dissemble, Sir, as best we may. What ho there! Mr. Reed.

REED. (*without*).   Yes, my dear!

MRS. R.   Is anything in sight?

REED.   Nothing, my dear!

MRS. R.   You may come down. He has been perched upon that bad eminence six hours and thirty minutes, a little rest perhaps will do him good. In twenty minutes up he goes again.

(*Mr. Reed clambers down rock.*)

REED.   Twenty minutes more and up I go again. Mrs. Reed — mercy!

MRS. R.   Never.

REED.   The air is cold up there, and the rocks cut like razors.

MRS. R.   Your duty is to keep a sharp look-out.

REED.   There's no doubt about its sharpness. Moody woman, will nothing touch your heart?

MRS. R.   Nothing — you have yourself to blame for all. Aye, Sir, yourself, yourself, yourself and several times yourself — that is, if you can be indeed yourself who are so frequently beside yourself.

REED.   But my dear, consider; it wasn't my idea to go on an Asiatic tour with "Ages Ago."

109

Mrs. R.   In truth that fortunate idea was mine.

Reed.   And coming home in the steamship after a profitable season was it *I* who insisted on playing "Ages Ago" in the Chief Cabin every evening till the passengers could stand it no longer and petitioned the Captain to put us all on shore on the first island he came to — Certainly not! It was your idea and you compelled me to carry it out. I expostulated but *you* insisted; when you *do* insist — oh Lord!

Mrs. R.   Enough of this recrimination, Sir, and understand me, German, once for all. You are my lord and master — yours the right to check a weak and inexperienced wife when she suggests an injudicious course (*shaking him*). You are a man; I, a weak woman, sir — your humble, truthful, timid little wife. You should exercise your influence to check me in my injudicious wish e'en to the length of physical treatment.

Reed.   My dear, I didn't think you'd like it.

Mrs. R.   Like! Ha, ha! like it? I do like that! What invalid likes medicine? Like it? Why, what matters that if it were good for me.

Reed. (*meekly*)   Yes my dear, but I *did* remonstrate and you threatened to get the Captain to put me in irons — that's all! You're very hard on me — you insist on making all arrangements yourself, and then you blame me when things turn out badly. It is all your fault that Arthur Cecil has the only part of the island on which anything will grow, for his share, while you and Miss Holland and I have to live on a barren rock and are entirely dependent on him for everything we eat.

Mrs. R.   I shared the island, Sir, in equal fourths. One fourth I gave you, and one other fourth I gave Miss Holland; one I took myself — and the remaining portion I assigned to that black-hearted monster, Arthur Cecil. This very just arrangement I designed when I imagined this isle was all rock — as our three fourths unfortunately are, and little dreamt the fourth that I assigned to Cecil was an Eastern Paradise, teeming with fruitful life of every kind, game of all kinds and Cochin China fowls — his shores abounding with the choicest fish — his beach encrusted with the rarest molusces, fine Aldermanic turtle, oysters, too, and the retiring periwink, while these our shores are naked as your hand — our pebble beach as hard as your heart — our glassy seas as empty as your head!

I am a weak and trembling girl, unfitted quite to combat with the world. You are a man — my husband — it was yours to check my wayward whim and set me right.

REED. Yes, go on, we are entirely dependent on him for everything we eat, and I did it all. He finds out what particular food we hate and feeds us on it, and I'm responsible. He makes us to sing carols to wake him in the morning, and it's my fault. He insists upon your speaking to him in blank verse, and it's all owing to me. He insists upon my keeping up perpetual conversation with him in rhyme, and I've no one to blame but myself. He compels Miss Holland to address him in recitatives, and I'm entirely to blame. Go on at me, I've no friends —

MRS. R. Rebellious insolent! Come, up you go. Resume your post this instant, sirrah, or —

REED. (*on his knees*). Forgive me — I apologise — I entreat — I'll say anything if you'll only let me stop and take my chance of what Arthur Cecil may give us for breakfast. I've eaten nothing since the day before yesterday, and I'm getting a little faint. Ha! here's Miss Holland. Good morning, Miss Holland. (*Enter Miss Holland with extemporised breakfast tray, and breakfast.*) And what have you got there?

MISS H. Ah, this is Mr. Cecil's breakfast — coconut milk, plover's eggs, fried soles, turtle fin, two pounds of ham, fourteen pork chops, and a roast pheasant. Don't it smell nice?

MRS. R. (*moodily*) In truth the viands have a goodly savour. Stay, think you that when eating pheasant men are prone to count the legs?

MISS H. Eh? How do you mean?

MRS. R. A pheasant, Miss, has two legs. Suppose we say (for sake of argument) its legs are two. If one were taken from it, do you think its absence would be noted?

MISS H. Oh, I'm sure it would — I wouldn't hear of such a thing. He feeds me on coconuts and bread fruit on condition that I cook his meals and if I allowed his breakfast to be tampered with it would be more than my place is worth.

REED. But you can explain that the pheasant had met with an accident — that it was a cripple — that it has been run over by an omnibus and wore a wooden leg — anything — for we are so hungry.

MISS H. Quite out of the question, but what's the matter with Mrs. Reed?

REED. Mrs. Reed has been talking blank verse all day and she's quite exhausted.

Miss H. But why does she talk blank verse when Mr. Cecil isn't here?

Reed. By way of keeping her hand in. She's always bothering *me* to talk rhyme when we are alone by way of keeping my hand in, but fortunately I have a wonderful gift of improvising and I've no occasion to practise.

Miss H. As for my recitation I take my chance about that. But it is time to wake the monster, and his breakfast is getting cold.

Reed. Well, I've written a new carol for him — he makes us wake him with a new carol every morning. Here are the parts — now then all ready! (*To Cecil's tent.*) Oh you double-dyed scoundrel!

[*Carol omitted in typescript.*]

(*Mr. Cecil comes from his tent yawning.*)

Cecil. That'll do, good people — bless you. Now, Miss Holland, breakfast.

Reed. But how about *our* breakfast? We have eaten nothing for two days.

Cecil. I thought I told you *always* to address me in rhyme.

Reed. Oh I beg pardon. Let's see —
We feel particularly hung(a)ry
And we should like a — a — a slice of Kungary.

Cecil. Kungary? Don't keep it.

Reed. (*explaining*). Kangaroo.

Cecil. You said Kungary.

Reed. Yes, local accent.

Cecil. Oh indeed? No, I can't spare you any Kangaroo. Do you like oysters?

Reed. Ugh! I can't bear oysters.

Cecil. Rhyme —

Reed. Keep 'em, and give 'em to — to — to — monks in cloisters.

Mrs. R. I cannot touch an oyster — never could.
Of all the shelly tribe an oyster is

The mollusc I do most abominate.
And when old age electrotypes my hair
With bands of silver —

Cecil. Very good — fine metaphor.

Mrs. R. (*haughtily*). I thank you, Sir!
— electrotypes my hair
With bands of silver, I shall hate it still.

Miss H. (*sings*).
I stand out for my share
Of womanly assertion,
And oysters I declare
Have been my pet aversion.
I've heard that oysters crossed in love may be,
And oysters I from babyhood have hated;
So should an oyster fall in love with me,
Its passion would not be reciprocated.

All.　　　I've　⎫
　　　　　　　⎬ heard that oysters, etc.
　　　　　She's ⎭

Cecil. Ha, that's unfortunate, for I've just discovered a bed of the very finest natives, and I intend to devote them to your exclusive sustenance.

Mrs. R. This is too much! Tyrant! thine hour has come — we throw off once for all thy hated yoke. No more we crouch beneath thy tyrant will. And Mr. Reed, Miss Holland, and myself resume once more the attitude of man.

Cecil. (*aside*). This is a crisis. Now, my favourite orb, this time to work thy spell.

(*He glares sternly at them — they quail.*)

Mrs. R. Ha! Ha! that eye!

(*Mrs. Reed glides off and Mr. Reed falls against a rock, overpowered by the brilliancy of Cecil's eye.*)

DUET.

Miss H. Oh Mr. Cecil, Sir, how can you?
Behold my tears, they should unman you.

And when the tear-drop in the eye
Is supplemented with a sigh,
A man must be devoid of feeling
Who can resist such mute appealing.

CECIL. Since England faded from my Dolland,
By Reed and Mrs. Reed, Miss Holland,
I've been invariably snubbed,
Against the grain most cruelly rubbed.
They've sowed their crop and they must reap it.
I've made a vow and I will keep it;
When e'er I think of it, I rage, I fume!

MISS H. From your emphatic manner I presume
You have some grievance, Sir.

CECIL. Precisely, Miss — I have a grievance.

MISS H. What's its nature?

CECIL. At all the best hotels and inns
I've spent enormous sums
While you have stayed with Mandarins
With Rajahs and Begums;
With Emperors and Royal Swells
You've managed all to stop
While I devoured in lone hotels
My solitary chop!

MISS H. But Emperors are hollow joys
And Mandarins are snares;
A Begum very quickly cloys,
She gives herself such airs.
You ask me why to kingly halls
Yourse'f we didn't bring?
We heard you were a Radical
That couldn't bear a King.

CECIL. However, my turn has come now and I mean to make the
most of it. This is a pleasant life, Miss Holland.

MISS H. (*recitative*).
I'm glad you like it — ah how glad!
But 'tis a life of which a little
Goes a long — long — long, long way.

CECIL. There's an easy abandon about this island life that suits me down to the ground. Lovely climate — plenty to eat and drink — nothing to do except to eat and drink it — three intelligent persons to amuse me — no Gallery of Illustration — and nothing to pay.

MISS H. (*recitative*).
    And yet I've heard you sigh, I've seen you weep;
    I've seen you plunged in meditation deep,
            Ah me! how often.
    And I've said when I have heard you sigh
    And seen the tear-drop glisten in your eye,
            His heart will soften.

CECIL. (*aside*). Shall I confide in her? She seems sympathetic — I will! (*to Miss H.*) Listen. I am the victim of a hopeless passion.

MISS H. A hopeless passion? How romantic!

CECIL. Yes — do you like anchovy with fish?

MISS H. Yes, pretty well. (*aside*) What a strange question!

CECIL. I adore anchovy sauce. Every day it occupies my thoughts; every night I dream that I am a young man at Burgess's, dwelling so to speak in a harem of anchovy sauce. But why should I intrude my sorrows on you? The subject is a painful one. — Talking of fish, you have cooked this sole like a Francatelli.

MISS H. (*recitative*).
    I'm glad you like it,
    Very, very, very glad.
    (*aside*) Oh, Monster!

CECIL. And by way of recompense I'll dispense with recitative at present.

MISS H. Very well and now that I'm allowed the free use of my tongue, allow me to express my opinion of your conduct towards us and let me tell you I think it is simply infamous. It is barbarous, monstrous, utterly and unspeakably monstrous. Now that's what I think of you and you may make the most of it. (*aside*) Ha! that eye!

(*He gazes sternly at her, and she quails.*)

CECIL. (*aside*). My favourite orb has done its duty well.

MISS H. Mysterious man, what is the secret of the influence that attaches to that extraordinary eye? Its wild lustre dazzles me. (*As if fascinated.*) Oh, thou mysterious orb.

CECIL. (*aside*). She little thinks that it is a glass one.

REED. (*from above*). Hallo! all of you!

(*Enter Mrs. Reed.*)

MRS. R. What's the matter? Anything in sight?

REED. Yes.

MRS. R. A sail! A sail! We are saved! saved!

TRIO.

Hurrah, a sail!
Blow, gentle gale,
And fan it to our shore;
Upon this isle
In savage style
We rusticate no more.

Our troubles end,
And we shall spend
This night on yonder ship;
We'll celebrate
Our happy fate
With hip! hip! hip! hip! hip! Hurrah!

(*Reed has descended during this trio and gazes on them in astonishment.*)

REED. I didn't say there was a sail in sight, my dear. I said there was *something*. It isn't a sail, it's a cask, apparently a provision cask, which is floating to our shores.

MRS. R. (*to Cecil*). Mind, if it's cast upon our shores, the cask belongs to us.

CECIL. Certainly — and to *me* if it is cast upon *my* shores.

MRS. R. Agreed! (*The cask is seen floating in the distance.*)

[*A quartette is indicated but omitted in the typescript.*]

(*After Quartette, the cask is cast on Reed's shore.*)

REED. It's ours. (*He rolls it on shore.*)

MRS. R. Now, Minion, the days of thy oppressive dynasty are numbered. At last we are independent of thee.

CECIL. I beg your pardon, but will you celebrate your freedom in blank verse as per agreement.

MRS. R. Never!

CECIL. This is rebellion.

MRS. R. It is!

CECIL. Let me understand what you want. Now pray be distinct.

MRS. R. I will be distinct — so distinct!

(*They wag their heads.*)

CECIL. Their manner is very extraordinary. It cannot be that anything has disagreed with them. I must again resort to my invaluable eye.

(*Melodramatic stare as before.*)

MRS. R. Ha! ha! I anticipated it. We are prepared.

(*Mr. and Mrs. Reed and Miss Holland put on green spectacles and return his stare without shrinking.*)

CECIL. Ha! Baffled!

MRS. R. The spell's broken — we are free.

REED. But, my dear, consider. Isn't it rather rash to —

MISS H. Don't interfere, Mr. Reed. You know you're always in the wrong.

REED. But —

MRS. R. Silence, sir. We may now be free. This cask contains provision enough to last us a month; before that time has elapsed a vessel will have sighted us and we shall be saved.

REED. But allow me, my dear, to suggest —

MRS. R. Will you be quiet, sir! (*Shaking him.*) We are no longer dependent for the food we eat on the whims of a capricious tyrant. We are free agents, disestablished, and we hereby renounce all allegiance to him. (*Mr. Reed's head in the cask.*)

REED. But —

MRS. R. Will you do as I order you! Meat, meat, meat in abundance, meat for breakfast, meat for dinner, meat for tea! Oh, we will have such meals! (*Reed stares in the head of the cask.*)

MRS. R. What is it?

REED. Anchovy sauce.

CECIL. Ah! Can it be?

MRS. R. Well, Mr. Reed, a nice mess you've made of this.

REED. I've made of this! Come, I like that!

MRS. R. Upon my word, Mr. Reed, you've involved us in a very pretty predicament.

REED. I involved you, my dear? You did it all yourself.

MISS H. And pray, Mr. Reed, I should like to know whether you expect Mrs. Reed and myself to live for a month on nothing but anchovy sauce.

REED. But you *would* declare our independence before you knew what was in the cask.

MRS. R. I *would*! I *would*! And pray what were you about all the while you allowed me to do so? I am a mere woman, a poor, weak, helpless woman. If I make mistakes it is your duty in right of your superior knowledge of the world to correct me.

REED. My dear, I said it was injudicious.

MRS. R. You said — words — words. Pitiful man, you should have *acted*; you should have choked my mouth when you heard me making injudicious remarks, and if that had not the effect of stopping me, you should have carried me bodily away.

(*In the meantime Cecil has been tasting the anchovy as an epicure tasting curious old port.*)

CECIL. (*aside*). Admirable — the bouquet is perfect. (*aloud*) Stop, I have a suggestion. You have a cask of anchovy sauce, I will purchase a quart of it with any produce my share of the island supplies.

REED. Agreed!

MRS. R. Stop! Mr. Reed, how dare you interfere? Leave this to me. (*to Cecil*) No sir, we are not retail traders — the whole cask or none.

CECIL. Good. How much?

MRS. R. Our terms are these — we exchange shares of this island. You take our shares, we take yours.

REED. But, my dear, now don't be rash.

MISS H. There you are, Mr. Reed, you must interfere. Mrs. Reed is quite able to take care of herself.

MRS. R. We must have full control over all the produce of your shares; you may have full control over the barrel of anchovy sauce. Moreover, we will undertake to supply you with any animal or vegetable food you may require.

REED. Mrs. Reed, I must protest against our entering into this agreement rashly.

MRS. R. Silence, sir; attend to your own business and leave me to manage mine.

CECIL. Are these your unalterable terms?

MRS. R. They are.

CECIL. I agree on one condition — that you surrender those green spectacles.

MRS. R. Good. There they are. (*Hands them over.*)

REED. Oh, but I say, you know —

MRS. R. Silence, sir, the thing is done, and we take possession. Mr. Reed, you will call every day on Mr. Cecil for orders.

(*They take formal possession of Cecil's share; he takes theirs.*)

[*A quartette is indicated but omitted in the typescript.*]

(*After Quartette, exeunt Mr. and Mrs. Reed and Miss Holland.*)

CECIL. Here I am at last in undisputed possession of a cask of my only weakness — a whole cask of anchovy sauce. What a treat to a man whose views of anchovy have hitherto been limited to half pint bottles and cruet stands. Shall I draw it as I want it from the wood, or bottle it off and lay it down against my sons' (if ever I have any) coming of age? I will think it over.

(*Enter Reed as a butcher.*)

REED. Cher!

CECIL. (*startled*). Eh!

REED. Cher! Any orders?

CECIL. Oh, you're the butcher. Yes, very good — let me see — what have you got today?

REED. Very nice wild pig, sir. Have a haunch of wild pig? Kangaroo steaks, sir.

CECIL. Any monkey?

REED. No monkey to-day, sir. Just out of monkey — plenty next week. We kill a very fine gorilla this afternoon. Shall I put you down a leg to salt?

CECIL. Well, yes, for this day week; and to-day I'll have kangaroo ham, and you say you have wild pig?

REED. Very fine wild pig, sir.

CECIL. Then I'll have some wild pork chops — six.

REED. Very good, sir. Anything else?

CECIL. Oh yes, some cocoanut milk and butter.

REED. Beg pardon, sir, very sorry — but that's the milkman. I'm the butcher.

CECIL. Oh to be sure — well, that's all to-day. Good morning.

REED. Good morning, sir. (*shouts*) Miau! Miau! (*as milkman*).

CECIL. Eh!

REED. Miau!

CECIL. What's that?

REED. Milkman, sir. Any orders to-day?

CECIL. Oh, I see — well, I told you cocoanut milk and cocoanut butter.

REED. Beg pardon, sir, didn't tell *me*. Think I heard you tell the butcher, sir.

CECIL. Oh I understand — very good, I should like a sweetbread.

REED. That's the butcher, sir — stop a bit, sir — I'll manage it. (*as butcher*) Cher! Sweetbread, sir, yes, sir.

CECIL. And a fine new-laid ostrich egg.

REED. One moment. (*Miau, as milkman.*) Now then, ostrich egg, sir, yes, sir.

CECIL. You have sugar canes, I think?

REED. Grocer has, sir.

CECIL. Then bring me half a dozen pounds of sugar.

REED. Grocer! (*as grocer*) Half a dozen pounds of sugar, sir; very good, sir; anything else, sir?

CECIL. Nothing else. You can go.

(*Enter Mrs. Reed and Miss Holland.*)

MRS. R. Mr. Reed, a sail.

MISS H. A sail — we are saved!

MRS. R. A large three-masted ship is laying about three miles off the shore. I have signalled her; she has seen us and has just put off a boat. If you come here, you can see her distinctly.

REED. So we can. Cecil, we are free!

CECIL. Well, we needn't have troubled ourselves to change sides if we had known this ten minutes since.

MRS. R. Mind, Mr. Cecil, the exchange holds good; the fourth of the island is ours.

REED. But what's the good of it, my dear, now we are saved?

MRS. R. Good of it? As soon as I get back to England I shall establish a "Tropical Produce Supply Company Limited," and I'll send you here as resident manager. The profits will be gigantic.

CECIL. But what can I do with my three-fourths?

MRS. R. That's your affair. You can form a "Building Society" and parcel it out in villa residences.

CECIL. But it's all solid rock. Look here.

(Detaches a piece of rock; it rolls forward and is seen to be a piece of solid gold.)

Why, what's this?

REED. Gold!

MRS. R. Solid gold!

REED. Unspeakable happiness!

MISS H. Astounding, overwhelming discovery!

MRS. R. We shall be the richest people in the world!

MISS H. I shall buy the Koh-i-noor and wear it in my hair!

MRS. R. I shall buy the United States and establish a despotism!

REED. I shall buy Ireland and evict everybody!

CECIL. I don't want to interfere with your rapture, but you seem to forget the golden portion of the island belongs to me; we exchanged half an hour ago.

MRS. R. But you will surely, sir, allow us to share it.

CECIL. On no account whatever.

MRS. R. But the division into shares was a temporary arrangement intended only to last till we were taken off the island.

CECIL. Oh, I don't think so. You forget the contemplated "Tropical Produce Company" that you intended to establish.

MRS. R. There! Mr. Reed, a pretty bargain you made in changing shares with Mr. Cecil. Upon my word, you've given up a pretty property.

REED. But, my dear, you forget you wouldn't let me interfere, you *would* do it.

MRS. R. Bah! the old excuse. How often am I to tell you that you are my lord and master and that a husband is responsible for his wife's arrangements.

REED. But you *will* settle everything yourself and you won't let me have a voice in anything.

MRS. R. I don't think you need choose this moment for complaining of me. If it hadn't been for me that ship would never have been seen, and we might have remained here for the rest of our days. At all events I suppose you will allow that you have to thank me for your rescue.

MISS H. Here's the boat. There is only one man in it!

MRS. R. The boat! saved! saved!

> (*They sing the refrain of "Hurrah a sail" with great animation. Enter Captain Bang, a melodramatic Pirate, black flag with a skull and cross-bones in his hand.*)

SONG. — CAPTAIN BANG.

Oh, tremble! I'm a Pirate Chief;
Who comes upon me comes to grief,
For I'm a murderer and a thief;
A Pirate Captain, I.
I spare nor age nor sex nor rank,
For every one my fetters clank,
Until they're made to walk the plank,
A Pirate Captain, I.

I'm a hardy sailor, too;
I've a vessel and a crew,
When it doesn't blow a gale
I can reef a little sail.
I never go below
And I generally know
The weather from the "lee,"
And I'm never sick at sea.

When I've a victim in my pow'r
I grant no quarter, no, not I,
Except the quarter of an hour
Which must elapse ere he must die.
I fly at his throat thus,
On his terror I gloat thus,
I finish his life
With a sweep of my knife
Which I wipe on the sleeve of my coat thus.

I'm Captain Byng,
The Pirate King, etc.[1]

(*After song, during which Mr. and Mrs. Reed and Miss Holland have been extremely terrified, Bang drops his ferocious demeanor, and falls sobbing onto a piece of rock.*)

BANG. (*mildly*). I hope I have not frightened you.

REED. (*in great terror*). Oh no, not a bit; we are glad to make your acquaintance.

BANG. I'm so glad. (*Taking* REED *aside.*) Do you ever suffer from remorse?

REED. Never! Perhaps my wife does; if she don't, she ought to.

BANG. Why?

REED. Because it's all through her we've fallen into your hands.

MISS H. Oh, sir, be merciful. Spare us!

BANG. (*in tears*). Spare you! I can't. I am the Pirate King of the southern seas.

MRS. R. Are then our lives to pay the penalty of our capture?

BANG. (*miserably*). That's it, ma'am — oh isn't it dreadful?

MRS. R. Upon my life I think it is.

BANG. I mean my life, ma'am, a Pirate's life. Oh, I am so ashamed of it. (*Weeps bitterly.*)

MRS. R. I don't want to appear inquisitive, but if you don't like the profession, why don't you leave it?

BANG. That's it, I can't — I'm bound to it. I'm the tenderest fellow on the face of the earth — I had a good father and a good mother who brought me up carefully and gave me a good musical education, but the force of circumstances has forced me into a line of life for which I am not by education qualified or by inclination intended. To think that before the sun sets I am bound to shoot you all.

---

[1] Isaac Goldberg, *The Story of Gilbert and Sullivan; or, The 'Compleat' Savoyard* (New York: Simon and Schuster, 1928), pp. 112–13. Goldberg prints the pirate's name as Byng, but the typescript of the play never makes it anything but Bang.

MRS. R. Oh spare us, sir.

MISS H. Mercy! we are women.

BANG. What, both of you? (*indicating Reed and Miss Holland*).

REED. Yes, both of us.

MISS H. No, no. That lady and I (*indicating Mrs. Reed*).

MRS. R. I, sir, am a woman.

BANG. I felt sure of it; but I can't help it, you must all die.

CECIL. But consider, sir, the awful character of your threat. Consider the ladies, their feelings, sir.

BANG. Oh bother their feelings. What are their feelings to mine? They've only got to be killed — I've got to kill 'em. They've the satisfaction of knowing that whatever happens, it isn't their fault. Now *I* haven't that satisfaction.

REED. I don't want to appear inquisitive, but if you're so tender-hearted, how came you to adopt piracy as a profession?

BANG. Listen, I will tell you my history and the history of my family. Shall I begin at the beginning?

REED. Do.

BANG. I will. In the reign of Edward III, there dwelt in a small village in Suffolk, a poor but honest cottager.

REED. Never mind the history of your ancestors; we'll take that to-morrow.

BANG. You shall. Tomorrow you will be in a position to hear it from their own lips. I will confine myself to my personal history. I was the only son of a kind indulgent father and a kind indulgent mother, whose only care was to gratify my smallest whim. On my seventh birthday my kind father asked me what I would like to be. I had always a hankering for a sea-life; at the same time I didn't want to leave them for long, for oh, I was an affectionate son. So I told them I should like to be a pilot. My kind papa consented and sent me with my nurse to the nearest sea-front, telling her to apprentice me to a pilot. The girl — a very good girl, but stupid — mistaking her instructions, apprenticed me to a pirate of her acquaintance and bound me over to serve him diligently and faithfully until I reached the age of twenty-one. We sailed that evening, and I have never seen my native land since.

Reed. But since it appears that it was all a mistake, why don't you give it up?

Bang. What? Break my articles? Never! I have promised to work them out, and I must keep my word. But when they expire I intend to renounce my dreadful life for ever!

Reed. Your story fascinates me strangely. Tell me where — where did you live?

Bang. Greenwich.

Reed. And your father's name was —?

Bang. German Reed.

Reed. Ha! Ha! my long lost boy!

(*Mr. and Mrs. Reed fall on his neck.*)

Bang. Then you are?

Reed. German Reed.

Bang. And you?

Mrs. R. Mrs. Reed.

Bang. My father and my mother! (*They embrace.*)

Reed. This is indeed a happy occurrence. We will all go home together, and we will never, never be separated again.

Bang. But you forget my dreadful duty.

Cecil. Miserable man! You surely won't put your threat into execution against your own father!

Reed. Surely, surely you won't put your threat into execution against your parents. The lives of these two (*indicating Cecil and Miss Holland*) will satisfy you.

Bang. Oh, but I have no alternative. By my articles of apprenticeship I am bound to slaughter every prisoner I take. You wouldn't ask me to break my articles?

Reed. No, no, I see your difficulty. What is to be done?

CECIL. When do your articles expire?

BANG. Tomorrow!

ALL. Tomorrow!

BANG. Tomorrow. Tomorrow I am twenty-one. Painful, isn't it?

MISS H. But is there no way out of the difficulty?

REED. None. He is quite right.

MRS. R. Quite.

REED. I wouldn't have him break his articles of apprenticeship on any account. I always taught him a scrupulous adherence to his engagements, and I am glad — very glad — Edward (*shaking Bang by the hand*) to see that you have not forgotten my precepts.

CECIL. Stay! An idea occurs to me by which the difficulty may be evaded.

MRS. R. Indeed! State it then!

BANG. My dear Sir, if you can show me any legitimate way in which I can conscientiously evade the discharge of my painful duty, I shall be extremely grateful.

CECIL. Good. You are twenty-one tomorrow?

BANG. At a quarter to five tomorrow morning.

CECIL. You were born at Greenwich?

BANG. Greenwich.

CECIL. On the meridian. Good. We are here in longtitude 50 east of Greenwich.

BANG. Exactly.

CECIL. Then, allowing for difference in longitude, you came of age twenty minutes ago.

ALL. Ha!

BANG. Quite true. That never occurred to me till now.

REED. My preserver! (*shaking Cecil by the hand*).

BANG. That consideration removes all difficulties; the pirate's conscience is satisfied. He is out of his articles and he proposes from this moment to atone for his involuntary misdeeds by an immaculate life.

REED. And you will take us home on your ship?

BANG. I will.

REED. Hurrah!

MRS. R. Hurrah!

CECIL. Hurrah!

FINALE.

(Air "Hurrah a sail")

Away we sail.
Blow gently, gale,
And fan us from the shore;
Upon this isle
In savage style
We rusticate no more.

Our troubles end,
And we will spend
This night on yonder ship;
We'll celebrate
Our happy fate
With hip! hip! hip! hip! hip! Hurrah!

THE END

A Sensation Novel

IN THREE VOLUMES

Characters

VOICE

AUTHOR ⎫

SIR RUTHVEN GLENALOON ⎬ *Baritone.*

BUS CONDUCTOR ⎭

GRIPPER ⎫
⎬ *Bass.*
THE SPIRIT OF ROMANCE ⎭

HERBERT — *Tenor.*

LADY ROCKALDA — *Mezzo or Contralto.*

ALICE GREY — *Soprano.*

The Characters in Brackets may be taken by one Performer.

VOL. I

Frontispiece: A crazy room on Bankside, overlooking the *Thames. Moonlight.*

No. 1.— *Music for Curtain.* The Author *discovered seated at a table writing. He has finished his first volume, and is at a loss how to begin the second.*

Author. I do not know how it is, but I cannot get on with this novel. I've been nearly a week at work, and I have only just finished the first volume. A week! why, I ought to have finished three volumes in a week! Am I not assisted by supernatural agency? Have I not entered into a compact with the Demon of Romance, by which I am able to turn out fifty, three-volumed novels per annum? And, on the strength of that compact, haven't I entered into an agreement with my publishers to supply them, under a heavy forfeiture, with that number of sensation novels every year till further notice? To be sure I have. But here I am in a fix. Well, shall I hesitate to summon my ghostly adviser to my aid? Certainly not! Now for the incantation that will bring him to my side.

(He takes a huge saucepan and places the following ingredients into it during the Incantation.)

No. 2. — INCANTATION.

Spoken through music.   Take of best quill pens a score,
               Take of ink a pint or more,
Take of foolscap half-a-ream,
Take, oh take, a convict's dream,
Lynch pin, fallen from a carriage,
Forged certificate of marriage,
Money wrongly won at whist,
Finger of a bigamist,
Cobweb from mysterious vaults,
Arsenic sold as Epsom salts,
Pocket-knife with blood-stained blade,
Telegram, some weeks delayed,
Parliamentary committee,
Joint stock panic in the city,
Trial at Old Bailey bar,
Take a Newgate Calendar,
Take a common jury's finding,

Take a most attractive binding,
Hold the saucepan by the handle,
Boil it on a penny candle.

(THE SPIRIT OF ROMANCE *appears.* AUTHOR *falls on his knees, terrified.*)

SPIRIT. I am here!

AUTHOR. You are!

SPIRIT. What do you want with me?

AUTHOR. Help, I have just finished the first volume of my novel — and I don't know how to begin the second. By our compact, I had leave to summon you whenever I found myself in a difficulty, and you promised to help me out of it.

SPIRIT. Have you employed the characters I have lent you? — the virtuous governess, the unemployed young Sunday school teacher, the sensation detective, the wicked baronet, the beautiful fiend with the yellow hair and the panther-like movement?

AUTHOR. I have!

SPIRIT. You have made the virtuous governess in love with the Sunday school teacher? You have made her persecuted by the wicked baronet?

AUTHOR. Yes!

SPIRIT. The yellow-haired fiend with the panther-like movement is his accomplice?

AUTHOR. She is!

SPIRIT. Have you made *her* fall in love with the Sunday school teacher?

AUTHOR. Head and ears.

SPIRIT. And he treats her with disdain?

AUTHOR. He does!

SPIRIT. Humph! Have you obeyed my advice as to diet and eaten nothing but pork chops and cold plum pudding?

AUTHOR. Nothing! Look at me.

SPIRIT. You have slept with your head lower than your body?

AUTHOR. Every night.

SPIRIT. You have put live shrimps down your back to make your flesh creep?

AUTHOR. Pints of them! There are some there now (*wriggles*).

SPIRIT. You have read the "Illustrated Police News"?

AUTHOR. Through and through.

SPIRIT. You are in my power! These creatures whom I have lent you are slaves to my will. Refuse to obey me, and I withdraw them altogether. They are accepted types, and you can't get on without them.

AUTHOR. True! But tell me, what is the nature of the power you exercise over them?

SPIRIT. It is very peculiar. They are all creatures who, in their mortal condition, have been guilty of positive or negative crime, and they are compelled to personate, under my direction, those stock characters of the sensation novelist which are most opposed to their individual tastes and inclinations.

AUTHOR. Then they have an existence apart from that with which they are endowed in the novel?

SPIRIT. They have! Apart from it, but eventually subject to it; that is to say, they have wishes, schemes and plans of their own, but the fulfilment of these wishes is, for the time being, in the hands of the Author, to whom they are entrusted. They have the power of coming to life at the end of the first and second volumes, and immediately before the last chapter of the third, to talk over the events that have taken place, and to arrange plans for the future — plans which are too often frustrated by the Author's arbitrary will. This is not generally known.

AUTHOR. Do I understand you to say that at the end of the first volume they come to life?

SPIRIT. They do!

AUTHOR. I have just finished the first volume.

SPIRIT. It is now five minutes to twelve — at twelve they will be here!

AUTHOR (*going*). I've an appointment in the City which I had entirely overlooked.

SPIRIT. Won't you stay and see them?

AUTHOR. Thanks, no. One supernatural being is as much as I feel
equal to at a time. I'd rather go.

No. 3A. — DUET. — SPIRIT and AUTHOR.

SPIRIT.   In half a minute they'll be here!

AUTHOR.   I shake and quake with sense of fear!

SPIRIT.   The Baronet — the maiden fair,
                The Panther with the yellow hair;

AUTHOR.   The Tutor, too, with fate ill-starred,
                Detective, too, from Scotland Yard,

BOTH.   All will be here!

SPIRIT.   They'll be plotting — they'll be planning —
                With the cunning of a Canning,

AUTHOR.   All my plans they'll be upsetting,
                Novel schemes they'll be begetting,

SPIRIT.   Both the baronet and the maiden,
                And the tutor, sorrow-laden,

AUTHOR.   And the panther with invective,
                'Gainst the Scotland Yard detective,

BOTH.   All will be here!

AUTHOR.   And is this so?

SPIRIT.   Yes! to the letter.

AUTHOR.   I think I'll go!

SPIRIT.   I think you'd better!

BOTH.   They will be here.

                                          [*Exeunt.*]

No. 3B. — MELODRAME.

Enter LADY ROCKALDA.

ROCK. So the first volume's at an end, and once more we, the puppets
of a sensation author's will, are launched upon our eventful careers. In

the course of the ten years during which I have been compelled to obey my prolific author's will, I, the beautiful yellow-haired fiend of sensational fiction, have worked my wicked way through no less than 75 sensation novels! I shudder when I think of the amount of evil I have done. I shudder still more, when I think of the amount of evil I have still to do! But I must not repine for I have deserved it all. When I was a mortal I was the indulgent mother of five unruly boys, an easy-going peace-loving mother. I allowed them to have their own way, and as a punishment for my culpable neglect I am compelled to serve my Author's will, during the term of his natural life! It's a hard fate, but I have deserved it, and I must not repine.

No. 4. — SONG. — LADY ROCKALDA.

I

Like a motherly old lady,
    With demure old-fashioned ways,
In a cottage snug and shady,
    I should like to spend my days.
Through the village I could toddle,
    To relieve the old and lame;
I would be the very model
    Of a motherly old dame.

II

But my tastes and inclinations
    Must be hidden out of sight;
Oh! forgive my lamentations,
    I am miserable quite.
For propriety's affliction
    Guilty deeds I must prepare;
I'm the lovely fiend of fiction,
    With the yellow, yellow hair.

III

With voice and gait mysterious,
Expression fixed and serious,
And manner most imperious,
    I work my charge.
In love unbridled, as in hate,
I wheedle, coax, and fascinate,

Then murder, rob, assassinate
Mankind at large.

IV

Like a motherly old lady,
With demure, old-fashioned ways,
In a cottage snug and shady,
I should like to end my days.
But for innocents' affliction
Guilty deeds I must prepare;
I'm the lovely fiend of fiction,
With the yellow, yellow hair.

No. 5. — MELODRAME.

Enter Sir Ruthven Glenaloon, *dressed as an Officer of Footguards.*

RUTH. Rockalda, this is a melancholy meeting.

ROCK. It is, but we have deserved it all.

RUTH. We have, but it is very hard to be a wicked baronet against one's will. Why, I was the softest hearted fellow alive — when I *was* alive.

ROCK. But soft hearted as you were, you did a deal of mischief in your time.

RUTH. I did! Let me confess my misdeeds: I never saw a beggar in the streets but I gave him a penny — shocking, wasn't it?

ROCK. Terrible, indeed! But you did worse than that — you — you encouraged organ grinders.

RUTH. I did, I did! but spare me your reproaches, for I now see the enormity of my misconduct, and I am undergoing a bitter expiation.

ROCK. Yes, you are the wicked baronet of sensational fiction, and it serves you right.

RUTH. But where are we?

ROCK. This is a ruined summer house, overlooking the Thames. The river runs under the window and beneath the floor, which is full of traps — which open with springs, and many murders have been committed in this very room.

RUTH. But why does the Author live here?

Rock. This room stimulates his imagination. The first volume treats of dark mysterious deeds, done in the vilest haunts of the most abandoned ruffians he could find.

Ruth. Then the abandoned ruffian has abandoned it for the present?

Rock. He has! Have no fear.

Ruth. I don't like this. I'm a timid, nervous man, and I don't feel at all comfortable in the place.

Rock. Take comfort. The second volume will treat of high life. For that, he has secured part of Windsor Castle. The third will take place in Africa, and we shall then find ourselves in Barbary. It is his way, and we are all the slaves of his fancy.

Ruth. But where's the good young man of the novel? He ought to be here!

No. 6a. — MELODRAME.

Enter Herbert, *dressed in semi-clerical fashion, with a very sanctified appearance.*

Herbert. He is here! my Rockalda!

Rock. My Herbert! (*They embrace.*)

Herbert. At last we meet. Let me see, the last time we met was at the end of the Indian novel — "Black as a boot is he!"

Rock. It was. You were then a mild young artist traveling in India.

Herbert. I was; and you were the yellow-haired Begum of the Rajah of Babbetyboobledore.

Ruth. And I — ha! ha! I was Nana Sahib! It's some comfort to reflect that I am to go through this novel with a clean face.

Herbert. But with very dirty hands.

Ruth. Yes, that's my invariable fate. Oh, I say, ain't I a bad character!

Rock. Shocking!

Ruth. We've only got to the end of the first volume, and I've already committed a burglary, a forgery, a falsification of a baptismal entry, and I'll lay twenty to one I try to murder you, Herbert, before I'm done.

Herbert. I'll take you twenty to one you don't succeed.

RUTH. No, you're the good young man, and it wouldn't do — you've got to marry Alice.

HERBERT. Bah! Don't remind me of that.

RUTH. My Alice, whom I love so devotedly, and who loves me.

ROCK. Yes, *out* of the novel.

RUTH. Exactly! *In* the novel she detests me. Fortunately, we have an opportunity at the end of each volume of shaking off the detestable attributes with which the Author invests us, and of appearing for an hour or so in our own true light. In my true light Alice worships me.

HERBERT. Well, we've deserved it all.

RUTH. We have, we have. What did you do on earth?

HERBERT. I! Listen. I frequented music halls and sang comic songs, and as a punishment I have to represent the author's good young man during the term of his natural life. Horrible, isn't it?

ALL. Most horrible!

ROCK. Well, I don't complain, only it was too bad to make a girl of twenty of me.

HERBERT. A girl of twenty! You're a girl of a thousand.

ROCK. My love!

RUTH. Yes, you look more than twenty.

ROCK. More than twenty? Why, I'm five and forty if I'm a day.

RUTH. No, forty — I should say.

ROCK. Forty-five — upon my honour.

HERBERT. You will always be young in *my* eyes.

ROCK. Under these circumstances I shall be content to live in them for ever.

RUTH. But the necessities of the story require that you shall pass yourself off for twenty. You know that you, the grown-up daughter of Tom Sittybank, the bus conductor, passed yourself off as the daughter of the Duke of Ben-Nevis, Lady Rockalda, whom you brought up as Alice Grey, the foundling, so you *must* pass yourself off as a being no older than the so-called Alice Grey, whose title and position in society you have assumed.

ROCK. And then to make me fall hopelessly in love with Herbert, hopelessly! He spurns me — loads me with reproaches, and tells me he is familiar with the details of my disgraceful career!

HERBERT. But I only spurn you *in* the novel — *out* of the novel I worship the very ground you walk on. It is an agreeable relief after making love for a whole volume to that ridiculously insipid creature, Alice Grey — I say it is a relief to find yourself in the society, though for a few moments, of so superior and well-matured a person as my Rockalda. (*They embrace.*)

No. 6B. — MELODRAME.

Enter ALICE GREY, *a very demure modest-looking governess.*

ALICE. Ha! Ha! My devoted Herbert in the arms of the detestable Lady Rockalda! What would the Author say?

No. 7. — QUARTET. — LADY ROCK., ALICE, SIR RUTH. *and* HERBERT.

ALICE   Goodness gracious!
        How audacious!
           What deception you disclose!
        My adorer
        On the floor-er,
           At the base Rockalda's toes!

{ HERB., ROCK.   Ah confusion!
    AND   } This delusion!
 SIR RUTHVEN. }   Will destroy her, goodness knows!
        It's affecting
        Her detecting,
        { Me }
        { You } preparing to propose.

ALICE   I will go and bring my action,
        I will bring it, I declare!
    Oh, despair! Oh, distraction!
        Oh, distraction! Oh, despair.

THE OTHERS. She will go and bring her action, etc.

HERBERT. Now look here! Alice, I've been spooneying after you, writing poetry to you, and kissing your *carte de visite* through the entire length of a whole volume, and to-morrow morning I shall have to begin again. Do, for goodness sake, let me enjoy myself during the few minutes of relaxation that are permitted me between the volumes.

ALICE. My good soul, don't suppose for one moment that I intend to interrupt you. Let us make the most of these happy intervals, for I'm sure you will marry me at the end of the third volume.

HERBERT. Horrible prospect!

ALICE. Horrible, indeed!

RUTH. But, Alice, you may not marry him after all. He may prove unworthy of you.

HERBERT. That's not likely. I'm dreadfully good — I feel it!

ALICE. Oh! Ruthven, my love, when the Author set you on to persecute me with your attention and contrive all sorts of plans to carry me off and marry me against my will, he little dreamt how ardently I hoped that your nefarious schemes would be successful. But, no, that irritating Curate whom I love so desperately *in* the novel, and detest so heartily *out* of it, always interferes to balk your plans.

HERBERT. Yes, I am a donkey *in* the novel.

ALICE. A donkey! You're a bashful noodle!

HERBERT. I was rather bold in the scene with you in the pine forest — don't you remember? Where's the MS.? Oh, here it is — (*Reads*) "Miss Alice," said Herbert —

ALICE. *Miss* Alice! In a pine forest — by moonlight, too. *Miss* Alice, oh, you great donkey!

HERBERT. Oh, but I warmed up afterwards. (*Reads*) "Miss Alice, I fear your stoney-hearted guardian will never relent."

RUTH. That's me; I'm the stoney-hearted guardian.

HERBERT (*reads*). "You are very formal, Herbert, replied Alice."

ALICE. Yes, I should think so, Sir Ruthven would have known better — Wouldn't you, dear?

HERBERT. But you were so confoundedly proper. Besides, I was only putting out a feeler. (*Reads*) "Miss Grey — Alice, dear Alice, dearest Alice, I *may* call you dearest — Alice may I not?" That was warm.

ALICE. Not a bit too warm after the demure encouragement I gave you — go on!

HERBERT (*reads*). "I may call you dearest, Alice, may I not?" "I cannot help what you choose to call me, said the pretty girl." Pretty girl, I like that.

ALICE. So do I!

HERBERT (*reads*). "They were alone — with the moon. They heard the throbbings of each other's hearts, which beat like rival watches, wound up in each other! He drew her gently towards him, and imprinted a solitary kiss on her soft —

ALICE (*taking the MS. from him*). "On her soft little hand!" Oh you goose!

ALL. Ha! Ha! Ha!

ALICE. But that's nothing to what followed, listen! (*Reads*) "She turned away, Oh, Herbert, said she, bashfully raising her purple eyes to the spot where he had been sitting — but he was gone." There! Left me alone in the pine forest at midnight.

HERBERT. But I heard footsteps and ran, that you might not be compromised. It was very considerate.

RUTH. The footsteps were mine.

ALICE (*fondly*). They were.

RUTH. I behaved better than he did in the scene that followed, didn't I?

ALICE. You did. It was rapture.

RUTH. (*taking the MS.*). "Alice, said the Baronet, his cold, evil grey eye lighting with a horrible fire. At last you are in my power! I heard you were in the forest, and I determined to find you. Alice covered her eyes with her hands. She tried to scream, but terror had rendered her speechless."

ALICE. Yes, it was delightful. I remember it all. Let's go through it again.

RUTH. You were alone with that penniless curate.

ALICE. I was.

RUTH. You love him.

ALICE. I do. Why should I blush to own it? But how know you this?

RUTH. I lay concealed beneath yon blackberry bush, and I overheard all.

ALICE. Then it was unmanly done.

RUTH. Not so, pretty one, for I also love you, and in love, as in war, all schemes are fair. (*Taking her round the waist.*)

ALICE. Unhand me, monster!

RUTH. Not so, pretty one. Listen! A coach and six is in readiness in the thickest part of the forest, and I have minions who will drive you where I will. Salisbury Plain is barely fifty leagues away, a clergyman in full canonicals, and an aged pew-opener are awaiting us at Stonehenge, and he will speak the words that will make you mine.

ALICE. Unhand me, coward, or my shrieks shall bring those around you who will make you repent the day you laid a hand on old John Grey's daughter, help! help! help!

HERBERT (*rushing forward and seizing* SIR RUTHVEN). Monster! unhand that lady!

ALICE. There! (*Aside.*) You were always interfering when you were not wanted, just as we were getting on so comfortably together.

HERBERT. Well it's the Author's fault — (*resuming*) Monster! unhand that lady! Alice, has he dared to offer violence?

ALICE. He has!

HERBERT. Ha! Then let this deadly blow avenge the dastard outrage (*prepares to strike*).

RUTH. Ah! never mind the deadly blow.

HERBERT. I delivered it right from the shoulder between the eyes.

RUTH. You did, I remember it perfectly.

HERBERT. I hope I didn't hurt you much?

RUTH. Ah, well, never mind, it's a painful subject; at all events I got over it, but wasn't it a delicious scene?

ALICE. Heavenly. Oh! Ruthven, if that donkey hadn't interrupted us we should have been comfortably married at Stonehenge and all would have ended happily.

HERBERT. I'm sure I wish it had.

ROCK. So indeed do I. *We* might have been happy. Do you remember the chapter in which I first fell in love with you?

HERBERT. Perfectly! It was at the old limekiln.

ROCK. It was. Sir Ruthven set me on to lure you to the limekiln, with my panther-like movement and the lurid fascination of my yellow hair.

RUTH. I did! "Rockalda," said I, "engage him in conversation at the brink of the limekiln. I will come upon him from behind, and, having stunned him with one unerring blow, I will consume his body in the lime, and not so much as a button shall be left to tell the tale."

ROCK. Yes, but I wouldn't agree to that. "No, Sir Ruthven," I said; "if there is murder to be done, I will do it alone." I lured you to the limekiln under a promise that when I had got you there I would reveal the secret of my birth.

HERBERT. You did! I came! "Madam," said I, "I am here at your request. You have a secret that concerns me intimately."

ROCK. I have!

HERBERT. Why turn your face away from me?

ROCK. No matter — it is my whim. (*Aside.*) I dare not look upon him, or he will read my deadly purpose in my eyes.

HERBERT. You tell me that you possess the secret of my birth? Oh, madam, reveal it!

ROCK. Listen, and I will reveal all! I have brought you here to murder you. Tremble, for your last hour has come. (*She turns and seizes him by the throat. A ray of moonlight falls on his face.*) Merciful heavens! how lovely!

HERBERT. I did not expect this. Strike, woman! if you have the heart to do so.

ROCK. Heart! I never had a heart till now. (*Aside.*) It is the face of an angel.

HERBERT. Unfortunately I am a Sunday school teacher or I would resist.

ROCK. Resistance were useless. Feel that arm!

HERBERT. The muscles are of steel.

ROCK. Exactly; listen! I am here to kill you, but I have seen your face and I love you. Marry me and your life is spared; refuse and I toss your body into the middle of yonder limekiln, and every trace of you will be consumed.

HERBERT. Marry you! Never! Strike if my hour is come. (*She raises dagger.*) Now, we can't get on without Gripper, the detective.

ROCK. Ah! where *is* Gripper? He ought to have been here before this.

ALL. Gripper! Gripper! Gripper!

No. 8. — MELODRAME.

(*Enter* GRIPPER *dressed as a Grand Turk.*)

GRIPPER. Here I am! How de do?

ROCK. You're late, Gripper?

GRIPPER. Well, I'm afraid I am; but then I am a sensation detective, and sensation detectives always *are* late. The reason's obvious enough. If the detective of a sensation novel were not always just too late, the novel would come to an end long before its time. If I bring to justice all the villains of the novel in the course of the first volume, what's to prevent the virtuous governess marrying the good young curate at once, and if she does that there's an end of everything.

ALICE. Of course! Why if Gripper hadn't been just too late throughout the first volume all would have ended happily at once; I should have married the man of my choice and been miserable for life fifty pages ago.

HERBERT. My dear Gripper, we ought to be very much obliged to you. The longer you can delay that catastrophe the better pleased we shall all be. But why are you dressed like that?

GRIPPER. It is a disguise, that I may follow you about without attracting too much attention.

ALL. Ridiculous! preposterous!

ROCK. I don't complain, I don't care what happens so that I am not separated from the good young curate.

HERBERT. And I don't care what happens so that I am not removed from my yellow-haired panther.

ALICE. And I don't care so that I continue to be persecuted by the infamous Sir Ruthven.

RUTH. And I don't care so that I am allowed sometimes to see the spotless innocent Alice.

GRIPPER. Very well! then don't complain of my being always too late. If I am only once in time — *only once* — there's an end of everything, and the governess marries the curate on the spot.

ALICE. Horrible!

HERBERT. Horrible indeed!

ALICE. (*to* HERBERT). I hate you more than ever!

HERBERT. Believe me, your sentiments are sincerely reciprocated.

ALICE (*to* RUTHVEN). But there is still hope, dear Ruthven; after all the Author may intend us for each other. The virtuous young woman has so often been married to the good young man that the public must begin to tire of the incessant repetition.

RUTH. Yes, but you see I'm such an awful villain!

ALICE. So you are! But couldn't I convert you?

RUTH. *You* could — if any one could. But I'm afraid I'm too far gone for that — No, you'll have to marry the Curate, and live happily ever after.

HERBERT. Marry and live happily ever after! And this is a novel that pretends to give a picture of life as it is. Yes, I'm afraid, Alice, we are booked for one another.

ROCK. But how much better it would be — how much more original if Alice were to reform Ruthven, and you were to reform me. You two good people would be of some use then.

Herbert. Ah, I'm afraid there's no chance of reforming *you*, my love — You don't feel it coming on, do you?

Rock. Not a bit — I'm worse than ever.

Gripper. Still there are two volumes to come, and who knows what may happen.

Rock. Yes, but if we are to be reformed, what's the use of you?

Gripper. Just what I want to know! One thing is quite certain. As long as I go on, assuming these preposterous disguises I shall never contrive to bring you or anybody else to justice. Why, I am as conspicuous as the Crystal Palace fireworks.

(Clock strikes one.)

Rock. One o'clock! Our time is up, and we must retire into our sensation characters. Good-bye, Herbert, we shall meet again at the end of the second volume. Ah, who knows what may happen in the interval.

Herbert. Whatever happens *in* the novel nothing can alter my sentiments towards you, *out* of it.

Ruth. Alice, farewell, Alice, my own, my loved one.

Alice. Farewell, Ruthven; we shall meet at the end of the second volume. In the meantime, persecute me, Ruthven, as much as you please. You can't think how much I like it.

No. 9. — FINALE TO VOL. I. — ENSEMBLE.

Alice.
Increase my woes,
My best of foes;
Oh, follow me, worry me, harry me,
And if you can,
Cut out that man;
And marry me, marry me, marry me!

Ruth.
With dark design,
To make you mine;
I'll follow you, worry you, trouble you!
So single stay,
If I've my way,
I'll double you, double you, double you!

HERBERT.	Oh, panther fair, With yellow hair, And beauty almost magical, If we should part, 'Twould break my heart; Ah, tragical, tragical, tragical!
ROCK.	Oh! you who rule A Sunday school Of babes in their minority, Though forty-four, I bow to your Authority — thority, thority!
GRIPPER.	Go on, my friends, Pursue your ends; I'll keep an open eye to you! Alas, if I'm But once in time, Good-bye to you, bye to you, bye to you!

END OF VOL. I

VOL. II

No. 10A. — INTRODUCTION.

FRONTISPIECE. — *The top of the Round Tower of Windsor Castle.*

No. 10B. — MELODRAME.

Enter LADY ROCKALDA.

ROCK. Well, here we are at the end of the second volume, and a nice time I've had of it.

Enter SIR RUTHVEN (*languidly*).

RUTH. Eh! What's the matter?

ROCK. Matter? Matter enough. Why, as you know, Herbert was

sent off at the beginning of the second volume as a missionary to Central Africa and he hasn't returned yet.

RUTH. Poor Rockalda.

ROCK. I wonder how much longer I'm to be kept without him.

RUTH. Well, but he's not much good to you, you know. He despises your love and avoids you whenever he can.

ROCK. I know he does *in* the novel, but still it is something to be with him and to see him sometimes, and we had to do without him for a whole volume. Ah, here he is! My Herbert!

HERBERT. My Rockalda! At last we meet!

ROCK. Tell me when — oh, when do you return from Central Africa?

HERBERT. Alas! Not for several chapters.

ROCK. This is indeed hard. I don't like this novel at all.

HERBERT. It's shameful! The publisher told the Author that I was getting so confoundedly insipid that no reader would stand me, and he must get rid of me somehow, so he sent me to Central Africa for seven years. I'm there now, and I am very much afraid I shall not return till the last chapter. Transportation for seven years is rather too serious a punishment. Is Alice all right?

RUTH. Yes, and more lovely than ever.

HERBERT. Oh! I'm sorry for that. You haven't carried her off and married her?

RUTH. No, not yet.

HERBERT. What a fellow you are! I've been out of your way all the volume. You might have done that for me.

RUTH. I'd have done it for myself with pleasure, but I'm not a free agent. I did try.

ROCK. That he did, and I helped him.

HERBERT. Bless you! Tell me all about it.

RUTH. What! don't you know?

HERBERT. How should I? I've been out of the volume altogether.

148

RUTH. True! Alice, as you are aware, was to have gone to Africa with you.

HERBERT. Yes! she was to have joined me at Liverpool, but by some fortunate chance I was spared that infliction — She never turned up and I sailed without her.

RUTH. Exactly — I managed that — You see that both Rockalda and I were interested in preventing that. I, because I loved Alice. Rockalda, because she loved you. She was to travel by the 9 o'clock express to Liverpool from London, so what do you think I did?

HERBERT. Sent her a Bradshaw perhaps to confuse her and make her miss her train.

RUTH. No, better than that. I slew the pointsman at Rugby Junction and turned the train on to the Midland line.

HERBERT. How good of you, well, what followed?

RUTH. I don't know, for just as I had accomplished my object a Red Indian struck me on the head with his tomahawk and I fell senseless to the ground.

ROCK. I can tell you what followed — I was in the train — After the train had been turned on to the Midland line I crept cautiously along the carriages as we entered the tunnel, strangled the engine driver, dressed myself in his clothes, and drove the train safely to Leeds.

HERBERT. You changed in the tunnel? (*Horrified.*)

ROCK. Yes, it was quite dark.

HERBERT. Very thoughtful of the Author. My dear Rockalda, I owe you an unspeakable debt of gratitude. But what followed?

ROCK. A fearful discovery. On arriving at Leeds, as the girl's ticket was for Liverpool, she was brought face to face with the station-master, who turned out to be — start not — her father, the Duke of Ben-Nevis, who for purposes of his own, had quitted his own lofty station for a *station* of a totally different description.

HERBERT. And he recognised her?

ROCK. He did.

HERBERT. But how? for he had always accepted you as his daughter.

Rock. By a singular family feature, hereditary in every direct female member of the Ben-Nevis line, the back hair of all the daughters of the Dukes of Ben-Nevis has always grown in the form of a ducal coronet. He recognised her at once, and discovered that I, who had all along passed as his daughter, was an impostor.

Herbert. Strange! But I noticed the same ducal peculiarity in your own back hair.

Rock. Yes, that puzzled his Grace at first. "How is this?" said he, "I have but one daughter, and yet here are two daughters whose back hair grows naturally in the form hereditary in our family. Which of them is mine?" And he wept bitterly.

Herbert. Poor old gentleman; and how was the matter decided?

Rock. "Stay," said he, "a thought"; and so saying he clutched at Alice's back hair, which strongly resisted his efforts. He then clutched at mine. Alas! it came off in his hand.

Herbert. Merciful powers! then that mass of yellow hair is —

Rock. A considerable portion of it, false!

Herbert. You never told me this.

Rock. Attribute my reticence to maidenly reserve; it were unmaidenly for a girl to refer to any details of her toilet in the presence of a Sunday school teacher.

Herbert. Quite out of the question. But what became of Alice?

Rock. She fled, alarmed at the Duke's extraordinary behaviour, and she has never been heard of since.

Herbert. Then she does not know she is his daughter?

Rock. Not yet.

Ruth. (*madly*). Ha! Ha! Ha!

Herbert. What is the matter with *you*? Is your back hair false too?

Ruth. No, no; but still I am desperately unhappy.

Herbert. Because you haven't yet persuaded Alice to marry you?

Ruth. No, not that! I can't expect to bring that about; she loathes me *in* the novel, but I did think we would have been happy *out* of it.

Rock. Well, can't you?

Ruth. I'm afraid not. I'm afraid that Alice is not the Duke's daughter after all. A fearful presentiment suggests to me that Alice, the lovely, the divine Alice, whom I worship with a devotion absolutely unparallelled, is — ha! ha! — my grand-daughter!

Herbert. Then you would be —

Ruth. Her grandfather! I've just recollected that in the first chapter of the novel your sister — that is to say, my second daughter — had a daughter of her own, a baby whom she deserted when only three days old. She left her on a doorstep in Belgrave Square, and I am ashamed to say she did it at my suggestion.

Herbert. You're a bad lot!

Ruth. Ain't I? Desperate! However, there was one redeeming point in her conduct, her choosing Belgrave Square. "Lucy," said I, "leave it on a doorstep in Seven Dials." "Never!" said she. "I love my babe better than life itself. Its happiness is everything to me, and its prosperity in life is my most anxious care. It shall be launched on its career under the most fashionable circumstances, and I should be neglecting my duty as a mother if I did leave it on any doorstep short of Belgrave Square." She left it in Belgrave Square, and the babe was adopted by a nobleman. Herbert! Rockalda! I'm very much afraid that the Lady Rockalda, who was put out to nurse with us, and whom you are personating, is that unhappy babe.

Herbert. Terrible!

Ruth. Hush! she comes! Leave us!

Enter Alice.

Alice. Ruthven! (*They embrace.*) Why turn from me so coldly? We have not met since the end of the first volume. Let us make the most of the short time during which we can be together.

Ruth. Alice, had you ever a father?

Alice. No!

Ruth. Nor a mother?

Alice. Never!

RUTH. Are you sure of that?

ALICE. Quite.

RUTH. Then I must have been mistaken. It has occurred to me that I might have been your grandfather; now, a woman, so I have heard, may not marry her grandfather.

ALICE. You have been rightly informed.

RUTH. But as the grandfather is the father of the father, and you have never had a father for me to be father of, it is impossible that I can be the father of the father you never had. And yet, on the other hand, if you never had a father or a mother, who were your parents?

ALICE. That is a question that has haunted me night and day.

No. 11A. — BALLAD. — ALICE.

I

ALICE.   No father's care, that I'm aware,
                Have I been cherished by;
            No mother's smile did e'er beguile
                My joyous infancy.
            That I'm alive, and grow and thrive,
                I know, indeed, full well;
            But how, alas! it came to pass
                I cannot, cannot tell.

II

            A father's pinch might make me flinch,
                As you're no doubt aware;
            A mother's tweak upon the cheek
                Is very hard to bear;
            But harder yet to owe a debt
                To no progenitor;
            I would die content, if I
                Could be accounted for.

RUTH.   Let me unveil a frightful tale —
                A tale of fraud, a tale of crime!

ALICE.   If aught you find upon your mind,
                Proceed —

No. 11B. — SONG. — Ruthven.

I

Well, once upon a time —
A nobleman dressed in a close-fitting mask,
His figure a domino mantling,
Brought a child to my cottage and gave me the task
Of rearing the poor little bantling.
Oh! you were that babe, as you shortly will see
(My sin this the time to retrieve is);
The mysterious noble who brought you to me,
Was the eminent Duke of Ben-Nevis!

II

My daughter, though twenty years older, or so,
Was extremely like you in the face, miss;
So she popped herself into the cradle, you know,
And passed herself off in your place, miss.
'Twas Rockalda, my daughter, who did it, I say
(Which a terrible crime to achieve is)!
And you, who have hitherto passed as Miss Grey,
Are the child of the Duke of Ben-Nevis!

[*Exit* Sir Ruthven.]

Alice. Upon my word, this is a pretty state of things! So it seems that I, who have had to pass through two volumes as a quiet, humble nursery governess, am a lady of rank and fortune! This must be enquired into.

No. 11C. — MELODRAME.

Enter Lady Rockalda.

Alice. So ma'am! you're an impostor! It seems that you have passed yourself off as the daughter of the Duke of Ben-Nevis, and caused me, his real daughter, to be brought up as an obscure and penniless governess.

Rock. My dear Alice, don't excite yourself. You have been recognised by the Duke as his daughter, and throughout the next volume you will no doubt occupy your proper station. If you hadn't run away just as the discovery was made you would have been reinstated long ago.

Alice. No doubt, but I did not know till a minute ago that it was through your agency that this shameful imposition was brought about.

Rock. Now don't be unreasonable, are we not all in the Author's hands?

Alice. Certainly! But you might have told me of this before!

Rock. The secret was not mine. It was the Author's!

Alice. But dear Ruthven has just revealed it.

Rock. Then it was very unprofessional of him. He was bound in honour to keep the Author's secret. It is not at all like Sir Ruthven to commit a breach of trust *out* of the novel.

Alice. However, as you have admitted the fact, I insist on taking my rank immediately.

Rock. But, my dear girl!

Alice. Menial! How dare you address me — *me* in such familiar terms? I am the Lady Alice.

Rock. Now don't be unreasonable.

Alice. Begone, omnibus conductor's daughter. If you dare to address me again in such terms, this dagger, which I wear as a protection against my darling Sir Ruthven, shall teach ye better manners.

No. 12A. — DUET. — Alice and Rockalda.

Alice. With rage infuriate I burn!

Rock. My wishes on the point you spurn.

Alice. Come, hand the jewels over please!

Rock. What! these — and these — and these and these?

Alice. Yes, all; that brooch, those earrings fair,
The tiara that decks your hair!

Rock. If I refuse?

Alice.   This dagger blade,
I straightway summon to my aid.

(Lady Rock. *gives jewels to* Alice — *she puts them on.*)

In rarest jewels brightly shining,
With diamonds upon my brow,

In humble garb no longer pining,
I take my true position now.

Rock. Those jewels ill befit your tatters —
Oh! dread, oh! dread the Author's rage!
For you're anticipating matters
By many and many a stirring page.

Both. $\begin{Bmatrix} \text{Though} \\ \text{Those} \end{Bmatrix}$ jewels ill befit $\begin{Bmatrix} \text{my} \\ \text{your} \end{Bmatrix}$ tatters,
I do not dread the Author's rage;
I like anticipating matters
By many and many a stirring page.

No. 12B. — MELODRAME.

Enter Gripper *dressed as a North American Indian.*

Gripper. I beg your pardon — I'm afraid I am late again.

Rock. You are! If you had been here a minute sooner, you would have been able to prevent a most outrageous robbery.

Gripper. Dear me! I am very sorry, but I am a detective and must act up to my character.

Rock. Surely it's part of a detective's duty to prevent the commission of crime!

Gripper. Oh dear no, quite the reverse! It is a detective's duty to encourage the commission of crime, that he may detect it after it has been committed and that, just too late to bring the perpetrator to justice! Why, you might as well expect a sportsman to banish pheasants from his preserves, that he may not be put to the trouble of shooting 'em. Who has been robbing you?

Rock. Alice Grey! She compelled me at the dagger's point to hand over all my jewelry.

Gripper. Indeed! Place the matter in my hands, and I'll detect her with pleasure. You are certain Alice Grey committed this robbery?

Rock. Quite!

Gripper. (*takes out note-book*). Then I have no hesitation in saying that suspicion points very strongly to Alice Grey.

Rock. You don't say so! Intelligent officer! Then there she is! You'd better arrest her!

Gripper. Arrest her! No, no, no. We don't do business like that. Arrest her! Why any fool could do that. No, I must track her down.

No. 13. — SONG. — Gripper.

I

When information I receive that Jones has been a-forging,
And on the proceeds of his crime is prodigally gorging,
Do you suppose I collar my friend and take him to the beak, ma'am?
Why, bless your heart, they wouldn't retain me in the force a week,
ma'am.

II

In curious wig and quaint disguise, and strangely altered face, ma'am,
Unrecognised I follow my prey about from place to place, ma'am;
I note his hair, his eyes, his nose, his clothing and complexion,
And when I have got 'em all into my head, I set about detection.

III

I take his servants, one by one, and bring them all to book, ma'am,
Both man and maid of every grade, particularly his cook, ma'am;
His tradesmen then I call upon, examine 'em on their oaths, ma'am;
And the elderly man, of the Hebrew clan, who buys his left-off clothes,
ma'am.

IV

His father-in-law, perhaps, is buffalo hunting in the Prairies,
His aunt may keep a lodging-house in the ocean-girt Canaries;
His uncle's out in Honolulu, his niece in arctic zones, ma'am,
I find them out and talk to them before arresting Jones, ma'am.

V

And when my call is quite complete, and home again I fly, ma'am,
I find that Jones has gone abroad, some people are so sly, ma'am;
But I've this consolation — all the facts that I've collated,
Would surely have convicted Jones — if Jones had only waited.

Enter Sir Ruthven.

Ruth. (*rushing at* Gripper). Ha! You are the North American that sprung upon me just as I had shunted the train, with Alice in it, on to the Midland line! You struck me a deadly blow.

GRIPPER. I did; I hope it didn't hurt you much! It wasn't my fault! I was in the Author's hands.

RUTH. True, I beg your pardon.

GRIPPER. You're extremely ungrateful! I didn't come upon you till you had shunted the train and done all the mischief.

RUTH. True. You were just too late. If you had been one moment sooner —

GRIPPER. Your base design would have been frustrated! Alice would have gone on to Liverpool! She would have sailed to Australia with Herbert and married him on the voyage, and where would you have been?

RUTH. My benefactor!

ALICE. My preserver!

ROCK. My best friend!

HERBERT. My truest ally!

RUTH. Gripper, tell me one thing. I've some reason to fear that my darling Alice, whom I worship so tenderly, and who loves me so fondly, turns out to be — ha! ha! my grand-daughter!

GRIPPER. No, I fancy not; I can't be sure; but if you ask *my* opinion, I fancy not.

RUTH. My daughter deserted her little girl twenty years ago, and she hasn't turned up yet.

GRIPPER. I have thought over the matter very carefully, and putting that and that together, I have some reason to believe that I am she!

ALL. You?

GRIPPER. Yes, extravagant, isn't it? See, here is the MS., read my description. (*Reads*): "Gripper, the most celebrated detective in the Metropolitan force, was at the same time the youngest member of it. Although of commanding stature, his face was extremely fair and his features most delicately chiselled; his hands were as soft as down, his figure was slight, indeed, almost girlish, and his voice had a touching accent in it that was invaluable to him in his assumption of female characters." That looks like it, doesn't it?

Ruth. It does! My long-lost-grand-daughter! (*Embraces him.*)

Gripper. Of course, I can't be sure, but we will hope that I am mistaken.

Rock. Well, time is up! The hour is about to strike! Next time we meet we shall probably know our destinies.

No. 14. — FINALE to VOL. II. — ENSEMBLE.

We must depart, our masters call us,
  Alas, 'tis useless to rebel;
Oh! who shall say what may befall us,
  Our destiny what tongue can tell?
With $\left\{ \begin{array}{l} \text{my} \\ \text{his} \end{array} \right\}$ adored $\left\{ \begin{array}{l} \text{shall I} \\ \text{will he} \end{array} \right\}$ be mated,
Or $\left\{ \begin{array}{l} \text{shall I} \\ \text{will he} \end{array} \right\}$ wed $\left\{ \begin{array}{l} \text{my} \\ \text{his} \end{array} \right\}$ direst foe;
Oh, how we all may be related,
  Upon my word, I do not know!

End of Vol. II

VOL. III

Frontispiece. — *Interior of a Hut in Barbary.*

No. 15a. — INTRODUCTION.

Enter Herbert *in wedding attire.*

No. 15b. — RECIT. AND SONG. — Herbert.

Oh, agony! and oh, despair!
My misery I cannot bear!
The novel's all but ended now,
  All hope has fled!
The girl I hated — you know how —
  I'm doomed to wed!
But when with me the Author's done,

And Alice Grey and I are one,
  I rather think my wife
Will have good reason to regret
The luckless day when first we met!
  I'll lead her such a life!

I

I'll sulk, and I'll fidget, and worry, and frown,
The housekeeping money I'll daily cut down;
And very poor dinners I'll make her purvey,
And someone shall dine with us every day;
I'll annoy her by superintending her rig,
Her boots shall be several sizes too big;
Her bed shall be apple-pie, sprinkled with crumbs;
Her gloves shall be cheap ones, and split at the thumbs!

II

Her silks shall be such as a tally-man hawks,
And I'll never allow her to bend as she walks;
High heels to her boots I shall not let her wear,
And nothing whatever shall stuff out her hair;
In second-hand bonnets my Alice shall show,
That went out of fashion a season ago;
She shall drink out of pewter, and eat out of delf,
And as for her dresses — I'll make 'em myself!

(*After Song, enter* ALICE *hurriedly, in wedding dress.*)

ALICE. It's infamous!

HERBERT. It's disgraceful!

ALICE. Here we are at the last chapter, and I'm just going to be married to the man I abominate!

HERBERT. And I to the woman I detest!

ALICE. And to bring me out here to Barbary, an outlandish place, with an insufficiently-clad population, and after *you*! After a milksop, who can't say bo to a goose! Oh, my friend! I'll give you such a time of it when we are comfortably married!

HERBERT. Now don't be unreasonable, Miss Grey. We are desperately in love with each other. Why should we quarrel? The remedy is within reach, I'll treat you abominably and we will be divorced.

ALICE. You promise sincerely (*shaking his hand*). You're a good-natured man after all. Forget what I said just now. Let us make the best of a bad job. How did you get from Central Africa to Algiers?

HERBERT. I walked across the desert. Didn't you read the chapter which describes my journey on foot and alone, bareheaded and bare-footed from the Mountains of the Moon across the Desert of Sahara!

ALICE. No!

HERBERT. Oh it was powerfully told. For eight and forty weeks I wandered over those scorching plains supporting life on nothing particularly worth mentioning. One evening as the sun was setting in golden splendour I lay me down to die in the desert; suddenly I remembered a strange legend that the unprovided traveller need never starve in the desert of Sahara. I endeavoured to recall the rest of the legend which gave the reason why, but in vain, but seeing a caravan of Arabs in the distance I staggered towards them, and addressing their Sheik I implored him to tell me why an unprovided traveller need never starve in the desert of Sahara. "Tell me," I said, "the secret of life and the orphan's blessing shall be yours."

ALICE. And he said?

HERBERT. "That it couldn't be done for the money. The secret of life is Allah's and must be bought with a price." I tried the other Arabs one by one, but they said, "It must be bought with a price." At length I came to a swarthy Ethiopian, whose high shirt-collars and correct evening dress indicated that he was, at least, partly civilised; he wore a large frill to his shirt, and in his hands were the rib-bones of some slaughtered animal, which he rattled briskly together, as he danced wildly in the rear of the procession. I addressed him in his native language. "Thanks," said I (*imitating nigger*), "Can you tell dis child why a hunprovided traveller need never starve on the desert of Sahara? Can you told me dat?" "Iss, massa," said he, "I know dat. Yah! Yah!" "Tell me," said I, "the secret of life, and an orphan's blessing shall be yours." "Dat very old conundrum," said he, "a man need never starve on the desert of Sahara because of the *sand which is* there. Yah! Yah! Yah!" I fell fainting on the ground, for I had staked my existence on a riddle.

ALICE. And a very old one!

HERBERT. And you! How came you to Algiers?

ALICE. After I had been recognised by my father, the Duke of Ben-

Nevis, I was removed into a sphere of life in which it was considered impossible for me to marry a Sunday school teacher. For a time I was happy, and thought it possible I might be intended for the infamous Sir Ruthven after all — but no, that irritating Author would not hear of it, and sent me here after you, and out I came to Algiers as — what do you think? — a female missionary to teach the dirty little black boys to read and write.

HERBERT.   And what has become of the ex-Lady Rockalda?

No. 16. — MELODRAME.

Enter ROCKALDA, *meanly dressed.*

ROCK. (*meekly*).   I am here!

HERBERT.   My Rockalda! and how changed! And why have you been brought out here?

ROCK.   I expect I am to turn up at your wedding. I rather think that stricken with remorse, I worked my passage out here as a stewardess that I might stagger into the church as you are being united, and tell you that you are no other than Sir Ruthven Glenaloon, and that he who has hitherto passed as that baronet is only poor Tom Sittybank, the bus-conductor.

HERBERT.   Then I am a baronet!

ROCK.   You are! but you won't know it till the end of the chapter.

HERBERT.   And the Sir Ruthven to whom Alice is devoted is only a mere omnibus conductor. What do you say to that, Miss Grey?

ALICE.   Say! Why let me tell you a truer and a prouder heart may beat beneath the Somerset House badge of the poor omnibus conductor than beneath the lordly forehead of the haughtiest baronet. Baronet or busman, I love him, and when we are divorced he shall be mine. Where is he?

ROCK.   I don't know. Hasn't he come yet?

ALICE.   No! It was understood that we were all to meet here just before the last chapter, and here (*turning to MS.*) is the heading of the last chapter, and that's all.

HERBERT.   I hope nothing has happened to him.

ALICE. Happened to him! Don't say that he is dead!

ROCK. Dead! I most sincerely hope not. Are you in the chapter that has just been written?

ALICE. No!

ROCK. Nor you?

HERBERT. No!

ROCK. Nor I! Let's see what it was about. (*Takes MS.*) It's all about Sir Ruthven (*reads*). Ha! My poor girl (*to* ALICE). I don't like you at all, but I can't help feeling for you; accept my condolences and prepare for the worst.

ALICE. The worst! Oh, read on!

ROCK. Listen! (*Reads*) "Now, said Sir Ruthven, when he had ascertained by passing his thumb over the edge of the hatchet that it was sufficiently sharp for the work before it. — Now, said he, to end a life that has long been too burthensome to bear."

ALICE (*terrified*). Ha!

ROCK. (*reads*). "He locked the door, and going up to a cheval glass, took one long look at the magnificent but diabolical face, which had worked so much mischief in its time. As he looked he saw one solitary tear trickle from his left eye and course its way down his detestable cheek. It is the first said he, and it shall be the last. And so saying he swung the ponderous axe three times round his head and towards the middle of the third swing the blade shot like lightning through the thickest part of the bad man's neck. The head bounded into the air and fell heavily on the floor. The lips still moved spasmodically. With a frightful effort, they managed to hiss out the dreadful words 'a very neat blow' when the jaw fell, and the vital spark departed never to return."

HERBERT. Poor Ruthven, he was a good fellow *out* of the novel.

ALICE. Now, look here, I propose we don't stand this — I propose we rebel. Let's summon the Author and have it out with him. Let's insist that the novel shall end as *we* like.

HERBERT. We will!

ALL. Author! Author!! Author!!!

AUTHOR *enters and they attack him vociferously.*

162

AUTHOR. Now, ladies and gentlemen, what is it?

ALICE. You have killed Sir Ruthven!

ROCK. You have murdered a true gentleman, and we insist on his being restored to life. If you don't we will never work for you again. We are conventional types; you can't get on without us.

AUTHOR. But reflect! He was such an awful scoundrel.

ROCK. What he was, you made him.

AUTHOR. Well — but — (*to* HERBERT) You don't want him back, do you?

HERBERT. Most certainly!

AUTHOR. What! your hated rival, the inveterate persecutor of your beloved Alice.

HERBERT. I entirely object to his being slaughtered on my account.

AUTHOR. Magnanimous Herbert! Oh! you're a beautiful character.

ROCK. Once for all, he must be restored to life.

AUTHOR. Rockalda! Consistent to the very last. She misses the abettor of all her schemes, and is helpless without him. I can quite understand it, but it can't be done.

ALICE. Oh, please give me back my love!

AUTHOR. Your love! What are you talking about? Why, he's your persecutor.

ALICE. True, but you can't think how I love him.

AUTHOR. Alice Grey! What does this mean? You are a quiet, virtuous, amiable young heroine, deeply in love with Herbert, who is a beautiful character.

ALICE. In love with Herbert! Pooh! Sir, I despise him!

AUTHOR. Oh, ridiculous!

ALICE. The man *I* love is a totally different character.

AUTHOR. But he's amiable, constant, philanthropic, mild, kind, good-tempered and (*whispers*) I'll tell you a secret — he comes into a baronetcy in the last chapter.

ALICE. I don't care; I hate mild and amiable men! I like a handsome rover, a scapegrace, a moral brigand, who sets all law at defiance. Do you suppose I'm going to marry that person? I insist on marrying Sir Ruthven, and, as a first step, he must be restored to life.

AUTHOR. But I've chopped his head off; I can't stick it on again.

ALICE. Science can do anything. Invent a process if you have it not, and if any of the critics doubt its operation, offer to prove its efficacy upon any one of them.

AUTHOR. Very good. Is there anything else?

HERBERT. Yes! I must marry Rockalda.

AUTHOR. What! the yellow-haired fiend with the panther-like movement?

HERBERT. Certainly!

AUTHOR. But you're a Sunday school teacher!

HERBERT. I don't care!

AUTHOR. I don't see how it is to be done. Will you reform her?

HERBERT. I'll try.

AUTHOR. Very good! I suppose I must give in — I don't know what my readers will say.

No. 17. — MELODRAME.

Enter GRIPPER *dressed as a beadle.*

GRIPPER. One moment, if you please! I wish to speak to you about my fate —

AUTHOR. Oh you're too late! We've settled everything.

ROCK. Don't interfere, Gripper! You're too late. If you had been here in time you might have been consulted.

GRIPPER. But I'm bound to be late, I can't be in time. Hang it, Sir —

AUTHOR. Don't use such awful language. You don't know who you are. If you did you would be more guarded in your expressions.

GRIPPER. Then I do turn out to be somebody else?

AUTHOR. I should think you did. There's such a surprise in store for you. Listen! You are here in Algiers disguised as a protestant beadle to arrest the wicked Rockalda immediately after she has informed Herbert in the Church that he is no other than Sir Ruthven. Well, to the surprise and consternation of the clergyman and the intense delight of yourself, you turn out to be no other than —

GRIPPER. Sir Ruthven's abandoned granddaughter!

AUTHOR (*surprised*). Yes! How did you know that?

GRIPPER. I guessed it.

AUTHOR. That was rather sharp for a detective. Yes, you are the granddaughter. Now ain't you sorry you said, "Hang it"?

GRIPPER. No, sir, I am not, I protest against such a discovery; it's ridiculously absurd. I've been a man all my life and I protest against being changed into a woman at my time of life.

AUTHOR. But you'll be a very fine woman!

GRIPPER. I'd rather be a very fine man.

AUTHOR. You shall marry an earl.

GRIPPER. I prefer a countess!

AUTHOR. Will you let me leave it doubtful?

GRIPPER. On no account. If I am not allowed I'll never work for you again. I'm a sensation detective and you can't get on without me.

AUTHOR. Very well; I give in. You shall continue to be a man, a very fine man. That's settled. I'll alter the last chapter. Herbert shall marry Rockalda; Ruthven shall be restored to life and marry Alice; and Gripper shall turn out to be Sherlock Holmes in disguise. (*Going off.*) There! What do you say to that? (*Exit.*)

No. 18. — FINALE to Vol. III. — LADY ROCKALDA, ALICE, HERBERT, GRIPPER.

ALL. I'm delighted; I'm delighted;
      All will have a happy ending.
      They will ⎱
      We shall ⎰ shortly be united,

        Their ⎱
        Our ⎰ lives together spending.

HERBERT.	My Rockalda!
ROCK.	Oh, my Herbert!
HERBERT.	I'll reform your taste for malice,
ALICE.	And Sir Ruthven, dear Sir Ruthven,
	Shall be married to his Alice.
ALICE & {	To our task together warming,
HERBERT. {	In a manner most decided,
	We will set about reforming
	Both our lovers so misguided.
ALL.	To their task, &c.

Enter SIR RUTHVEN *as a bus conductor.*

RUTH. (*Rataplan*). City — Bank —— City — Bank, &c., &c.

ALL.   I'm delighted! I'm delighted, &c.

END OF VOL. III

CURTAIN

Happy Arcadia

Characters

STREPHON —————————— *A happy Arcadian, betrothed to Chloe.*

LYCIDAS —————————— *The handsomest man in the world.*

COLIN —————————— *A virtuous old peasant, father of Chloe.*

DAPHNE —————————— *An elderly Arcadian, Chloe's mama.*

CHLOE —————————— *A happy Arcadian, betrothed to Strephon.*

ASTROLOGOS —————————— *A blighted Bogy.*

SCENE: *Exterior of* STREPHON's *cottage. Entrance to cottage R. Large tree C., with seat round it. Pretty Arcadian landscape, cornfields, water, etc.*

STREPHON *and* CHLOE *discovered.* STREPHON *seated beneath tree, playing on flageolet.* CHLOE *dancing with pet lamb, decorated with ribbons.* THEY *are dressed as a "Watteau" shepherd and shepherdess.*

DUET. — STREPHON *and* CHLOE.

Let us sing,
Let us dance,
And deck our existence with flowers.
And our joy
To enhance
We'll live but in arbors and bowers.
And we'll ne'er
Turn a glance
On palaces, temples and towers.
Oh, that all
Had a chance
Of a life that's as happy as ours!

(*After song* CHLOE *sits down impatiently.*)

CHLOE. Oh, bother!

STREP. (*sulkily*). Certainly. Bother!

CHLOE. "A life that's as happy as ours!" What nonsense it is! Why, I'm miserable!

STREP. So am I. Utterly, completely and intensely miserable. Bored beyond expression. Utterly, unmistakably bored!

CHLOE. Look at this disgusting little lamb that I'm obliged to go about with all day! I, who hate lambs!

STREP. And look at this irritating pipe that I'm obliged to play upon from morning to night! I, who hate music!

CHLOE. I always pinch my lamb when nobody's looking.

STREP. And I always play out of tune when nobody's listening.

CHLOE. For matter of all that you were playing out of tune just now.

STREP. Well, *you're* nobody.

CHLOE. Oh, I could shake you for saying that!

STREP. Ah, you're a nice girl to be engaged to.

CHLOE. So everybody says.

STREP. I wish everybody had an opportunity of trying.

CHLOE. Oh, you great hulking booby, I wish I'd never seen you!

STREP. Pity you didn't say so when our parents proposed to betroth us!

CHLOE. I was only three days old, but I remember I *thought* so.

STREP. (*furiously*). Look here — let's break it off!

CHLOE. By all means.

STREP. Upon my word I can't stand you.

CHLOE. I assure you, you are absolutely insupportable.

STREP. You're a flirt —

CHLOE. You're a booby.

STREP. You are plain.

CHLOE. You are hideous.

STREP. You — you are not as young as you were.

CHLOE. I am!

STREP. You're not.

CHLOE. I am — you — you — you — (*bursts into tears, then suddenly*) Here's somebody coming.

(STREPHON *and* CHLOE *resume their singing and dancing as*
DAPHNE *enters, with lamb.*)

DAPHNE (*speaking very rapidly*). Oh, what pretty, pretty little birds! Oh, what a happy little man, and, oh, what a happy little maid! Ah, innocent, innocent little people, with their little hearts overflowing with love, and their little bodies moving in harmony with the pretty little songs they sing to one another! Oh, happy, happy, happy little birds!

CHLOE (*relapsing*). Oh, it's only ma! Never mind ma!

STREP. Oh, it's only aunt — never mind aunt!

DAPHNE. Oh, what pretty little happy innocent —

STREP. Oh, nonsense. Drop it — we're quite alone.

DAPHNE. Why — bless my heart alive, you've never been quarreling — and in Arcadia — happy, happy Arcadia. Oh, naughty, naughty, naughty! Oh, fie! fie! fie! Oh, that isn't pretty behaved at all, at all, at all!

CHLOE. Oh, Strephon *is* such a donkey!

STREP. So I am — a donkey. A patient, faithful, docile, ill-used, meek, long-suffering — abominably treated animal — a donkey! So I am! Yah!

(Kicks open door of cottage, passionately, and exits in a furious rage.)

DAPHNE. Ah, deary, deary, deary, times are dreadfully changed since I was a girl. Those were the early days of Arcadia, and everybody was really happy and contented. But now it seems that nobody is satisfied — even your poor dear papa, who has been an Arcadian for fifty years — and is looked upon as a patriarch by other Arcadians — even he is discontented!

CHLOE. Why, what's the matter with papa?

DAPHNE. Why, he's got all sorts of fancies into his poor old head — he's always wishing he was somebody else. What do you think is his grievance now? Why, that he can't be a woman! He actually and positively wishes he was a woman! I'm sure I'd do anything to make him comfortable, but there are some things I cannot and will not do, and that is one! Hush! here he comes.

(THEY retire behind tree C. as COLIN enters.)

(COLIN is a very ugly and remorseful looking man. HE enters singing and playing on a pipe. HE leads a lamb and dances with great difficulty.)

COLIN *(singing)*. "Let us sing — let us dance," etc. *(Sees that he is alone.)* Oh, no one here? *(Relapses.)* Ah! *(Sighing and wiping his eyes.)* Here's a miserable object for you! Here is a miserable object for you! Born with a natural taste for crime — nursed in a stolen cradle — weaned upon abstracted pap — my schooling paid for with bad sovereigns — I was taught from my infancy to look upon fraud and dishonesty as the legitimate means of earning a dishonorable competency! Looking forward, as I always did, to retiring in middle life into a condition of guilty respectability, how is it that Fate has so far interfered with my intentions as to turn me into a simple and unsophisticated shepherd of Happy Arcadia? Forty years ago, in sportive mood, I forged a poor little will. It was a very small will, and the testator was dead; still, people were annoyed, and to avoid the consequences I fled to Arcadia, where for forty years I have been compelled, against my will, to lead a life of absolute innocence. I hate innocence — I abhor respectability, and I would return at once to the happy iniquitous world if it were not that my doing so would involve immediate arrest, followed by fourteen years penal servitude. Oh, that I were a woman! Women have such privileges, such immunities! A woman forges a will — she pleads ignorance of business — and she is acquitted. She steals silk dresses or Dutch cheeses, and she pleads kleptomania — and she is acquitted. Oh, woman, woman, if you only knew how to work the prerogatives you possess, you might all retire on a comfortable and dishonest fortune in rather less than no time!

SONG. — Colin.

"Only a Woman."

From the first it was always the same,
    And many before me have said it —
Where men are all saddled with blame,
    A woman gets nothing but credit.
Though life's a toss-up for our sins,
    The toss always falls as she chooses —
If it's "heads" the poor little maid wins —
    If it's "tails" — her antagonist loses.

    For though she is only a woman,
    A poor, inexperienced woman —
        She feathers her nest
        With the softest and best,
    Poor timid and innocent woman!

In business a woman beyond
    The reach of all business-like men is —
She fastens you down to your bond
    Like the Jew in the "Merchant of Venice."
And when she believes there's a flaw,
    She violates every condition;

172

And if then you appeal to the law,
She answers with seeming contrition

That please she is only a woman —
A helpless and innocent woman —
You *must* be a brute
If you enter a suit
'Gainst a weak and unbusinesslike woman!

(*At end of song* COLIN *bursts into a loud hysterical wail, which brings every one in in great alarm. He has sunk on the seat round the tree, but on their entry he springs up and sings:*)

"Let us sing — let us dance," etc.

CHLOE (*approaching* COLIN *kindly*). Papa! Are you not well?

COLIN (*smiling seraphically*). Well? Who is *not* well in Arcadia?

DAPHNE. Perhaps you are unhappy? If there is any silent sorrow tugging at your poor old heartstrings — tell it, oh, tell it to me — my bosom is easily lacerated — and the tear of sympathy is ever ready to bedew the eye of conjugal affection. *Are* you unhappy?

COLIN. Unhappy? In Arcadia? For shame! Is not our life the purest and happiest that the intellect of man can devise?

ALL. It is!

COLIN. Are not the very breezes scented with innocence?

ALL. Invariably!

COLIN. Don't buttercups and daisies grow wild in the open air?

ALL. To be sure!

COLIN. Don't the oaks and the elms flourish without the assistance of so much as a watering pot?

ALL. Certainly.

COLIN. Isn't it summer throughout June and July?

ALL. As a rule.

COLIN. And lastly — and chiefly — and above all — don't the — don't the — (*bursts into tears*). Oh, it's no use — I've done it for fifty years and I can't do it any longer! I do believe I'm the most miserable old dog in existence!

STREP. But what's the matter with you? Can it be remorse?

COLIN. It can! More — it is!

DAPHNE. But bless us and save us, what in the world has the poor man been and done?

COLIN. Nothing! That's it! For fifty years I have done nothing but dance and tootle on a pipe. Think of what I might have done in fifty years if I had been permitted to wallow in native wickedness — to coruscate in congenial crime. But circumstances have compelled me to become an Arcadian and now, in my old age, I begin to lament my misspent manhood and to groan over the wasted years that can never be recalled! Ah! It's a weary world!

DAPHNE. I have no sympathy with your views, but it certainly is a very weary world!

CHLOE. I repudiate your sentiments, but it is a very, very weary world, indeed.

STREP. I am aghast at the state of your morals, but it certainly is a confounded ill-contrived, three-cornered, square-peg-in-a-round-hole sort of a world and I wish I was well out of it altogether! Ah!

ALL (*sighing heavily and shaking their heads*). Ah!

(ASTROLOGOS, *a very pale, lank, disconsolate person, dressed in black, puts his head out of an upper window. He plays a flageolet very badly.*)

COLIN (*suddenly*). There's somebody looking! (*They all spring up and take up refrain of song, "Let us sing — let us dance,"* COLIN *and* STREPHON *playing, while* DAPHNE *and* CHLOE *dance with lambs.*)

AST. (*at window*). Oh, my! Here's a state of innocence for you! Oh, my goodness! Ain't this a state of innocence for you?

ALL. It is!

AST. Ain't you all happy neither?

ALL. Ain't we just!

AST. Ah, don't I wish I was as happy as you!

DAPHNE. Ah, but you see you're not an Arcadian.

COLIN. You're a miserable dweller in cities and know nothing of the beauties of rustic life.

AST. And don't I wish I could play the pipe in tune?

STREP. You're only a lodger — a tourist — an excursionist — you cannot expect to play the pipe in tune, unless you're a naturalized Arcadian! (ASTROLOGOS *disappears from window.*)

(*During this dialogue the Arcadians have been dancing and tootling, but when* ASTROLOGOS *disappears they relapse.*)

COLIN. He's gone!

STREP. That's an agreeable person. He's occupied my first floor for the last three months. I hate filthy lucre, but he hasn't suggested anything in the shape of rent.

DAPHNE. Well, why don't you ask him for it?

STREP. An Arcadian dun a lodger for rent? He wouldn't do it. He's too unsophisticated. Hang it all, I hope I haven't come down to hankering after dross. I trust I'm too unworldly to do that. I merely mention, as an incidental fact, curious in itself but of no special importance whatever, that up to the present moment he hasn't suggested anything in the shape of rent.

COLIN. Ha! Strange!

DAPHNE. Droll — very droll.

STREP. Yes, as a matter of fact it is droll — that's just what it is — it's droll.

ALL. Ha! ha!

(*Enter* ASTROLOGOS. *He is very dismal and lank. He is playing on a pipe and leading a lamb with a ribbon. He goes up to* DAPHNE, *then to* CHLOE, *then to* COLIN. *Each walks off, much alarmed, in succession.* STREPHON *remains.*)

AST. (*in tears*). The simple shepherds seem afraid of me.

STREP. Well, you're not a pleasant person.

AST. I'm afraid I'm not. I've such odd ways, haven't I?

STREP. Your ways *are* odd.

Ast. I'm always thus. You will never find anything in the shape of change about me.

Strep. I regret to hear it.

Ast. To tell you the truth I don't believe I'm human.

Strep. That idea has already occurred to me.

Ast. I believe I'm a sort of demon. Now, would it astonish you to learn that there's a very long and interesting tale attached to me?

Strep. Not a bit — though it's wonderful how you stow it away.

Ast. (*shaking his head*). Ah, I could joke like that once — but I don't mean "tail" — an appendage. I mean "tale" — a history.

Strep. Oh!

Ast. I'll tell it to you. A quarter of a century ago, I was younger than I am now by some years. The first thing I can remember is being a good young man in spectacles.

Strep. Weak eyes?

Ast. No — capital eyes, but serious disposition. But everybody ridiculed me, especially little boys.

Strep. I should have smacked 'em.

Ast. So I did, but the cowards kicked me. But I was even with them, for I went to Merlin and asked him to make me a bogy.

Strep. Couldn't you have taken a mask and some straw, and made one for yourself?

Ast. No, no — to make *me* a bogy — *me*, you know — to frighten little boys.

Strep. I see — but your conversation is not very lucid.

Ast. Sloppy, ain't it? Well, he made me a bogy and taught me all sorts of conjuring tricks. Dreadful, ain't it?

Strep. It's appalling.

Ast. Don't be frightened.

Strep. I'm not.

Ast. Now, it's a proud distinction to be a bogy, but it ain't all pleasure. For instance, I had to live in a coal cellar.

Strep. I see — to be called out by nursemaids to frighten naughty little boys.

Ast. No — that wouldn't have been so bad — I wasn't called out at all — I was there to be alluded to.

Strep. But they could have alluded to you without your being there, couldn't they?

Ast. Ah, but that would have been a deception.

Strep. So it would.

Ast. I hate deception. I wouldn't deceive a nursemaid. Are you fond of nursemaids?

Strep. (*shocked*). No — are you?

Ast. Ain't I just! Well, I remained in the cellar for twenty years and amused myself conjuring with bits of coal. Can you conjure with bits of coal?

Strep. No — can you?

Ast. Can't I just! It's very simple — you take a big bit of coal in your right hand and a little bit of coal in your left. Then you put your hand behind your back and you ask the company which hand the big bit is in. If they guess rightly you slyly change the pieces behind your back and confound them. It frightens them horribly.

Strep. I should conceive that it was calculated to strike them with unspeakable terror. But if you are alone?

Ast. Ah, then you must be the company as well. I used to conjure and guess too, and I always took care to guess wrong, which made my tricks very successful, but I was obliged to give it up, it unnerved me so. In fact, the excitement of the life was too much for me and I had to retire.

Strep. And how do you live?

Ast. Well, at first I did very well. Merlin had given me four magic talismans — a cap, a cloak, a ring and a stick. Whoever possesses any one of these articles has the right to have one wish granted — but only one.

So, as I possessed all four, I had four wishes — and I wished four times for beef (of which I am fond), and I got it and I eat it up and now I have no more wishes left, and no more beef. Well, then I earned a living by conjuring. You haven't seen my great feat?

STREP. Oh, yes, I have — and I was very glad to see that they *were* feet and not hoofs.

AST. That's an amusing joke, but it isn't what I mean. I mean my great trick — with the coals. I can't do it here, because there are no coals in Arcadia. It's a pity, because it earns me a deal of money, and if I could only find some bits of coal I should be a made man.

STREP. But won't other things do as well as coals?

AST. Such as what?

STREP. Such as stones for instance — or money (*aside*) — that's a good idea — (*aloud*) Money, such as a sovereign and half a sovereign, or a fifty-pound note and a hundred-pound note.

AST. Of course — a fifty-pound note and a hundred-pound note will do capitally — I've got the very thing. (*Producing notes.* STREPHON *very keen after them.*) I'll go this very day.

STREP. I must drop a hint about that rent. Stop — I know a song with a hint in it. I'll sing it to him. (*Aloud.*) Before you go I should like to sing to you a little thing of my own — a simple little thing — just a suggestion of an idea — nothing more.

AST. I should like to hear it very much. (*Sits.*)

STREP. (*aside*). I've got him now. (*Sings.*)
 Fair love —

AST. (*interrupting*). Eh?

STREP. Fair love — (it's supposed to be sung to a lady)
 Fair love, assuage the wearing woe
  Within this bosom pent;
 Thou tellest me that thou must go
  Because thy heart is rent —
 Is rent — is rent, rent, rent — is rent — (*Ad lib.*)
 Because thy heart is rent. (*Pauses significantly.*)

AST. Exactly — you mean torn, I suppose. You don't mean ha! ha! the hire of a house.

Strep. No, no — of course not. Torn — broken —

Ast. I declare, I thought you meant the rent of a house.

Strep. Oh, no — nothing of the kind — torn. Well, it goes on like this: (*Sings.*)

> Rent though that heart may be,
> Rent though that heart may be —
> *Rent* though that heart may be —

Ast. Exactly. Rent though that heart may be —

Strep. (*sings*). Why, give it, love, to me.

(*Holds out his hand as for money.* Astrologos *shakes it heartily.*)

Ast. Capital — excellent. Only —

Strep. Yes?

Ast. Don't you think you've got rather too much "rent"?

Strep. Well, do you know, I was thinking I hadn't got quite enough.

Ast. Too much. I should reduce my rent. Good-morning.

(*Exit* Astrologos.)

Strep. He's gone. Now, anybody but an Arcadian would be disappointed. I couldn't help throwing out a hint just to see if he would take it — and he wouldn't. It's very shabby, because he can't *know* that I don't care about money. That's the great beauty of being an Arcadian — one can't be sordid even if one wants to. Thank goodness I'm a true Arcadian! It is a happy life, after all, and I wouldn't change it for any consideration.

SONG. — Strephon.

> There's naught but care, and toil, and strife
> For him who leads a city life;
> He dines each day in tip-top fig
> On dainty meats — the nasty pig —
> And finishes — unhappy brute —
> On first-rate wine and hothouse fruit.
> If first-rate wine were given me
> How miserable I should be!
>> For I'm a simple, simple swain,
>> Who treats such things with much disdain.

Such matters have no charm for me,
A simple swain of Arcadee!

The wretched fellow, you will find,
Gets up just when he feels inclined,
And always takes his nightly rest
At any hour that suits him best.
Whene'er he walks abroad, I vow,
The common people scrape and bow.
If common people bowed to me
How miserable I should be!
　　For I'm a simple, simple swain, etc.

He goes to opera, ball and play,
(Disgusting joys!) and every day
Some unforeseen enjoyment brings.
Now, there's a dreadful state of things!
And spite of old duennas grim,
Fair maidens fall in love with him.
If maidens fell in love with me
How miserable I should be!
　　For I'm a simple, simple swain, etc.

(*Enter* Daphne, *very excited.*)

Daphne.　Oh, my! Oh, there now! Oh, I've such news! Colin! Chloe!
I've such news!　　　　　　　　(*Enter* Colin *and* Chloe.)

Colin (*shaking her*).　Speak out, woman, can't you? What's wrong?

Daphne.　Nothing. Everything is right. Lycidas — the handsome,
wealthy, gifted Lycidas — has determined to renounce the vanities of a
worldly life and is going to become an Arcadian!

Strep.　And who is Lycidas?

Colin.　Lycidas is the richest man in the world!

Daphne.　Lycidas is the noblest man in the world!

Chloe.　Lycidas is the handsomest man in the world!

Colin.　Ha! ha! I was all that once!

Daphne.　And why — why do you think he is coming? Because he
has taken a fancy to — who do you think?

Strep.　You?

DAPHNE.   No. Because he has taken a fancy to Chloe! There!

CHLOE.   To me! Oh, how delightful! How do I look?

COLIN.   To Chloe! My dear child! My darling child! This, indeed, is happiness.

STREP.   But here — I say — it don't seem to occur to you that there is a little difficulty in the way. Chloe is betrothed to me.

COLIN.   Don't let that distress you — set your mind at rest. I shall offer no obstacle to the betrothal being cancelled.

STREP.   Oh, yes — but I say —

DAPHNE.   Lycidas is so handsome — *he* is!

COLIN.   And such a gentleman — he is!

CHLOE.   And so rich — he is! Not that *that* matters in Arcadia.

DAPHNE.   No, that don't matter in Arcadia.

COLIN.   Money is vanity — dross — rubbish.

CHLOE.   I'm sure *I* despise it; still, as a matter of fact — curious in itself, but having no special bearing on the case — Lycidas *is* rich.

STREP.   Look here. I'm an Arcadian, and as an Arcadian I'm bound to give every stranger a welcome. But if this stranger is coming after Chloe I'll give him the sort of welcome he don't expect.

DAPHNE.   An Arcadian bearing malice! Oh, there now!

STREP.   I won't be an Arcadian any longer. I'll resign. I'll go in for athletic exercises. I'll practice night and day with Indian clubs, dumb bells, chest expanders and boxing gloves. My temperament is naturally fierce — it shall have full swing; my disposition is pugilistic, it shall revel unrestrained. I'll — I'll smash this fellow — (*Suddenly.*) Here he comes!

(*All take up pipes and sing.*)

ENSEMBLE.   Welcome to this spot,
Free from care and danger,
Welcome to our humble cot,
Welcome, little stranger!

(*Enter* LYCIDAS. *He is magnificently dressed and leads two lambs decorated with ribbons. As he sings he accompanies himself on a pipe.*)

SOLO. — Lycidas.   (*Very melodramatic*)

Far away from care and strife,
Far from busy pillage —
I will lead a simple life
In this happy village.

ALL. Welcome, welcome to this spot,
Free from care and danger,
Welcome to our humble cot,
Welcome, little stranger —
In this little village of ours!

Lycidas. In this little village of theirs!

ALL. Our life is all honey and flowers,
Untainted by sorrow or cares!

QUARTETTE.

Colin. On the banks of every stream
Are pleasure-boats ready to launch.
Our cows give nothing but cream,
Our mutton's all saddle and haunch.

ALL. In this little village of ours!

Lycidas. In this little village of theirs!

ALL. Our life is all honey and flowers,
Untainted by sorrow or cares!

Strep. And every night there's a moon,
And figs grow thistles upon,
And the little pigs squeak in tune,
And every goose is a swan.

ALL. In this little village of ours!

Lycidas. In this little village of theirs!

ALL. Our life is all honey and flowers,
Untainted by sorrow or cares!

ALL. In this little village of ours!

Lycidas. In this little village of theirs!

ALL.	Our life is all honey and flowers,
	Untainted by sorrow or cares!
DAPHNE.	Asparagus all the year round,
	And apples that eat like a peach;
	And gloves are a penny a pound,
	And bonnets a half-penny each.
ALL.	In this little village of ours!
LYCIDAS.	In this little village of theirs!
ALL.	Our life is all honey and flowers,
	Untainted by sorrow or cares!

(DANCE.)

LYCIDAS (*impetuously*). This is the life for me. I see plainly that this is the life for me. I will be a simple shepherd and come and live with you. Oblige me with the address of a house agent, a field, a fold, a flock of sheep and a list of local charities.

COLIN. It is indeed a charming existence. Beautiful climate — unlimited health — nothing to do.

CHLOE. Lovely things to wear.

DAPHNE. Envy, hatred and malice unheard of.

STREP. And money a drug.

DAPHNE. A drug.

COLIN. A drug.

LYCIDAS. I am sorry to hear that. I am wealthy, and as I pride myself on the completeness with which I do everything I undertake, I had provided myself with money with which I should have liked to pay my footing (*producing bags — three small, one large*).

STREP. A stranger's whim is sacred. We thwart him in nothing.

DAPHNE. In nothing.

CHLOE. In nothing whatever.

COLIN. In nothing at all.

LYCIDAS. Good. (*He distributes the bags. All endeavor to get the big one, which falls to* STREPHON's *share.*)

DAPHNE (*opening bag*). Gold!

CHLOE (*opening bag*). Gold!

COLIN (*opening bag*). Gold!

STREP. (*opening bag*). Copper!   (*Disappointed.*)

LYCIDAS. And now, leave me alone with her.

(*Indicating* CHLOE.)

STREP. But I say —

COLIN (*To* DAPHNE). The gentleman wishes us to leave him with Chloe. Come, Daphne.

DAPHNE. But —

COLIN. Let us humor the young people. Incredible as it may appear, you were once young yourself.

(*Exit with* DAPHNE.)

LYCIDAS (*to* STREPHON, *who remains*). I said I would be alone with *her.*

STREP. Yes, that's all very well, but —

LYCIDAS (*sternly*). It is the stranger's whim!

STREP. Oh, of course, if it is the stranger's whim.

(*Exit. Bus.*)

LYCIDAS. Now we are alone.

CHLOE. So we are.

LYCIDAS. Maiden, hear me. I am a man of few words — hot, rash, impulsive. I am a whirlwind — a cataract — a volcano. That being so, you will be prepared to hear that I worship you fondly, madly, recklessly. Be mine.

CHLOE. Really this is so sudden.

LYCIDAS. As I said before, I pride myself on the completeness with which I do everything I undertake. That being so, I shall be glad to hear the names of your dressmaker, jeweller, confectioner, livery-stable keeper and favorite clergyman.

CHLOE. But before I reply —

LYCIDAS. Ha, an evasion! Then I have a rival! His name and those of his physician, family undertaker and monumental mason!

(*Enter* STREPHON *with stick, unobserved.*)

CHLOE. No, no — you are too impetuous. It is true there is a great hulking, foolish, awkward booby always bothering me, but he is nothing.

LYCIDAS. He shall be less than nothing. I will grind him to gray powder and take him in jam. Where is he?

STREP. (*coming forward*). He is here. (LYCIDAS *alarmed.*) Perhaps you would like to apologize?

LYCIDAS (*meekly*). You anticipate my fondest wish. To a true gentleman there is nothing humiliating in a frank confession of error. Favor me with the name of your daily paper, its charge for advertisements, and your favorite form of retraction.

STREP. But one moment.

CHLOE (*aside to* LYCIDAS). You had better go, I think. You can return in half an hour.

LYCIDAS. Sir, I retire gracefully. Take the maiden. She is not good enough for you. She is not young enough for you. She is not pretty enough for you — but take her nevertheless. She may improve. (*Aside to* CHLOE.) In half an hour. (*Aloud.*) Good-morning!

(*Exit* LYCIDAS, *followed by* STREPHON, *shaking his stick significantly.*)

STREP. And now, miss, understand me. I am no longer an Arcadian. If that fellow presumes to address you again, I will smash that fellow. You understand — I will smash him! It's painful, but it must be done.

(*Exit* STREPHON.)

CHLOE. It's very hard. The gentleman is handsome, which is a recommendation, and he's affectionate, which is agreeable, and he's wealthy, which don't matter, and he makes love in the manner which of all others I prefer. I like a man who comes to the point at once. Ah, that's the way to woo!

(*Enter* STREPHON *in great agitation. He staggers to a seat.*)

STREP. He's gone! Gone! Gone! Ha! ha! ha!

CHLOE. Who has gone? Not Lycidas?

STREP. Lycidas? No, Astrologos! He's vanished! Disappeared! And he owed me three months' rent! It's of no consequence whatever, but as a matter of fact, or rather as a don't matter of fact, he certainly did owe me three months' rent! Ha! ha! ha! (*Weeping hysterically.*)

(*Enter* DAPHNE *and* COLIN.)

DAPHNE. Strephon, my dear Strephon, here is a little parcel which has been sent to you by Astrologos; the wretch has gone, but who knows what this may contain? It's not a matter of any interest to an Arcadian, but I shouldn't be at all surprised if it's an equivalent for the creature's rent.

STREP. Perhaps. Who knows? If it is, it would serve him right to keep it. Just to punish him, you know.

COLIN. Yes, to punish him.

DAPHNE. Exactly, to punish him.

STREP. I'll open it. (*Does so.*) A stick, a ring, a cloak, and a cap! — and a note addressed to me. (*Opens and reads.*)
"These things are no longer of any use to me.
There is a mystic power attached to them.
Distribute them as you think fit. ASTROLOGOS."
Come, that's something!

COLIN. You are to distribute them as you think fit.

(*Holding out his hand.*)

STREP. Yes, and I think fit to distribute them by auction.

ALL. Good — by auction.

STREP. (*Table is brought.*) That's it. Now then, ladies and gentlemen, allow me to submit —

ALL. No, no — sing it, sing it.

QUARTETTE.

STREP.   Good people all, attend, attend to me,
               While I submit the stranger's kit,
               Which here displayed you plainly see,
               To public competition.

A cap, a cloak, a ring, a cloak, a ring, a box,
And everything in excellent condition.

COL., CH. AND D.　　　　In excellent, in excellent condition.

STREP.　　　In excellent condition.　　　　　*[Takes cap.]*
You place it thus upon your head,
And everywhere you hear it said
That you're a clever, knowing man,
With wit to plot and plan.

COL., CH. AND D.　　　You place it thus, and as I live
An air of innocence 'twill give.
The craftiest man, by such a rule,
Will look a simple fool.

STREP.　Now, what shall we say for this little cap?

COL., CH. AND D.　Now, what shall we say for that little cap?

CHLOE.　A penny!

DAPHNE.　Two pence!

COLIN.　Three pence!

CHLOE.　Four!

STREP.　Any more, any more, any more, any more? Four pence —
Any advance upon — going, going, going, going, gone!

OMNES.　Hurrah! hurrah! it's Chloe's cap, it's Chloe's cap,
it's Chloe's cap.
It's a kind of wide-awake, for it hasn't got a nap.
Hurrah! for Chloe's cap!

STREP.　Good people all, attend, attend to me,
While I submit the stranger's kit,
Which here displayed you plainly see,
To public competition.
Now, here's a little cloak,
Such a nice little, sweet little cloak,
Such a dear little, grey little, red little cloak I never
did see.

COL., CH. AND D.　Come, we must try ere we can buy.

STREP.　Yes, you shall try, and then you'll buy;
Believe me, for I do not joke,

187

I never saw so lovely a cloak.
'Twill keep the rain-drops from your pins,
And hide a multitude of sins.

COL., CH. AND D.   You place it thus, all square and true,
And you're a merchant, well to do.
You place it thus — you're taken for
A base conspirator!
Now, what shall we say for that little cloak?

[STREPHON.]   Now, what shall we say for this little cloak?

DAPHNE.   A penny!

COLIN.   Two pence!

CHLOE.   Three pence!

DAPHNE.   Four pence!

STREP.   Any more, any more, any more, any more?
Four pence! Any advance upon?
Going, going, going, gone!

OMNES.   Hurrah! hurrah! it's Daphne's cloak,
It's Daphne's cloak, it's Daphne's cloak.
She's very wide-awake, with a feeling for a joke.
Hurrah! for Daphne's cloak!

STREP.   Now, here's a lot that must, that must be sold,
A snuff-box, made of solid gold.
Now, make an offer, if you please —
It's not a thing at which to sneeze.
Now, what shall we say for this affair?
What shall we say for the tabatière?
What shall we say for this tabatière
Of solid gold?

COL., CH. AND D.   Now, make a bid for this affair.

STREP.   Such a nice little box I never did see.
Now, make an offer if you please —
It's not a thing at which to sneeze —
A snuff-box made of solid gold,
Of solid gold.

COL., CH. AND D. Now, make a bid for this affair.
What shall we say for this affair?
This gold tabatière, what shall
We say for this affair?

STREP. Now, what shall we say for this little box?
Now, what shall we say for this little box?

COLIN. A penny!

DAPHNE. Two pence!

CHLOE. Three pence!

COLIN. Four pence!

STREP. Any more, any more, any more, any more?
Four pence — any advance upon?
Going, going, going, going, gone!

OMNES. Hurrah! hurrah! it's Colin's box,
It's Colin's box, it's Colin's box,
It's all of solid gold, he's a very sly old fox.
Hurrah! for Colin's box.
Hurrah! hurrah! hurrah! hurrah!
He bid away, away,
Hurrah! hurrah! hurrah! he'll never rue this day.
Hurrah! hurrah! hurrah! hurrah!

(*Exeunt.*)

DAPHNE (*examining cloak*). Well, there now, I declare, it's not such a very bad bargain. It's not very handsome, but then four pence isn't much, and altogether I've no reason to complain of my bargain. (*Takes out knitting.*) So that disreputable old gentleman declared that whoever possessed one of these things should have one wish granted, did he? And there are some donkeys who'd believe that nonsense! Have a wish granted! Why, bless us and save us, don't we live in Arcadia, where nobody has anything to wish for? But some people are never satisfied. You may take a man and make kings and queens of him, and he'll grumble because you haven't made him emperors and empresses! Ah, well — people never seem to know when they're well off. There's my old man — healthy old gentleman — plenty to eat and drink — nothing to do — nothing will satisfy him short of being a woman. There's my nephew Strephon — fine, muscular lad — good-looking, too — *he's* always grumbling and wishing he was somebody else. Ah! I wish I'd as little to grumble at as he has! There'd be some excuse for a poor feeble old lady — but a fine handsome lad just beginning life! Ah, I wish I was in his shoes.

(*Passes behind tree C.* Strephon *comes from other side to convey the idea that the change has been effected. He wears the red cloak and knits a stocking.*)

Strep. (*with manners of* Daphne). I'd soon show them that there was little to grumble at! (*Sees coat.*) Eh! What? Why, what an extraordinary thing. Why, bless us and save us, if I haven't come out in Strephon's coat. Now, that's a most extraordinary mistake to have made. Why, what a foolish old woman I must be! Now, how could that have happened? Let me see. (*Passes hand over chin in considering — finds it rough.*) Dear me! (*Rubs it.*) How rough my chin is! It must be the cold wind that has chapped it! (*Feels for pocket in skirt to replace knitting. Finds that he has no skirt.*) Why — oh dear! Oh, bless me! Oh, I must be dreaming! If I haven't got on a pair of — Oh! (*Sits and endeavors to hide his legs under seat.*) Oh, Dame Daphne! Dame Daphne! (*Sees legs again.*) Oh! How shocking! I couldn't possibly have put on a pair of — a pair of — a pair of these things without knowing it! Oh, I daren't look at 'em. I'm sure I don't know which way to look! (*Pulls handkerchief out of pocket to cover knees. Sees* Strephon's *name on it.*) Why, it's Strephon's handkerchief and Strephon's clothes (*looks in glass*) and Strephon's face. Oh, there now! If I'm not Strephon! I wished to be Strephon and I'm become Strephon. Why, I declare I'm a young man. Bless me, how very embarrassing. But if I'm Strephon, what in the world has become of me? I must have disappeared — vanished from the face of the earth!

(*Enter* Daphne, *striding about the stage with the manner of* Colin *and exhibiting in pantomime great remorse.*)

That's what it is — I'm dead! Deary, deary me! Well, *I* was a good old soul, and he was very fond of me! Deary, deary, deary me!

Daphne (*laughing remorsefully*). Ha! ha! ha! Oh, remorse! remorse!

Strep. (*without looking round*). So you're there, Colin, are you? Well, poor old Daphne — she's dead!

Daphne. Daphne dead? What do you mean? (*Roughly.*)

Strep. (*turning round*). Why, most extraordinary thing.

DAPHNE. What's the matter with you? Ain't you well?

STREP. (*much puzzled*). Well, thank'ee, ma'am, I'm *not* altogether myself this morning. (*Aside.*) It *is* a *most* extraordinary thing! If I, who was Daphne, am now Strephon, the question arises, who is the person who is now Daphne? I don't quite like the idea of my poor old body being inhabited by a total stranger. (*Aloud.*) I beg your pardon, ma'am — I don't know whether you're aware of it, but that's *my* body you've got on!

DAPHNE. Your body? It seems to me it's my wife's body. At all events I married it.

STREP. Why, what in the world do you mean?

DAPHNE. Mean? Why, I was thinking just now that I'd had enough of this innocent Arcadian existence. I've been good for fifty years, and I determined to begin from that moment a career of blood-curdling crime.

STREP. Gracious! How horrible!

DAPHNE. The only drawback is that a man's so soon found out. Now, there's my missus, said I, she's a good, homely, simple, harmless body — no one would suspect *her*. Why wasn't I my own missus? — and then — presto, will you believe it, all at once I became her!

STREP. Why, that's just what happened to me! I wished to be Strephon and I became Strephon!

DAPHNE. Why, then you are —

STREP. Daphne! And you?

DAPHNE. Colin!

STREP. My husband!

DAPHNE. My wife!   (*They embrace.*)

STREP. This is really very curious.

DAPHNE. It's the queerest start I ever knew.

STREP. Queerest start! I don't quite like that expression. It isn't exactly ladylike.

DAPHNE. But there's such a plaguey lot of things to put on, and I don't know how they come!

STREP. And there's so few things for me to put on, and they're not at all the sort of things I've been accustomed to. There now, I never, never *can* show myself in such an extremely scanty dress.

DAPHNE. Go and change those things directly. I don't approve of my wife going about in those clothes.

STREP. Well, but I'm not your wife now, dear — I'm your husband.

DAPHNE. I don't care. I insist on your wearing a petticoat.

STREP. But people will laugh at me. If I'm a man I must dress as such —

DAPHNE. Can't go into that.

(*Takes out pipe and puts it in her mouth.*)

STREP. Oh, please don't smoke. I never used to smoke when I was you.

DAPHNE. Can't go into that. I'm not going to change my habits for any one. Can't do without my pipe and glass of grog, you know.

(*Prepares to take snuff.*)

STREP. Oh, dear! oh, dear! what will people say?

DAPHNE. Hallo! What's the matter with this tooth?

STREP. Oh, please be very careful. That tooth is — I never liked to tell you, but it isn't quite real. If you must smoke, please smoke on the *other* side of your mouth. (DAPHNE *makes the change.*) Thank you, oh, *so* much. (*She takes out knitting and begins to knit.*) And while I am about it, I should like to tell you of two or three little things that any one who inhabits *my* body will have to attend to. In the first place that right shoulder will want rubbing every morning with Friar's Balsam and nine oils for seven minutes and a half. Please be very careful, as it gets dreadfully stiff if it's neglected. Then, in doing your hair be very careful to change the parting every two days, because it's spreading, and — and — if you please, I don't think I ever mentioned it before, but some of it takes off for convenience, and while I am about it I may mention that just a little tiny wee suspicion of complexion laid on very lightly with a piece of new cotton wool does one's self no harm and gives pleasure to others, and if it isn't done it might be missed!

(*Enter* COLIN, *skipping girlishly with the manners of* CHLOE.)

COLIN (*running to* DAPHNE). Oh mamma! mamma! I'm so frightened! Oh, dear! oh, dear! I'm so terrified!

DAPHNE (*roughly*). Hullo! Why, this is me! What do you mean by being me? Who are you? Can't you speak?   (*Shakes him.*)

COLIN. Oh, don't, you hurt me! Please don't be angry but, if you please — you wouldn't think it, but I'm — I'm Chloe!

DAPHNE. ⎱
          ⎰ Chloe!
STREP.   ⎱

COLIN. Yes, such a wonderful thing has happened! I was so angry with Strephon for having quarreled with me about Lycidas, and so angry with Lycidas for having made me quarrel with Strephon, that I began to wish I wasn't a pretty girl at all! "There now," said I, "I declare that sooner than be tormented with all these tiresome admirers, I'd sooner be a grumpy, ill-conditioned old bear like papa and — and — if you please, I became a bear like papa without knowing it. It's so dreadful for a young lady to be her own papa! And — and — please forgive me, Strephon, for it must be a dreadful disappointment to you!

STREP. Disappointment? Oh, dear, no!

COLIN. What?

STREP. Oh, by the bye, I forgot to tell you, it's an awkward thing to admit, but I'm your mamma!

COLIN. Oh, nonsense. This is my mamma; are you not my dear, dear, kind, indulgent mamma?   (*Fondling her.*)

DAPHNE. Get out! I'm your father.

COLIN. My father?

DAPHNE. Yes, I am the grumpy, ill-conditioned old bear in question.

STREP. We've all been wishing and we've all got our wishes, and a very pretty kettle of fish we made of it!

COLIN. Oh, dear! oh, dear! oh, dear!   (*Crying.*)

ALL. What's the matter?

COLIN. If you're my papa and you're my mamma, what's become of my Strephon?

(*Enter* CHLOE *with boxing-gloves.*)

CHLOE. Here he is! (*Hitting out.*) One! two! three! four!

ALL. Are you Strephon?

CHLOE. Yes, I am. (*As before.*) One! two! three! four!

DAPHNE. But how did it all come about?

CHLOE. Oh, simplest thing in the world. One, two, three, four — everybody seemed to dislike me — one, two — and everybody seemed to love Chloe — three, four — so I wished I was Chloe — one, two, three, four — and I became — one, two —Chloe — three, four — all at once — one, two, three, four!

COLIN. Then you are really my darling, darling Strephon!

CHLOE. To be sure; and you are —

COLIN. Chloe!

CHLOE. My love!

COLIN. My pet! (*They embrace.*)

DAPHNE. But what are you doing with boxing-gloves?

CHLOE. I'm practicing, to take it out of Lycidas — one, two, three, four — wait till I meet him; you'll see — one, two, three, four.

COLIN. Oh, don't hurt him; he isn't strong.

CHLOE. I passed my word that I would smash him, and smash him I will.

STREP. But a young lady — oh, I forgot, you are — I —

CHLOE. Yes, and he is me. (*Indicating* COLIN.)

DAPHNE. And I am he. (*Indicating* COLIN.)

COLIN. And I am she. (*Indicating* CHLOE.)

CHLOE. No, *I* am me.

COLIN. You can't be me, if I'm *me*.

DAPHNE. No, no, surely *I* am me.

STREP. So am I. But that's ridiculous, you know — we can't all be *me*.

DAPHNE. I've got it. I'm you, you're me, he's she, she's he — no, *she must be she.*

STREP. She must be she, he must be he, I'm I — I know I'm I.

DAPHNE. No, you're I — no, I'm you — no, I see very plainly that if we don't settle who we all are we shall make a precious mess of this.

IDENTITY QUARTETTE.

COLIN. The question of identity
Suppose we now discuss.
It seems that all of us are me
And neither of us *us!*

ALL. This interchange will surely be
A source of endless fuss,
If I am he and he is me,
And neither of us *us!*

COLIN. If I am she, and she is him,
And him is her, or me,
Arises then the question grim,
Why, who on earth are we?

ALL. Oh, that I'd never lived to see
This most unhappy day,
When none of us are he or she,
But each of us is *they!*

CHLOE. How horrid, if it should occur,
As it may seem to be,
That none of us are him or her
And all of us are we!

DAPHNE. If I am he — I should say she —
Dear madam — that is, sir,
And he is she — that's meaning *me,*
Pray, tell me, who is her?

ALL. Oh, some one please to tell us now,
If I am ma'am or sir,
Or if perchance I'm thee or thou,
Or if I'm him or her.

STREP.   It's very clear you are not me,
           You are not you — you say,
           You are not he, you are not she,
           Then, bless my soul, you're *they!*

DAPHNE.   There, you see, confusion from beginning to end. Now, I've an idea. Whoever possesses one of these talismans has a right to have one wish granted, but only one. Well, we've had that one, and a pretty mess we've made of it!

ALL.   We have indeed.

DAPHNE.   Then suppose we exchange. You take the cloak, you the ring, you the cap, I the stick,[1] then we can wish ourselves ourselves again.

ALL.   Capital!

STREP. (*to* CHLOE).   Allow me.   (*Giving cloak.*)

CHLOE (*to* COLIN).   Permit me.   (*Giving ring.*)

COLIN (*to* DAPHNE).   Suffer me.   (*Giving stick.*)

DAPHNE.   And here's my cap. (*Giving cap to* STREPHON.) Now! Wish! All at once — one, two, three!

ALL.   I've wished!

(*All resume their natural demeanor.*)

STREP.   Why, I'm Strephon again!

CHLOE.   And I'm Chloe!

COLIN.   And I'm Colin!

DAPHNE.   And I'm Daphne!

(*All embrace. Enter* LYCIDAS.)

LYCIDAS.   I've come to the conclusion that this is no place for me. I shall depart by the next train. Oblige me with a rug, a foot-warmer, a smoking carriage, a shilling for the guard, a cheap novel, and a railway time table.

---

[1] See Appendix A, pp. 245–46.

Strep. A railway time table? That's of no use nowadays. But if you are going, perhaps you'd like to take a few little souvenirs with you. We are about to dispose of some by auction.

Lycidas. Souvenirs of what?

All. Of happy Arcadia!

FINALE. — Strephon *and* Chorus.

In this innocent little vale,
Whenever we've chattels for sale,
We send for an auctioneer.
Now, what shall we say for this little lot?

Lycidas. A penny!

Daphne. Two pence!

Chloe. Three pence!

Lycidas. Four!

Strep. Any more, any more, any more, any more?
Going at four pence, four pence, four!
Four pence! Any advance upon?
Going, going, going, going, going, going, gone!

(*Knocks them down.*)

(Lycidas *takes things and puts them on.*)

All.   They go, en masse,
To Lycidas!
Alas! alas! alas!
To Lycidas!
Hurrah! hurrah! for Lycidas!

CURTAIN

Eyes And No Eyes

OR, THE ART OF SEEING

Characters

CASSANDRE	{ *A wealthy Farmer in love with Nicolette.* }	*Bass.*
COLUMBINE CLOCHETTE	} *His Nieces*	{ *Mezzo-Soprano.* *Soprano.*
ARLEQUIN PIERROT	} *Brothers*	{ *Baritone.* *Tenor.*
NICOLETTE	*An old Coquette*	{ *Contralto or* *Mezzo-Soprano.*

SCENE: *Exterior of* CASSANDRE'S *cottage. Cottage in flat with door and practicable window. Trees, &c. R. and L.* CLOCHETTE *discovered with Spinning-wheel.*

No. 1. — SONG. — CLOCHETTE.

As I at my wheel sit spinning,
I think of my maiden state,
For I am, at my life's beginning,
A thread in the hands of Fate.
Shall I dwell among crowds that flatter,
A robe for a king to bear —
Or a poor little rag of a tatter
A beggar would scorn to wear?
  As I at my wheel sit spinning
  I think of my maiden state,
  For I am, at my life's beginning,
  A thread in the hands of Fate.

Half-past one and Columbine not home yet. I hope no accident has happened to the old mare. If there has, I wouldn't be in Uncle Cassandre's way when he hears of it! There's a stingy cross old man for two dear little orphan nieces to have to live with. And when he's married to Nicolette — and he's to be betrothed to her to-day — the cottage will be unendurable. Here comes the conceited old maid. Well, as she's going to be my aunt, I suppose I had better be civil to her. (*Spins.*)

Enter NICOLETTE.

NIC.   Good-morning, my dear. Hard at work, I see.

CLO.   Oh yes, hard at work. No time to be idle like *some* people. No time to go gadding about setting honest folk by the ears like *some* people. No time for flirting and ogling, and making myself conspicuous and getting myself talked about like *some* people. Ugh! (*Aside.*) Must be civil to her.

NIC.   Ah, well, I like to see little girls busy. It keeps them out of all sorts of mischief. I often wish I could work too.

CLO.   Oh, but at *your* age, Nicolette —

NIC.   Exactly, as you say, at my age one's time's fully employed in receiving those little attentions which fall to the lot of an extremely lovely girl. Your time will come some day, but the men are terrible plagues, and you needn't wish you were me, dear.

CLO. I don't.

NIC. I'm not the gay and giddy young thing I look.

CLO. (*aside*). I know you're not! Made up old thing!

NIC. When you see me, the centre of an eager throng, vieing with each other as to who shall say the sweetest things to me; when you see me playing fast and loose with one, encouraging another, and sending a third about his business, broken-hearted, say to yourself, "I hope I may never, never, never be like Nicolette."

CLO. Believe me, it is my most earnest prayer.

NIC. For reflect — say I have a hundred admirers —

CLO. I beg your pardon — how many?

NIC. Say a hundred. Now out of this hundred I can only marry one.

CLO. Poor fellow!

NIC. Well — I declare myself in favour of that one, and what becomes of the other ninety-nine?

CLO. (*after a pause*). I give it up.

NIC. (*annoyed*). Why, they blow their brains out, of course!

CLO. What, right out?

NIC. Right out. Bang! Poof! and it's over. Now that's a fearful responsibility for a young woman to have on her mind.

CLO. Appalling! Oh, Nicolette, I do indeed hope more than ever that I shall never be anything at all like you.

NIC. Well, to do you justice, I don't think you ever will. You're a good girl, but you're not pretty, and if ever you're a full-grown woman like me, you'll be plain.

CLO. Yes — if ever I'm a full-grown woman *like you*, I shall be very plain indeed. And now, what can I do for you?

NIC. Do for me?

CLO. Yes, I suppose you've called about something?

Nic. No! Oh no — I've come to spend a long, long day with my two dear little friends, Clochette and Columbine.

Clo. Oh that is nice. I'm so glad, because it's so dull here without uncle.

Nic. (*taken aback*). Without uncle? Isn't he at home?

Clo. Oh no, he's out, and he won't be home for ever so long. You'll have us all to yourself, you dear old thing, and we'll be as happy as three little birds.

Nic. Oh. (*Getting up.*) Well, I must be off.

Clo. You're not going?

Nic. Oh yes I am. I can't stop chattering here all day. I'm very busy, very busy indeed. But before I go, I *should* like to break a bit of very bad news to you.

Clo. I'm sure you would.

Nic. Yes. It's about Pierrot and Arlequin. It's generally understood that they're in love with you and Columbine. My dear, they're not.

Clo. What do you mean?

Nic. They used to come and see you every day, I believe?

Clo. Yes.

Nic. But they haven't been for the last two days?

Clo. Well?

Nic. My dear, I'm very sorry for you, but — they've seen me!

Clo. You don't mean to say that you've frightened them away?

Nic. You are quite right, I *don't* mean to say it. On the contrary, I am very very sorry to say that they love me fondly. They told me so. I did all I could to persuade them to be true to you, but in vain. "Ah, Pierrot! Ah, Arlequin!" I said, "Moths about a candle — moths about a candle! how soon will ye burn your poor wings, and lie helplessly and hopelessly with a hundred others at my feet. Better, far better are the solid practical virtues of the homely Clochette than the superficial attractions of the beauty who, like the jewelled serpent, fascinates only to destroy." "Be pitiful, oh lovely Nicolette," said they. "I cannot," I replied, "I am a basilisk. I am Nicolette the Destroyer!"

No. 2. — SCENA. — Nicolette.

Yes, yes, I am that miserable Beauty,
    Whose lot it is to wither hearts and homes;
Who, in the course of her unhappy duty,
    Brings grief and misery where'er she roams.
        The man who on me sets his eyes —
            He is my prize!
        He can't escape — he pines and dies!
    This state of things goes on from bad to worse;
            I am so fair,
            So passing fair,
            So dangerously fair,
        That people call me the Domestic Curse!

Women avoid me like a plague,
For they have heard tales, strange and vague,
Told at the fire with bated breath,
Of beautiful witches who lure to death —
        Of husbands false and cheated wives —
        Of broken hearts and wasted lives —
        Of suicides in chill despair —
            Oh Society!
            Oh Society!
        Is it my fault if I am fair?
            Oh Society!
            Oh Society!
        That I am a Basilisk is too true,
            But, Oh Society!
            Oh Society!
        What in the world would you have me do?

I'll do anything you like, I'm sure!
    I'll dress in cottons and cheap serges,
Blacken my face like a Blackamoor —
    A Black-a-Moore-and-Burgess!
        Stroll in the park in a Life Guardsman's boots,
            Smoke cheroots,
        Pull out my eyelashes by the roots!
            Pad myself out
            Till I look stout;
            My H's drop,

Squint, limp, lollop and flop,
Go to dinner-parties in a great pasteboard nose
(Or one of gutta-percha plastic),
And shave off all my hair,
And walk about with my head bare,
And wear nothing on it but a rose
    On a piece of elastic!

Useless, alas, would be the vain endeavour,
    For if I did all this (though you may doubt me),
There'd still be something so remarkable about me
    That men would stare at me as much as ever!
For alas, I am that miserable Beauty
    Whose lot it is to wither hearts and homes;
Who in the course of her unhappy duty
    Brings grief and misery where'er she roams!
                        (*Exit* NICOLETTE.)

CLO. Poor dear old lady — it's very melancholy! So Pierrot and Arlequin have been amusing themselves by playing on the poor old thing's weakness, have they? I'm afraid they're a pair of terrible rakes. Well, a reformed rake is a useful implement of husbandry after all!

     Enter ARLEQUIN *and* PIERROT *suddenly, their arms about each other's necks. They strike an attitude.*

Oh, here you are, you two!

ARL. Yes, here we are, we two.

PIER. Oh yes, here we are.

ARL. What are you spinning?

CLO. Why, my wedding linen, of course.

PIER. Her wedding linen.

ARL. Oh rapture!

     (*They skip simultaneously and strike another attitude.*)

CLO. Yes, I believe one of you is going to marry me.

PIER. Yes, only one.

CLO. And the other is going to marry Columbine.

ARL. Yes — only the other.

CLO. By the bye, which other?

ARL. True. Pierrot, which other?

PIER. I don't care, I love 'em both.

ARL. So do I, madly.

PIER. After all, what does it matter? Our love is a grand love, a majestic love, a heroic love, a pyramidical love. We two love you two pyramidically. A love like ours cannot condescend to details. Let us leave the details to be settled by sordid lawyers.

CLO. Well, as long as you don't quarrel about us —

ARL. Quarrel? We never quarrel. We are twins.

PIER. Are we?

ARL. Certainly. Did I never mention it? Oh yes — I came into the world with you.

PIER. Did you? Sociable creature. (*Shaking his hand.*) How good of you. But, are you sure?

ARL. Quite. (*Beckoning to him mysteriously.*) I was there — you were not.

PIER. That settles it — if you were there you must know.

CLO. Why, bless me!

BOTH. What?

CLO. If you are both twins, that accounts for your being brothers!

ARL. Yes, we are rather remarkable people. We are called "The Coincidental Infants."

No. 3. — TRIO. — ARLEQUIN, PIERROT *and* CLOCHETTE.

ARL.   Of our parents each child is the son,

CLO.   Yet you had the same father and mother.

PIER.   In number we're two — I am one,

ARL.   And I, if you please am the other.

PIER.   Our lives did together begin,

CLO.   A fact they've no reason to smother —

ARL.   Moreover, each one is a twin.

PIER.   And each of the twins is a brother.

ALL.   Oh, pray to $\left\{ \begin{array}{c} \text{our} \\ \text{their} \end{array} \right\}$ history, hark!

$\left\{ \begin{array}{c} \text{Our} \\ \text{Their} \end{array} \right\}$ story is singular very,

And justifies well the remark,
    Oh, derry! oh, derry! down derry!

CLO.   They were born the same moment exact,

ARL.   Which, at times, sets us wondering whether

PIER.   That may not account for the fact

ARL.   That our birthdays come always together.

PIER.   We could walk when we grew to be men,

ARL.   But when we were born we were carried,

CLO.   And each was a bachelor then,
    For neither had ever been married.

ALL.   Oh, pray to $\left\{ \begin{array}{c} \text{our} \\ \text{their} \end{array} \right\}$ history, hark! etc.

ARL.   Astonishing questions occur —

CLO.   A solution, perhaps, I may render?

ARL.   If I had been changed to a her,

PIER.   And I had been female in gender;

ARL.   And both had been twins from our birth,

CLO.   But born of two different mothers,

ARL.   Whatever relation on earth

PIER.   Would each of us be to the other?

ALL.   On that point $\left\{ \begin{array}{c} \text{we} \\ \text{they} \end{array} \right\}$ are still in the dark,

> The query is singular, very,
> And justifies quite the remark,
> Oh derry! oh derry! down derry!

CLO. (*crying*). Ah, there are no coincidences in *my* family. *My* brother's a sister, and she's ever so much older than I am, and besides that, she was born first and at a different date too, and neither of us is a twin, and we are both girls.

ARL. This is bad news, Pierrot.

PIER. Very. I'd no idea they were *both* girls.

CLO. If that's an objection you'd better trot off to Nicolette. *She* is not a girl, and I know you've been flirting with her.

ARL. (*carelessly*). Oh yes, we've flirted with her. Lardy-da, Lardy-da —nothing more, 'sure you!

PIER. We flirt with all women. We love 'em all, on principle.

CLO. On principle? On want of principle you mean. You know you don't want to marry her.

PIER. Oh *dear* no! She's too old — and stout, and her complexion isn't what it was.

CLO. What, has she changed her perfumer, then?

ARL. Oh come, that's very good — oh dear me, that's very subtle!

CLO. But perhaps you're not aware that Uncle Cassandre is going to marry Nicolette — and then she'll be my aunt.

PIER. Why, then, if I'd married her I should have been your uncle. No, I'm wrong. But are you sure he's going to marry her?

CLO. Yes, he's to be formally betrothed to her this afternoon, and what's more he's sent Columbine to town to buy him a magnificent mantle to do it in.

ARL. A magnificent mantle?

CLO. Yes, cotton velvet trimmed with rabbit-skin, and I expect her home with it every minute.

PIER. You expect Columbine home? Beloved Columbine!

ARL. How we adore that girl.

PIER. We will wait for her.   (*They sit simultaneously.*)

CLO. Well, you won't have to wait long, for here she is!

Enter COLUMBINE.

No. 4.— QUARTETTE.

COL. (*agitated*). Well, here's a very pretty state of things,
        Upon my word I don't know what to do;
        Each day some fresh perplexing worry brings,
        Such terribly bad luck I never knew!

ARL. & PIER.   Oh, we love you fondly — madly,
        We would marry you most gladly;
        I adore you, so does he —

COL. (*irritably*). Go away and let me be!

CLO.   Why, what's happened? come, come, dry your eye!

COL. (*sobbing*). The cloak that uncle ordered me to buy —

CLO.   Yes, yes — I'm almost dying to behold it —

COL. (*sobbing*). A dozen crowns I paid to him who sold it.

CLO. It must be beautiful indeed to cost it!
        Come, show it me —

COL.   I can't.

CLO.   Why not?

COL.   I've lost it!

BOTH.   Lost it — lost it — lost the cloak —
        'Tis a very serious joke —

CLO.   Think of Uncle's awful rage.

COL.   How he'll bluster, stamp and scold.

BOTH.   Fix like this would madden sage,
        Who to tell him will make bold?

ARL. ⎫   Yes we love you fondly — madly,
AND   ⎬   We would marry you most gladly,
PIER. ⎭   I adore you, so does he.

Col. ⎫
and   ⎬ Go away and let me be —
Clo. ⎭ Well, here's a pretty state of things, etc.

Pier. ⎫
and   ⎬ Yes, we love you fondly, madly, etc.
Arl. ⎭

(*At end of ensemble,* Arlequin *and* Pierrot *exeunt into house.*)

Clo. Well, when Uncle Cassandre returns and hears that the cloak's lost, the village won't hold him.

Col. Oh yes it will, dear, I wish it wouldn't. But what on earth shall we do?

Clo. I can't think.   (Columbine *cries.*)
Now don't cry, let's try and find a way out of the scrape. Do you believe in fairies?

Col. No. Do you?

Clo. No, but I'm going to. Now listen, Pierrot is a flirt.

Col. No doubt.

Clo. Arlequin is an awful flirt.

Col. Awful!

Clo. Nicolette is a terrific flirt.

Col. Absolutely terrific!

Clo. And Uncle Cassandre is rather worse than all three put together.

Col. Uncle Cassandre would flirt with his own shadow.

Clo. Now this is my plan, we'll pretend that the cloak is a magic cloak, visible only to true lovers, and absolutely invisible to flirts of every degree.

Col. I understand. As they are flirts they won't be surprised at not being able to see it.

Clo. Exactly. Here come Pierrot and Arlequin, let's try it on them first; we'll pretend to be admiring it. We'll suppose we've got the cloak, now hold it out — there, so.

Enter PIERROT *and* ARLEQUIN *from house.* COLUMBINE *and* CLOCHETTE
pretend to be admiring the cloak. PIERROT *and* ARLEQUIN, *thinking
themselves unobserved, watch their proceedings with amazement.*

CLO. Well, there now, it is extremely pretty.

COL. Most sweet, most enchanting! Feel its texture.

CLO. Oh, what a lovely quality! I should so like to try it on.

COL. Should you? Then you shall. There (*putting it on*) stop a bit —
there, oh my, that *is* lovely!

PIER. (*whispers to* ARLEQUIN). What are they doing?

ARL. (*whispers*). Going mad.   (PIERROT *howls*.)

COL. Oh dear me, here are Pierrot and Arlequin who've been watch-
ing us all the time, and I promised Uncle nobody should see it. (*Pretending to snatch it off.*)

CLO. Oh my dear, you needn't be alarmed. They *couldn't* see it.

COL. Oh, of course, I forgot. *They* couldn't see it.

CLO. Not if they stared at it for a month.

COL. And propped their eyelids open with bits of lucifer match.

CLO. And wore telescopes in them.

COL. And ear trumpets.

CLO. And smelling bottles.

COL. Because *they* are flirts.

CLO. Yes, because *they* trifle with young confiding hearts.

COL. And because *this* cloak, being a magic cloak, is visible only to
true lovers.

CLO. Which you are not.

COL. And is *in*visible to flirts and popinjays.

CLO. Which you are. And *that's* why you don't see the cloak, and
that's why you never *will* see the cloak, no, not if you live to be as old as
Jerusalem. Neither of you! ugh!

PIER. Why, you don't mean to say you really believe we are not true to you? Oh Arlequin!

ARL. Oh Pierrot! (*They sob on each other's shoulders.*)

PIER. All our little jokelets about Nicolette taken in earnest!

ARL. All our little innocent attentions looked on as flirtations!

PIER. You, who are so true!

ARL. You, who are constancy itself. Oh Pierrot!

PIER. Oh Arlequin!

COL. Well, but *did* you see the cloak?

PIER. What cloak?

COL. There! he asks *what* cloak! He *didn't* see it! He couldn't see it.

PIER. But I don't know what cloak you're referring to.

CLO. Why, the magic cloak we had in our hands when you came in, to be sure.

PIER. Oh, the magic cloak! Oh yes, we saw the magic cloak. But you didn't say you meant the *magic* cloak.

COL. No, but did you *really* see it?

PIER. Did we really see it? Why of course we really saw it.

ARL. Do you think we are blind? We were admiring it as you spoke.

CLO. Oh Arlequin, I'm so sorry I doubted you.

COL. Pierrot, will you forgive me? For now I know you are true; if you hadn't been true you'd never have seen it.

PIER. Well, say no more about it, but produce it at once.

CLO. (*pretending to produce it*). There — isn't it a love?

PIER. No, no, I don't want to see *that* one, I want to see the invisible one.

CLO. This is the invisible one.

PIER. Well, but it can't be invisible if *I* can see it. Why it's as plain as Arlequin. Clochette, you're trying to deceive me. (*Hurt.*)

ARL. Columbine, you're practising on our inexperience. (*Hurt.*)

Col. No, *indeed* this is the one. Isn't it a beauty?

Arl. (*pretending to admire it*). Well, it *is* a beauty, to be sure.

Pier. Oh my! what a duck.

Arl. Put it on.

Col. To be sure I will! (*Pretends to put it on.*)

Pier. Well I never *did* see anything like it. Stop a bit, you've got it wrinkled on the shoulder. (*Pretends to smooth it.*) There — that's better.

Col. How do you like the colour?

Arl. Oh, it's a beautiful colour.

Pier. H'm — well, yes, — no, to my taste it's rather too — what shall I say?

Arl. Well, that occurred to me. It *is* rather — just the least thing too —

Clo.
and   } Yes — what?
Col.

Arl. Well, I should have thought red would have suited the old gentleman better.

Pier. Ah, now *I* should have thought yellow.

Arl. You are quite right; yellow would decidedly have been better.

Clo. Why that *is* good. Why, it *is* yellow! Ha, ha, ha!

Col. Ha, ha, ha!

Arl. Well, it's a *kind* of yellow.

Pier. A kind of reddish yellow.

Arl. Now, what material do you call this? Silk, isn't it?

Col. Silk! why it's the richest cotton velvet.

Pier. Ho, ho! that *is* good. Silk! He don't know silk from velvet. Why, you great donkey, anyone can see that it's the richest cotton velvet, trimmed with gold.

Col. Silver.

PIER. Eh?

COL. Silver.

ARL. Oh, he don't know gold from silver. Oh, he *is* a muff. He could see it was velvet, but he couldn't see it was silver.

PIER. How is a poor, friendless, destitute orphan to know gold from silver? Born before I was old enough to work for my bread; left to gain my living by my own native shrewdness; what chance have I of ever seeing either? Now, if it had been trimmed with ha'pence I should have known it at a glance. I'm a judge of ha'pence. So this is really silver, is it? Dear me, I've often heard of silver.

COL. There now, you've looked at it quite long enough; don't touch it or you'll tarnish it. (*Slapping his hands.*) We must fold it up and put it back in the parcel. Uncle will be furious if he finds we've opened it.

(*Exeunt* CLO. *and* COL.)

PIER. Arlequin, that's a remarkably handsome cloak?

ARL. Beautiful! Very tasty indeed.

PIER. I'm glad I was able to see it.

ARL. I'm glad *I* was able to see it.

PIER. I say, Arlequin —

ARL. Well?

PIER. I shouldn't have thought you and I were exactly what's called true lovers.

ARL. No, but we must be or we couldn't have seen the cloak.

PIER. We did see it, didn't we?

ARL. Distinctly. I can see it now.

PIER. So can I, as plainly as when I had it in my hand.

ARL. I should have thought that if there were two people to whom the cloak would have been invisible, you and I would have been those two people.

PIER. Yes, we do carry on.

ARL. Awfully. But in confidence, did you *really* see it!

PIER. What a question! Of course I did.

ARL. No, but honour?

PIER. Well, when I say I saw it, I've no objection to admit I saw it indistinctly. Now after that admission, how did it appear to you?

ARL. Foggy. Outline confused.

PIER. Sketchy, eh?

ARL. Very. In fact I could barely distinguish it.

PIER. And to me it was hardly perceptible.

ARL. I scarcely saw it — in fact, I may say I didn't see it.

PIER. So may I. *I* didn't see it. We both didn't see it. Shake hands.
(*Music.*)   (*Exeunt together.*)

Enter CASSANDRE *with whip.*

CASS. (*furious*). Clochette! Columbine! Why aren't you here to receive me? I've come back. Where's my dinner? I'm hungry. Oh, when I *do* catch you two young women! Well, I'm home at last. Home to discharge the most important duty of my career, for to-night I am to be formally betrothed to Nicolette. Thirty years ago I saw her, and then I didn't like her. People said she was an acquired taste, and so she was. I am fond of acquired tastes, and I determined to learn to love her. For thirty years I withdrew myself from my native village and set to work. In the first place, Nicolette was stout, so I began by trying to be fond of stout people, and I succeeded — the fatter they were the more I loved them. Nicolette was a chatterbox, I fell in love with all the chatterboxes I could find. Nicolette was vain, I became the slave of all the conceited young women for miles around. Nicolette was quick-tempered, there wasn't a cross-grained vixen in the province whom I didn't adore. But by this time Nicolette had grown elderly, so it became necessary to cultivate a taste for oldest inhabitants, and I succeeded so well that a troop of lovesick grandmothers followed me wherever I went. Having taught myself to admire all those qualities for which Nicolette is remarkable, I returned to her, and directly I saw her I fainted in her arms. What took place during the interval of unconsciousness I don't know, but it must have been something decisive, for when I revived I found myself engaged to her — engaged to the purest, properest, and correctest old lady in France. Oh, how correct is Nicolette!

Enter NICOLETTE.

NIC. And had it tum home to its little old lady, and was it a naughty, naughty old poppet to top away so long?

CASS. (*aside*). What fascinating innocence. (*Aloud*.) Yes, it *had* tum home again, and it had ordered its little niece to buy it a boofy mantle to make its little love in, that it might be a pooty pooty boy when it came to see its little pipsy wipsy.

NIC. (*doubtfully*). I don't understand what you mean by pipsy wipsy.

CASS. It's a term of endearment.

NIC. I never heard the expression.

CASS. It's Arabic.

NIC. Oh, if it's Arabic I don't mind.

CASS. (*aside*). How prudent and respectable she is. (*Aloud*.) Shall we resume?

NIC. Certainly, only pray be careful.

CASS. I will. And when will it make its little old gentleman the happiest old tootletum in the world?

NIC. It shall name its own little day, it shall, and they shall be married in a boofy little church and they shall be as happy as two tiny tiny little dicky birds.

CASS. Oh, it was a delightful little roguey poguey.

NIC. (*severely*). Roguey poguey? I am not familiar with that expression.

CASS. It's a term of general application signifying respectful affection. It's Scotch.

NIC. Oh. The Scotch are a moral people, and if it's Scotch I've no doubt it's correct.

CASS. She is indeed delightfully particular. Ah, Nicolette, how much more quickly time flies with some people than it does with others. When I first knew you we were the same age, I was then eight and twenty. (*Sighs*.)

NIC. So was I. (*Sighs*.)

Cass. And now I'm fifty-eight. (*Sighs.*)

Nic. And I am eight and twenty still. (*Sighs.*)

Cass. Then notwithstanding the disparity of our years you don't think I'm too old for you?

Nic. No, if you don't think I'm too young for you.

Cass. Not a day, not a day. I think I could love you if you were younger still.

No. 5. — DUET. — Cassandre *and* Nicolette.

Nic.
When you were eight and twenty,
  You were extremely wild,
Of wilfulness you'd plenty,
  A giddy thoughtless child.
All life seemed sugar candy,
Hardbake and balls of brandy,
A little jack-a-dandy,
  And quite unfit to mate.
'Twas dolce far niente,
When you were eight and twenty,
When you were eight and twenty,
  When you were twenty-eight.

Both.
'Twas dolce far niente, etc.

Cass.
But now I'm eight and fifty,
  I've reached the prime of life;
I'm sober now and thrifty,
  And fit to take a wife.
My boyish freaks are over,
No longer I'm a rover,
I'm fit to be a lover,
  I've come to man's estate.
I'm careful now and thrifty,
For I am eight and fifty,
For I am eight and fifty,
  For I am fifty-eight.

Both.
He's careful now and thrifty, &c. (*They embrace.*)

Enter Columbine.

Col. (*starts*). Oh, beg your pardon. I didn't know you were doing anything like that.

Cass. Ahem! allow me to present to you a new aunt.

(Nicolette *curtseys*, Columbine *also.*)

Col. She don't look new.

Cass. Cherish her, venerate her, for I love her. Columbine, respect that love, for it has taken thirty years to develope. My child, respect the labour of thirty years. (Columbine *kisses her.*)

Nic. My darling little niece.

Col. My pretty little aunt.

Nic. (*aside*). Affected little coquette.

Col. (*aside*). Old frump.

Cass. And now, where's the cloak, I'm dying to see it.

Col. Oh, but uncle –

Cass. What?

Col. I — that is —

Cass. That is what? That is *what*, I say? Now — now be careful. Don't say anything happened to it, I'm very delicate and easily excited, and if something was to give way —

Nic. Columbine, if anything snaps inside him, I shall hold you responsible. Now go on. (*Listens to hear if anything snaps.*)

Col. Oh, but nothing happened, dear uncle, only — *are* you *very* fond of Nicolette.

Cass. Of course I am, I love her madly — ducky, ducky, ducky!
(*Flirting with her.*)

Col. And are you *very* fond of uncle?

Nic. What an absurd question. Of course I am. Chucky, chucky, chucky! (*Flirting with him.*)

Col. Oh, I'm *so* glad.

Nic. What does the girl mean?

Col. I'm so glad you're so fond of each other, because the cloak is a magic cloak and is visible only to true lovers who never flirt. You're both sure to be able to see it.

Nic. *Are* we? (*Aside.*)

Cass. I doubt it very much. (*Aside.*)

Col. I bought it of a tall grim man with great flashing eyes and beautiful big teeth, and great horns sticking out of his head; he had the very thing, so I asked the price, and as soon as I bought it he disappeared in a whirlwind.

Cass. I see — before you paid for it.

Col. No, immediately after.

Cass. (*disappointed*). Oh! And where is it?

Col. (*aside*). I haven't the face to do it all alone. (*Aloud.*) Oh, Clochette's got it, she'll — she'll be here directly.

Cass. Very good. Nicolette, come into the house and read the contract; the lawyer will be here directly, and then —

Nic. Ah, Cassandre!

Cass. Yes —

Nic. There are no fools like young ones.

(*Exeunt into house.*)

Col. There's a pretty bunch of stories. Oh dear, oh dear, I hope I don't look as wicked as I feel.

Enter Clochette *with small basket.*

Clo. Well, I've good news for you, I've found the cloak.

Col. What?

Clo. You left it behind, at Hubert's, the blacksmith's, and he's sent it on and it's here. (*Opening basket.*)

Col. Oh, what a pity.

Clo. A pity!

Col. Yes, I've told Uncle and Nicolette that it's a magic cloak and visible only to true lovers. Now when they find that they can really see it they'll know I've been telling stories. And then he'll beat me —

Clo. Oh never mind a beating, dear — bear it.

Col. Yes, but he'll beat you too.

Clo. Oh my dear, we must hit on another plan. Tell him you made a mistake, and that it's visible to flirts and coquettes but invisible to true lovers; then when they see it, they'll be convinced of its supernatural character. Oh, here they are.

Enter Cassandre and Nicolette.

No. 6. — CONCERTED PIECE. — Cassandre, Nicolette,

Columbine *and* Clochette.

Cass.   Now, Columbine, the magic cloak produce,
      This mystic robe I'm dying for to see!
(*aside.*) Although, alas, it's very little use,
      For it will be invisible to me.
         For, oh, I am such a terrible rake,
         For every girl my heart does ache;
         Of wicked old men I am the pink,
         I flirt, I ogle, I leer, I wink.

Nic.   Come, let the cloak instanter be displayed,
      Its gorgeous beauties please at once unfold!
(*aside*). Alas, alas, I'm very much afraid
      That magic cloak I never can behold.
         For, oh, I am such a wicked old maid,
           Whatever its age, whatever its grade,
         On every heart at once I seize,
           I giggle, I flutter, I flirt, I tease.

Clo.   But, Uncle, I admit with terror
      That I have made a serious error.
      I've made the very greatest of mistakes —
        I said 'twas visible to lovers true —
      It's only visible to flirts and rakes,
        And therefore won't be visible to you,
        And therefore won't be visible to you.

Nic.
and } Why, what d'ye mean, the truth, come quickly tell!
Cass.

COL.   To all true lovers it's invisi-bell.

NIC.   Then, alas, alas, it can never be
AND   Visible unto you or me.
CASS.   For I am a lover, a lover true,
         It cannot be seen by me or you.
(*aside.*)   This is as right as right can be,
         This magical cloak I'm sure to see.

CASS. (*aside*).   For, oh, I am such a terrible rake, &c.

NIC. (*aside*).   For, oh, I am such a wicked old flirt, &c.

COL. (*aside*).   For, oh, he is such a terrible rake, &c.

CLO. (*aside*).   For, oh, she is such a wicked old maid,
         Whatever its age, whatever its grade,
         On every heart at once does seize,
         To giggle, to flutter, to flirt and tease.

CLO. (*opening basket*).   There, there it is. (*Showing cloak which is in basket.*)

CASS. (*looking in*).   Where?

NIC.   I don't see any cloak.

COL.   No, I told you you wouldn't be able to see it.

CASS.   Pooh, pooh! there's no cloak here. (*Aside.*) Oh remorse, I see it plainly.

NIC. (*aside*).   Agony! It's as plain as a pikestaff.

CLO.   But if you can't see it, you can feel it.

CASS.   I do, I feel it very much.

CLO.   But I mean the cloak.

CASS.   Oh, I beg your pardon.

(CASSANDRE *and* NICOLETTE *put their hands into basket.*)

NIC.   Dear me, there certainly *is* something here.

CASS.   Well, that's the most extraordinary thing I ever experienced. There certainly *is* a cloak, cotton velvet trimmed with rabbit-skin.

NIC.   Yes, and a very pretty cloak too.

Cass. (*suspiciously*). How do you know it's pretty?

Nic. Why, if it's cotton velvet trimmed with rabbit-skin, it must be pretty, mustn't it? Oh, Cassandre, do you doubt your particular and correct Nicolette?

Cass. Never! I believe it's as invisible to you as it is to me.

Nic. (*aside*). About.

Cass. But I should like to have just one peep at it.

Nic. Cassandre!

Cass. If I might be permitted to allow my thoughts to wander from you for one minute, only one —

Nic. Cassandre, if ever that cloak meets your eye, the consequence will be Death!

Cass. To you?

Nic. No — to you.

Cass. (*aside*). Then the sooner I go stone blind the better.

Enter Pierrot *and* Arlequin *staggering. They throw themselves on to a bank and weep.*

Nic. Why bless the boys, what's this?

Arl. It is remorse.

Pier. It is the voice of conscience. (*To* Cassandre) Listen, old man, we love your nieces — but we are unworthy of them. We found that out half an hour ago.

Cass. *I* found it out half a year ago.

Pier. On making the discovery we resolved to reform. For half an hour each of us has stood in a corner. Old man, we went into those corners reckless and light-hearted and triflers; we came out of those corners the repentant wrecks you see before you.

Arl. Old man, we have been thoughtless butterflies — we are now sober and highly respectable worms. We have winked much, but we will never wink again.

Pier. We have winked our last wink, we have squeezed our last squeeze, we have soft-nothinged our last soft-nothing.

Cass. If I could be sure that you are reformed characters —

Pier. Old man, we are indeed.

Arl. Old man —

Cass. (*furious*). *Do not* call me old man. I won't take your word for your reformation, I must have some proof. Call again in ten years.

Arl. Oh, Pierrot, this will break my heart.

Pier. Arlequin! (*Sobs on his breast.*)

Enter Columbine *and* Clochette.

Cass. Stay, I have a plan. (*Takes mantle.*) Can you see this mantle?

Pier. (*overjoyed*). I can. Ha, ha, ha! (*Hysterically.*)

Arl. So can I. Ha, ha, ha!

Cass. I thought so.

Pier. It is made of the richest cotton velvet.

Arl. Trimmed with the rarest rabbit.

Pier. Its colour — is yellow.

Arl. And it is trimmed with silver.

Cass. Scoundrels! Know that this mantle which you see so plainly is visible only to those that are faithless.

Arl. I beg your pardon — faith*ful*.

Nic. Oh no — faith*less*.

Pier. Faith*ful*.

Cass. Faith —

Arl. (*loudly*). Ful!

Nic. Less, I say.

Pier. Ful, I say.

Cass. Less.

Arl. Ful!

Nic. Clochette, Columbine — what is the truth of this?

Cass. We are both agreed that it is faith — on that point we are unanimous. The only question is, *is* it *ful* or is it *less*.

Pier.
and
Arl.
} *I* say *ful*.

Nic.
and
Cass.
} *I* say *less*.

Pier. The less you say the better.

Nic. What? (*Angrily.*)

Pier. Nothing.

Col.
and
Clo.
} Well, uncle, in a kind of way you're both right. It's visible to true lovers under thirty, and invisible to true lovers over thirty.

Cass. But — Nicolette saw it, and she is ever so much under thirty. Oh, cockatrice! (*To* Nicolette.)

Nic. (*kneeling*). Cassandre, listen to the confession of a guilty girl. I did indeed see it, but — I have deceived you as to my age. I was thirty the day before yesterday. (*Weeps.*)

Cass. Quite thirty?

Nic. Quite.

Cass. Well, you don't look it.

Nic. My own.

Cass. My love! Now to make the children happy. (*To* Arl. *and* Pier.) Here are my nieces. Which of them do you love?

Pier. (*With* Clo.) We don't know — we leave that to you. Only — we should like one apiece.

(Arlequin *is with* Columbine.)

Cass. You shall have one apiece. The simple halfpenny shall decide. Heads, Arlequin has Columbine; tails, Pierrot has Columbine. (*He tosses.*) Heads! Clochette, go to Arlequin; Columbine, go to Pierrot.

Arl. But —

Cass. Will you do as I tell you?

(Pierrot *has had his arm round* Columbine *and* Arlequin *has had his arm round* Clochette. *They exchange lovers unwillingly.*)

No. 7. — FINALE.

ENSEMBLE.

Pierrot, Arlequin, Columbine *and* Clochette.

Agony and fell despair!
This will end I know not where!

Pier. I believed until today
Both possessed this heart of mine,
Neither less and neither more;
Now that I have Columbine,
I've found (alack and well-a-day!)
It is Clochette I adore.

All. It is Clochette he adores.

Pierrot, Arlequin, Columbine *and* Clochette.

Agony and fell despair!
This will end I know not where.

Arl. I believed until to-day
On them both my heart was set,
Neither less and neither more;
Now that I possess Clochette!
I've found (alack and well-a-day!)
Columbine I do adore.

All. Columbine he does adore.

Pierrot, Arlequin, Columbine *and* Clochette.

Agony and fell despair!
This will end I know not where.

Clo. I believed until to-day
Both alike in love did shine,
Neither less, and neither more;

225

	Now that Arlequin is mine,
	It is Pierrot I adore.
ALL.	It is Pierrot she adores!

PIERROT, ARLEQUIN, COLUMBINE *and* CLOCHETTE.

Agony and fell despair!
This will end I know not where.

COL.   I believed until to-day,
That I loved them both so-so!
Neither less and neither more;
Now that I have got Pierrot,
Arlequin I do adore.

ALL.   Arlequin she does adore!

(CASSANDRE *and* NICOLETTE *come forward lovingly.*)

BOTH.   Happy, happy shall we be
You and I, and he and she.
Happy we and happy they
Sing a merry roundelay!

PIERROT, ARLEQUIN, COLUMBINE *and* CLOCHETTE.

(*Very dismally.*) Sing a merry roundelay!

CASS.
AND
NIC.   Dance and sing and flirt and quarrel,
Make it up and draw a moral,
Seal it with our lips of coral,
Sing a merry roundelay.   (*They retire up.*)

CLO.   If I wed Arlequin — my thoughts will range!

COL.   While they're not looking at us, let us change!
(CLOCHETTE *goes to* PIERROT, COLUMBINE *to* ARLEQUIN.)

ALL.   Happy, happy shall we be, &c.

CURTAIN

Appendix A

TEXTS AND VARIANTS IN
GILBERT'S GERMAN REED ENTERTAINMENTS

A NOTE ON TEXTS

EACH OF GILBERT'S GERMAN REED ENTERTAINMENTS exists in several versions, with the exception of *Our Island Home*, which was never printed. None, unfortunately, was printed in its entirety during its original production.

The earliest texts of the Entertainments are the four manuscript copies submitted for licensing to the Lord Chamberlain's Office and now deposited in the British Museum. That the two missing plays, *Our Island Home* and *A Sensation Novel*, were also submitted is attested by appropriate entries in the day book kept by the Examiner of Plays. *A Sensation Novel* is also listed in the index of its appropriate manuscript volume, although the play itself seems to have been cut out of its original place.[1] A typescript of *Our Island Home*, presumably made from the license copy sometime in the 1930's, exists in the British Museum,[2] but lacks the words to several songs. It is likely that the words had been written; they were probably attached at the end of the original manuscript as was occasionally the habit with pieces submitted by the Gallery. Indeed, the words to one of the songs are given in Isaac Goldberg's *The Story of Gilbert and Sullivan*. Goldberg was allowed to copy them from a manuscript libretto in the possession of Florian Williams, who also owned a MS score. These too seem to have disappeared.

The still extant license copies of *No Cards, Ages Ago, Happy Arcadia*, and *Eyes and No Eyes* are not in Gilbert's handwriting, although he did add a note to the upper margin of a page of *Happy Arcadia*, giving an

---

[1] Perhaps these copies may yet be found in the process of cataloguing this great mass of manuscripts, disordered by its peregrinations.

[2] Copies of this typescript are also in The Reginald Allen Collection at The Pierpont Morgan Library.

additional line of dialogue ("And young men were so polite — so atten-
tive then — / But that's all changed now") and indicating a song for
Daphne, the words of which do not appear in this manuscript, but are
included in the first printed version of the Entertainment (see below).
A second manuscript copy of *Eyes and No Eyes* is now in the Reginald
Allen Collection; it varies slightly from the Lord Chamberlain's copy
and has been annotated in pencil to show stage positions, presumably
during the original rehearsals.

The first printed texts of the Entertainments were books of the lyrics
published in London by J. Mallett, the Reeds' regular printer. These
libretti are undated, but were issued for sale in the Gallery of Illustration
during the original production of each Entertainment.[3] Dialogue is
missing, but there are brief synopses of action between musical numbers.
Gilbert himself may have been responsible for some of these synopses,
particularly those of *Happy Arcadia* in which "the Author" playfully
addresses his audience. For example, after the series of statements announcing that the members of the cast have been metamorphosed into
each other, an editorial aside comments: "*The Author is aghast when he
contemplates the unparalleled embarrassment that he has been the means
of introducing into three amiable families. It shall not occur again.*" [4]

The score of *Ages Ago* was published by Boosey & Co. "as first performed at the Gallery of Illustration November 22, 1869." Its words vary
slightly from the Mallett lyrics. No other score was published in full,
but isolated songs from some of the other Entertainments were published
as sheet music.[5]

Finally, the Joseph Williams Company, musical publishers, brought
out the full libretti, words and prose dialogue, in a series beginning
in 1895 when the deaths of Alfred Reed and Corney Grain closed the
Gallery, and ending in 1901. *A Sensation Novel* was re-issued in 1912.
Florian Pascal (the younger Joseph Williams) reset *A Sensation Novel*
and *Eyes and No Eyes*;[6] and the five plays (*Our Island Home* had still

---

[3] These "books of the words" also contain synopses of the rest of the bill:
always a monologue and a second dramatic entertainment.

[4] The metamorphoses are preceded by another comment: "At this point —
the audience will scarcely believe it, it is asking too much of them — she becomes
Strephon! Yes; incredible as it may appear, before the very eyes of the audience.
. . ." Later, when all "become themselves again!!!," the Author remarks, aside:
"*The news is immediately telegraphed to their disconsolate relatives.*"

[5] See Reginald Allen, *W. S. Gilbert: An Anniversary Survey* (Charlottesville:
The Bibliographical Society of the University of Virginia, 1963).

[6] He seems to have intended to set *Our Island Home* as well.

not achieved publication) were issued as part of *The German Reed Repertory of Musical Pieces* suitable for amateur production. *No Cards* was published with the notation "Music by L[ionel] Elliott," although Mallett's libretto gives German Reed as the composer. *Ages Ago* and *Happy Arcadia* retained their original Clay scores. Joseph Williams published the libretti separately, and their texts differ markedly from those printed by Mallett, which, in turn, often vary from the license copy manuscripts.

I have followed the Joseph Williams texts for *No Cards*, *Ages Ago*, *A Sensation Novel* (1912 text), *Happy Arcadia*, and *Eyes and No Eyes*. I have tacitly corrected obvious typographical errors and less obvious mistakes, using earlier versions as my guide to probable intention.[7] I have not attempted to regularize the texts completely when regularity would not affect meaning. The text of *Our Island Home* is taken, with much correction, from the British Museum typescript, which reflects the original's absence of punctuation as well as the twentieth-century typist's inability to decipher some of its handwriting. Throughout, I have taken clarity as the principle on which to make changes, and I have tried to preserve punctuation which seems to indicate how lines were meant to be spoken.

SIGNIFICANT VARIATIONS

IN THE LICENSE COPIES and the Mallett libretti there are many passages of dialogue and words for songs which disappeared before the 1895–1901 publication of the Entertainments. Mallett includes some lyrics not present in either of the other texts. Some of these passages may have been added or cut during the original rehearsals and production; others may have been tinkered out of existence later, when the Reeds changed the length of an "old" Entertainment to fit the altered schedule caused by pairing it with a new work. This is particularly true of *Ages Ago!!*, which was shortened to its most popular scene — the animation of the portraits — or arbitrarily ended after that scene while retaining the contemporary opening episode, as the exigencies of the bill demanded.

Some of the smaller changes in text are perhaps merely owing to a copyist's errors in transcribing Gilbert's handwriting hastily for the official copy. Thus the character later called Hebblethwaite in *Ages Ago* is regularly "Habblethwaite" in the license manuscript. Other minor changes are in the interests of topicality. For instance, Mr. Churchmouse's

---

[7] The printed texts of many Victorian plays are full of typesetters' mistakes, no doubt because these pieces were considered ephemeral. Nor did Gilbert and his copyist always write the clearest of hands.

list of conversable topics originally included "Disestablishment of the Irish Church" (later changed to "The return of the Jews to Palestine") and "Should Mr. Beales have a statue" (later omitted). Still other changes, making lines more singable, may have been made during the original run on the basis of practical experience. They make no real difference in the sense or effect of the individual works. Nor has anything essential been lost by the deletion of substantial passages of verse or prose from the first versions. Their absence does not alter story line or main comic development. Therefore, I have not returned them to their original places, but have left the Entertainments in the forms they finally achieved. Many of the omitted passages, however, are interesting enough both for their own sakes and as further examples of Gilbert's early work to warrant inclusion here.

In selecting the passages printed below I have not regarded insignificant variations in wording where style and sense remain the same; I have chosen only the most substantial and self-sufficient of the deleted prose passages; but I have given all the lyrics which were cut from earlier versions. I have not, however, attempted to straighten out the variant states of ensemble numbers where changes in wording or assignment to speaker make no substantial difference and possess no intrinsic interest for the reader. In all, I have supplied punctuation, from Mallett when possible, and corrected obvious errors.[8]

LC represents the original manuscript text as found in the license copy; *M*, the Mallett libretto; and *JW*, the final form published by Joseph Williams.

No Cards

The action, as synopsized in *M*, protracts the disguises of Ellis Dee and Churchmouse, who retain their false identities until just before the finale. Dee uses the false name of "Manfred Kettledrum," and Churchmouse, as "Universal Agent for All the Charities in Great Britain and Ireland," calls himself Mr. M. Poster. Mrs. Pennythorne's alias, "Salamanca Trombone," is in *M* the less euphonious "Salamanca Gamboge," and her imaginary kingdom is spelled Babbedyboobledore.

Mr. Churchmouse originally developed his topics of conversation at much greater length in *LC* by discussing one of them with his characteristic nervous variability.

---

[8] The license copies were almost entirely unpunctuated or used dashes of varying lengths to separate sentences. In verse, the position of the lines was evidently considered punctuation enough in itself.

Miss P.	And which of them is your favourite theme?
Mr. Church.	Well perhaps manhood suffrage, Miss Penrose? Give every low-born vagabond who can prove he's a highly respectable man a voice in the representation, Miss Penrose? Ridiculous — absurd! Allow every bricklayer's labourer & jobbing plasterer to say how he'd like to be governed? Preposterous — out of the question. You'll excuse my warmth but it's a subject on which I feel very strongly — and yet somehow there's a good deal to be said on the other side. It does seem hard that a decent bricklayer with a respectable character should not be allowed to express his opinion on so important a topic & simply because he's poor. I often think that it would only be right to let such a man have a vote even if he sleeps under a hedge. Right? it's more than right — it is the duty of every man in every station in life to take his part in the government of his country. If I had my way I'd make every man in the kingdom vote whether he liked it or not. What? Refuse an honest man the opportunity of saying how he'd like to be governed because he's poor. It's infamous, disgraceful, abominable. You'll excuse my warmth but it's a topic on which I feel very strongly. Ah, a piano.

A brief discussion of the piano follows, which *M* summarizes as "His views on Amateur Vocalization." After this in *LC*, Churchmouse sits and sings, the words of his song not being given. *M*, however, indicates that the song is "The Three Husbands," words by James Safe, Esq.! The words are not printed in *M*. It is easy to see that *No Cards* was very early Gilbert, for the interpolation of someone else's words would scarcely be tolerated otherwise. No doubt Gilbert's own Bab Ballad, "The Precocious Baby," which does not appear in *M*, rapidly became Churchmouse's only solo.

Mrs. Pennythorne's song "A great deal of experience in life I've had" was omitted in *LC* and in *M*. The former indicates a song, "The Young Man of the Period," at the appropriate place, but does not give the words; the latter has, instead, a solo for Annabella at this point: "Thady O'Flinn," set by James L. Molloy and published separately by Boosey during the preceding October.[9] This conventional Irish song lacks the metrical ingenuity of Mrs. Pennythorne's solo, but no doubt was inserted to display Rosa D'Erina's Celtic charm. As the *Daily Telegraph* re-

---

[9] The sheet music is dated October 7, 1868, by Reginald Allen, *W. S. Gilbert: An Anniversary Survey*, p. 25.

marked, she sang the ballad "with archness." The fact that an earlier Gilbert-Molloy song was imported into the Entertainment suggests that the score was indeed assembled by German Reed rather than composed.

BALLAD. — Mdlle. Rosa D'Erina.

Thady O'Flinn, agin and agin
    You said you loved me dearly,
And sorra a bit I doubted it,
    I thought you loved sincerely;
You said when we should married be,
    You'd make me quite a lady,
But now I find you've changed your mind,
    It's ugly Norah Grady.

At Phelim's wake I saw ye take
    Her hand with glances tinder,
Tho' sorra a bit ye fancied it,
    I saw ye through the winder;
Your arm you placed around her waist,
    It's little did she mind ye;
You call'd her dear right in her ear,
    I wish I'd been behind ye.
Thady O'Flinn, you vowed it thin
    You'd make me quite a lady,
But now I find you've changed your mind,
    It's ugly Norah Grady.

At Goolah fair, I saw ye there
    Along with Norah Grady,
It's sorra a bit ye fancied it,
    But I persaived ye, Thady;
I pity your taste, your love to waste
    On Norah so consaited;
Why! I declare you're muttherin' there,
    As if you'd been ill-treated.
There go your ways, yourself to plase
    You only need be troublin',
Ye think there's few as fine as you,
    From here away to Dublin.

There's Pat Malone, at least you'll own,
    And Mike and Clanty Brady,
And Barney Bourke, and Terry O'Rourke,

I'm not in earnest, Thady.
Now, Thady, dear, come sit ye here,
And listen awhile to raisin,
It's sorra a bit I mind the chit,
Sure I was only tazin.
It's you're the one to throw your fun
At ugly Norah Grady;
But don't begin and do it agin,
Now there's a darlin' Thady!

M follows *LC*'s version of the trio for Ellis Dee, Churchmouse, and Miss Penrose ("From this pretty bower hence"). This number originally bore the notation "Yankee Doodle" after Dee's first line: "Listen, this is my receipt." Such a direction further indicates that the music for *No Cards* was "arranged" and only infrequently original. Churchmouse's verse of the trio is completely different in the earlier versions and is followed by an ensemble:

MR. CHURCH. Mystic disguises
             Of various surprises[10]
                 I have close at hand —
             In manner elective
             Defying invective,
             Like any detective
                 In Pollaky's band!
             Pretty, pretty, pretty Pollaky!

MR. DEE.   Pretty, pretty, pretty Pollaky!

MISS P.   Pretty, pretty, pretty Pollaky!

ALL.   Pretty, pretty, pretty Pollaky
             On Paddington Green!
             He's a chrysalis or a butterfly,
                 As he changes his mien,
             Is pretty, pretty Pollacky[11]
                 On Paddington Green.

Paddington Pollaky, of course, reappears in *Patience*, while the parody of "Pretty Polly Perkins of Paddington Green" ("Beautiful as a butterfly

---

[10] In *M* this line reads "Of various sizes" and is followed by "Producing surprises."
[11] "Is pretty, pretty, pretty Pollacky" in *M*. The last four lines, sung here by all, are repeated by Miss Penrose in *M*'s version of the finale after all sing "Coodle-oodle-oodle" for the first time.

and as proud as a Queen") is a further indication that Reed relied heavily upon popular tunes. In fact, the change within a single musical number from one popular tune to another is very much a convention of the mid-Victorian musical stage. Another tune used in *No Cards* is indicated in the sub-title which Gilbert gave "An elderly person" when it appeared as a Bab Ballad: "The Precocious Baby /A VERY TRUE TALE / (*To be sung to the Air of the 'Whistling Oyster.'*)."

Ages Ago

This entertainment, like *No Cards*, presents some variation in names of characters. "Sir Cecil Blount"[12] (*LC* and *JW*) is "Sir Aubrey de Beaupré" in Boosey's score, and is sometimes "Sir Cecil" and sometimes "Sir Aubrey" in *M*. Dame Maybud is called "Rose" in the *LC* list of characters, but "Cherry" in the text, as in the other two texts. The anonymous Steward had a name in *M*: "Angus McTavish."

In *M*, Lady Maud's animation song had three stanzas, which have become two in the score and in *JW*. *LC* is the same as *M* except that it omits a line, evidently through carelessness. *M*'s version of the first two verses differs slightly from *JW*, notably in the first two lines, which *JW*, printing them as one, gives as "Moments so fleeting stern spirits give."

In the two earliest versions, Lady Maud sings:

> The time is fleeting
> That spirits give,
> My heart is beating,
> I breathe, I live!
> For three short hours,
> While darkness lowers,
> By mystic powers,
> I breathe, I live!
>
> Night's sombre awning
> Hath set me free.
> The daylight, dawning,
> Brings night to me.
> My heart is aching,
> For daylight breaking,

---

[12] In *LC*, "Mr. David" and "Mr. Connell" were first indicated for the role of Hebblethwaite–Blount. Their names were then crossed out in favour of "A. Cecil." "Lord Carnaby" is sometimes "Sir Carnaby."

All others waking,
Brings night to me!

What songs of glory
Might poets steal?
From many a story
I could reveal.
The silent pages
Of bygone ages
To poets sages
I could reveal!

In *LC* her speech then continues as in *JW*, but is longer and dwells further on the changes that four centuries have wrought. After observing that the portraits in her gallery are strangers to her, Lady Maud turns her attention to the grounds.

> (*sees window*) Ah! that window. I recollect. It looks out upon my pretty arbour (*looks out*) Why my arbour is gone — and the new tower I spent so much money upon is in ruins. The way the builders run these things up now a days is disgraceful and the trees are all changed. Who has stuck all those hoops in my beautiful lawn. And who has dared to plant those two extraordinary stumps with red blue green and yellow bands around them, and they filled up the pond I stocked with six dozen carp just before I died. . . .

Gilbert had already published a topical sketch on "Croquet" in the *Broadway Annual* for 1867. He uses the same sort of comedy which informs these lines of Lady Maud for Sir Cecil's and Maud's conversation a little later on. Sir Cecil tells her how he used to sit before her portrait, smoking.

LADY M.   Smoking! What do you mean?

SIR CECIL.   Smoking tobacco.

LADY M.   And what is tobacco?

SIR CECIL.   It's a West Indian plant & was brought to England in 1565 by Sir John Hawkins. You place a portion of the leaf in a receptacle at the end of a tube & set fire to it.

LADY M.   But don't it make you ill?

SIR CECIL.   It did, but I got used to it.

Sir Cecil's speech continues as in the 1895 version.
Preceding this, Lady Maud's ballad, "So please you, Sir," was con-

structed in stanzas of eight lines (*LC*) finally altered to stanzas of four long lines (*JW*) with slight changes in wording to suit the contracted rhyme scheme. Mallett follows *LC* but with occasional variations, as "while" for "whilst" and "lady" for "maiden." The first stanza indicates the difference between manuscript and final version:

> So please you, Sir, to listen to
> My story whilst I tell
> The happiness awaiting you —
> A maiden love you well.
> She's far too timid to declare
> The love that makes her sigh —
> And would you know that maiden fair?
> So please you, Sir, 'tis I.

The vocal score and *JW* substitute "hear" for "listen to"; "dares not" for ". . . 's far too timid"; *JW* omits the final "fair" in the penultimate line. The following duet, "A sweeter fate I never heard," was prose dialogue in *LC*, but had become verse by the time the score was published.

After all the portraits have been animated and Lord Carnaby has begun a quarrel with Brown on the grounds that he is a spurious ancestor, *LC* gives a trio for Carnaby, Dame Cherry, and Brown. It is introduced by the line: "I'm alluding to your body, Sir, not your setting."

TRIO

SIR CAR.   Come down, Sir,
                Come down, Sir,
                Now Brown, Sir,
                     Come down.

DAME CHERRY. Descend, Sir,
                Descend, Sir,
                Unbend, Sir,
                     Descend.

BROWN.   Oh, no, Sir,
                Oh, no, Sir,
                Below, Sir,
                     Oh no.

ALL.   { Now what can he mean by remaining up there
              { I'm safer, my friend, in this gilded affair
                Like Mahomet's coffin high up in the air.

BROWN.   My friend, you forget.
            You are dry in effect —
        I am not, I am wet,
            So of course I object
                To descend.
                For I fear
            I should end
                In a smear,
            And I do not,
            No, I do not,
            Do not wish
                To end in a smear.

        SOLO. — DAME CHERRY *to* LORD CARNABY.

        There was a time when *you* were wet,
            When gapers not a few
        Within your native studio met [13]
            (For you were then on view).
        Remember how you feared those men
            As rudely fast they scrubbed; [14]
        Remember how you trembled then
            For fear you should be rubbed,
        He's safer, my friend, in that gilded affair
        Like Mahomet's coffin high up in the air.

This trio does not appear in *M* or in the score. On the other hand, the
score includes the duet for Carnaby and Dame Cherry ("At twenty-three
Lord Carnaby") which is absent from *LC*, although contained in *M*
and *JW*.

Mallett's version of *Ages Ago!!* [15] contains three additional numbers
which do not appear in *LC* or *JW*; all are also present in the score.
These songs — a trio, duet, and solo — built up Mrs. Reed's first impersonation, that of Mistress Maggie McMotherly. The first opens the
Entertainment:

        TRIO. — ROSA, ANGUS, *and* MISTRESS MCMOTHERLY.

        Oh, fie! come dry your eye,
        He's gone, he's running along in the rain!

---

[13] *LC* has "studies," surely a copyist's misreading of "studio."
[14] *LC* has "scribbled."
[15] The title lost its *!!* by the end of the century; it had lost one *!* by the third
page of Mallett. The "a" of "Mac Motherley" was also variable.

He's off at last, he won't come back;
The train is fast, the night is black,
He'll catch, he'll catch the train.
I know he's running along in the rain,
No danger of missing, of missing his train.
He's gone, he's gone, he's gone.
Oh, fie! come dry your eye,
He's gone, he's running along in the rain.
Good bye, good bye!
Come dry your eye, he's gone!

Rosa.   'Tis not so clear,
           Dear Mrs. Mack;
         For listen here,
           The clock's put back.

The score adds: "It's half an hour too slow, it's half an hour too slow."
The second number followed some discussion, dialogue not given, of "The mystic Legend of the wicked Sir Roger de Bohun." It suggests the more highly developed macabre imagery of "When the night wind howls," Sir Roderic's song in *Ruddigore*.

DUET. — Mrs. McMotherly *and* Rosa.

When nature sleeps and slumber creeps
O'er[16] mortal eyes, then witches play;
An elf in every shadow hides,
On every cloud a warlock rides
      To hold his tryst
      In mountain mist;
The moon supplants the light of day
To light the warlocks on their way.

The third song is obviously an opportunity for Mrs. Reed to exhibit the middle-aged pertness she depicted so well. It is addressed to Sir Ebenezer Tare, but some lines are intended for Rosa. Mrs. Reed probably stood between them and turned appropriately to each. The song is a possible alternative for the long prose speech of Mrs. McMotherly, "Eh Sir! but ye ken weel. . . ." in *JW*.

What is it that ye say,
Ye maun let her have her way;
She's a varra puir old body, and she thinks like that?

---

[16] *M* has "on," but the score's "o'er" is clearly the better word.

Well! possibly it's true,
I am poor and aged too,
But my talking's nae a matter to be sneering at.

Ye may smirk and ye may twirl,
You're a varra naughty girl,
And you'll have to buy experience with sighs and tears.
But there's nae excuse for you,
You're an ancient body too,
You've been forty-three for rather more than fifteen years.

I'm blind enough, I know,
But I wasn't always so,
Though you treat your puir old Maggie as a jesting butt.
Ye'd have had an ugly throw,
Mony, mony years ago,
If she'd tottered through her duty with her eyelids shut.
Ye may smirk and ye may twirl, &c.[17]

When these songs were added is not clear. The license copy indicates that the Entertainment is to be produced on Monday evening, November 22, and it is endorsed "Read — L. Man / informed 21 Nov/ 69"; so it should represent as final a state as possible before actual production. The copy submitted was supposed to include everything in the work to be staged,[18] and the Examiner did not usually retain manuscripts for very long. Therefore, it seems reasonable to assume that the additions were made in the very last stages of rehearsal, almost necessarily during the last week or immediately after opening night at the latest, a period during which the later Gilbert habitually revised heavily. What is unusual here, however, is the addition of long musical numbers, all of which appear in the contemporary printed score. Clay must have possessed some of Sullivan's facility of last-minute composition. In 1895, when the need of enlarging Mrs. Reed's role was long past, the *JW* text returned to the same opening as in the license copy.

Of course, if the numbers did not do well on stage, they may have been cut very early, although Clay retained them in the score. How one member of the 1869 audience felt about them is indicated in a copy of

---

[17] There are insignificant variations in wording in the score; the only one of interest is "saucy" for "naughty" in the second stanza, a more appropriate adjective for Rosa's behavior.

[18] In practice it seems to have been sometimes possible to leave blanks to be filled in later.

Mallett in The Reginald Allen Collection. This libretto is marked in pencil, evidently by someone as he attended the performance. The anonymous theatre-goer thought the duet "pretty," but wrote "Not much" beside Mistress Mcmotherly's solo.[19]

A Sensation Novel

Although the license copy of this Entertainment is missing, it seems unlikely that it would show marked variation from the Joseph Williams version. The Mallett libretto differs from *JW* mainly in the point at which Alice learns that Sir Ruthven is "no Baronet, but only poor Tom Sittybank, the 'bus conductor, who, for purposes of his own, has assumed a title and social position to which he has no claim." In *M* this revelation comes in "Vol. II"; in *JW*, Rockalda tells the truth to Alice early in "Vol. III."

Mallett's Baronet is Glenalvon, a name beloved in romantic fiction and drama; *JW* burlesques it as "Glenaloon," but sometimes forgetfully allows "Glenalvon" to slip in. In *M*, Herbert has a last name — de Browne — and is always referred to as "the irreproachable tutor." There is no indication in *M* that he turns out to be the rightful Sir Ruthven, nor is there any evidence as to whether Gripper is Hawkshaw in disguise.

The other changes are a few insignificant variations in wording and a large number of alterations in punctuation, not systematically carried out.

---

[19] He became more enthusiastic as the piece progressed, writing "Excellent" beside Hebblethwaite's song; "Very good" beside both "Your room is old" and "We fly to fields of fancy," the latter winning the additional comment, "best yet." He also liked the quintet with which the pictures returned to their frames, and he found several other numbers "good" (as distinct from "Very good"). The trio "I stand on my authority" is annotated "Lively. 1st part very much like 'Who's to be the robber chief.'"

A playbill in The Reginald Allen Collection commemorates a wildly divergent, probably American version of *Ages Ago* at Bryant's Opera House, May 19th, city and year unspecified. In it, Mrs. McMotherly has become the sister of McTavish; Rosa and a new character, Maggie, are McTavish's nieces. Hebblethwaite is described as a poet and painter and has acquired a friend, Sir Fred Jaunty, who is in love with Maggie. Sir Tare [*sic*] has a servant named Burrampoota-al-Mahoun-Jamjee, while other "occasional characters" include Wild Mag, "a witch of several centuries." This idiosyncratic production must have been put together from a copy of the Mallett libretto, for only in *M* does the name "McTavish" appear for the Steward. It was undoubtedly a piratical precursor of the many unauthorized and botched versions of the Savoy Operas, also constructed from a copy of the libretto and a piano score.

The 1912 re-issue of *A Sensation Novel* includes two stanzas present in Mallett but omitted in Joseph Williams' first publication of this Entertainment (1897). These are the fourth stanza of Rockalda's song "Like a motherly old lady" and the second stanza of Sir Ruthven's song "A nobleman dressed in a close-fitting mask."

Happy Arcadia

The 1872 versions of *Happy Arcadia* were decidedly longer than the final one. Songs appear in both *LC* and *M* which have disappeared in *JW*; verses have been deleted, and there are minor alterations in wording for concerted numbers as well as in the order and assignment of verses. The first substantial difference is the appearance in *M* of Daphne's song "When I was Seventeen," only indicated in *LC* and absent in *JW*. This ballad for Mrs. German Reed followed Daphne's speech about the early contented days of Arcadia. The prose transition to the verses is indicated in *LC*'s marginal dialogue already quoted. In content, the song belongs to the same group of Gilbert lyrics as the later "Time was when Love and I were well-acquainted" (*The Sorcerer*) and "Silvered is the raven hair" (*Patience*).

When I was seventeen,
　　Young men were better bred;
They gave attention keen
　　To every word I said.
In every kind of way
　　They sought to be polite;
Such compliments all day!
　　Such serenades all night!
By Daphne's pretty eye
　　Young lovers used to vow;
I can't imagine why
　　They never do so now!
Ah! life seemed evergreen
When I was seventeen!

If Daphne caught a cold,
　　Or kept her little room,
There fell on every fold
　　A universal gloom.
Had I a broken rest,
　　Young men would sob and sigh;
A weight in every breast,
　　A tear in every eye!

Rheumatics through me fly,
And aches enough, I vow;
I can't imagine why
I don't affect them now!
Ah! life seemed ever green
When I was seventeen!

Colin's song, "Only a Woman," originally had six stanzas in *LC*, four in *M*, and had dwindled to two in *JW*.[20] In all three the song begins with the two verses retained in *JW*; in *LC* they are followed by four more, the last stanza being a repetition of the first: "From the first it was always the same." The three intermediate stanzas are as follows:

She makes a good thing of her loves,
Through a natural talent for betting;
And should you lose dozens of gloves,
She gives you no chance of forgetting.
And, oh! you'll find out your mistake
If bettor & owing her any,
You venture to ask her to take
A dozen, at one and a penny!
For though she is only a woman,
A helpless & innocent woman;
She'll haggle & chaff
Like a man & a half,
Poor weak inexperienced woman!

And if you imagine she lost
And rejoice in this lucky beginning,
In the end you will find to your cost
That her losing is very like winning;
That you've lost, you must always admit
And remember she's eyes like a glutton's
For the quality, maker and fit,
And she's strict on the number of buttons!
For though she is only a woman,
A helpless & innocent woman;
She's down on your tricks
Like a thousand of bricks,
Poor simple and innocent woman.

---

[20] According to its title page, *JW* printed *Happy Arcadia* "as performed in 1895."

In a crowd, she will struggle & squeeze,
   Then shoving, & pushing, and striking
With shoulders, & elbows, and knees,
   Till she finds herself placed to her liking.
And should you hold fast to your place,
   And hint at some care for each other,
She'll give you a slap in the face,
   And appeal to her husband or brother!
      For though she is only a woman
      A gentle, weak, timid young woman;
         There's always a band
         Of relations at hand
      To look after this timid young woman!

Mallett omits the "And if you imagine she lost" stanza and does not repeat the first stanza at the end of the song. The prose speech for Colin which preceded this number contained in *LC* a bitterly grotesque line, since deleted: "She smothers her babies & she pleads the expense of keeping them & she is acquitted."

Strephon's song, "There's naught but care," had a fourth stanza in both *LC* and *M*:

      Compelled to do — just what he likes,
      And forced to go — where fancy strikes;
      Obliged to revel like a king,
      And please himself in everything;
      Compelled to be in merry throng,
      As happy as the day is long.
      If such a life were forced on me —
      How miserable I should be!
         For I'm a simple swain, &c.

In both *LC* and *M*, there are additional verses for the entrance of Lycidas. After his first solo, "Far away from care and strife," all sing:

      Far away from city set,
         Coarse, unfeeling, brutal,
      Here upon $\left\{ \begin{array}{l} \text{his} \\ \text{my} \end{array} \right\}$ flageolet
      $\left\{ \begin{array}{l} \text{He} \\ \text{I} \end{array} \right\}$ will daily tootle
         Tootle! tootle! tootle!

Then Lycidas again:

      Sick of gaiety immense,
      Sick of balls and dinners;

I will live in innocence,
Far from polished sinners.

ALL.   Far away from city set, &c.

After this, *M* prints an additional chorus:

ALL.   Where innocent, harmless mirth
              Reigns everywhere supreme;
              Its eminent, sterling worth
              Shall always be our theme.
              In this little village of ours —

The following quartet gave Chloe a solo verse, which followed Strephon's in *LC*, but preceded Colin's in *M*. She sketches a feminine Cockaigne:

              In valley, & meadows, & plains,
                  We've afternoon teas and "at homes";
              Back hair grows wild in the lanes
                  Together with tortoise shell combs.

Chloe was also given a full-length solo number of her own, "The Way of Wooing," which came after her expression of admiration for Lycidas, ending "I like a man who comes to the point at once. Ah, that's the way to woo." This song, like "The Precocious Baby" in *No Cards*, is also a Bab Ballad under the same title and with a very few minor differences, attributable to the changes between lines to be read and lines to be sung. Since "The Way of Wooing" appears in the collected Babs, it seems unnecessary to reproduce it here.

Mallett, however, has a ballad called "The Way of Wooing" for Chloe which is not a Bab Ballad, although its meaning is similar.

              Little lady, tell me, pray,
                  How to gain a lover's end;
              Shall I win your heart away
                  If I bow, and if I bend?
              Shall I gain a kind assent,
              Paying formal compliment?
              Will you kindly hearing lend
              If I bow, and if I bend?
              "No, no, that will never do,
              That is not the way to woo!"

              Little lady, tell me, now,
                  Shall I sob, and shall I sigh,
              Uttering a timid vow,

With a tear-drop in each eye?
Shall I play a lover's part,
With a flutter at my heart?
Can you love me (if you try)
With a tear-drop in each eye?
"No, no, that will never do,
That is not the way to woo!"

"If you'd woo me well, indeed,
    Never mind what I may say!
Take a sword, and take a steed,
    Carry me by force away.
Let me sob, if so I will;
    Let me sigh, but take me still;
When you're wedded to me, why,
Time enough for *you* to sigh!"
Little lady's words were true,
That's the proper way to woo!

In the auction ensemble which closes the first act of *Happy Arcadia*, Colin acquires a stick (*LC*) rather than a gold snuffbox (*M* and *JW*).

STREPH. *(with stick)* Now here's a lot I recommend,
A good stout stick that will not bend.
Of equal worth, as I shall show,
To help a friend or thrash a foe.

ALL.   Of equal worth, &c.

STREPH.   Now make a bid, a bid, Sir, quick!
Now what shall we say to this little stick,
    This nice little stick,
    This big little stick,
Now what shall he say, Sir, quick, quick, quick!

CHLOE.   A penny, *&c as before*
    It's Colin's stick,
    It's Colin's stick,
It's very, very long
    And very, very thick;
Hurrah, hurrah for Colin's stick!

JW with characteristic absent-mindedness reverts to the stick for Colin in the final exchange. Mallett varies from both *LC* and *JW* in minor details and wording for this ensemble, and contains more lines descriptive of some of the articles. Of the cap, for instance, Strephon sings:

You turn it inside out in dirty weather.
Now what shall we say for this little cap,
For this little cap, for this little cap,
For this little cap and feather?

and

You place it thus, and — I declare —
It gives at once a rakish air;
And any stupid owlish log
Becomes at once a gay young dog.

In the lines dealing with the cloak, "A base conspirator" becomes in *M*
"A truculent conspirator"; and just before the bidding begins for this
article, Strephon has three additional lines:

You do not buy a pig in a poke;
Examine it well, and bid away —
You never will live to rue the day.

The prose dialogue of *LC* contains a long scene between Lycidas and
Strephon, who has taken on Chloe's form. Gilbert very likely cut this
passage because he had made enough comedy from the confusion of
identities and from theoretical transvestism. The lines are amusing
enough, however, as when Strephon–Chloe says,

Well, as I'm Chloe — as I'm Chloe you understand — I forgive you this
time but if ever I'm Strephon again, I shall certainly smash you. You've
had an uncommonly narrow escape — Now be off.

This scene is synopsized in *M*:

Re-appearance of Lycidas, who is unaware of the change that has taken
place. His astonishment at the ruffianly reception he receives at the hands
of the lady who was once the gentle Miss Holland. His confusion
heightened by the arrival of the gentleman who was once the brutal
Arthur Cecil.[21]

There is a "running gag" of "Chloe" making statements applicable
to Strephon and then exclaiming, "You're quite right — I forgot —
Strephon one minute — Chloe the next — one gets confused you know."
Daphne in the form of Strephon enters this scene and Lycidas expects
a fight, but Daphne calls him a slyboots. Lycidas encounters Colin as

---

[21] Here and in *Our Island Home*, Gilbert could not resist the opportunity of
describing Cecil (in reality the mildest and most amiable of actors, praised by reviewers for his gentlemanliness) in terms applicable to a bully. No doubt the
Gallery audiences appreciated the "family" teasing.

Daphne and leaves in bewilderment, a cumulation which suggests the convergence of the enchanted five upon the old fairy in *Creatures of Impulse*.

In *LC* and *JW*, the Entertainment concludes with Lycidas' exit, carrying all the magic appurtenances. But *M* gave the author's last word on his plot:

> The talismans, that have been the cause of so much inconvenience, are sold to Lycidas, who probably puts them to the very worst use. But at this point history becomes so uncertain, that the Author prefers to leave the consequences to the imagination of the audience.

Gilbert's revisions for *Happy Arcadia* characteristically leave plot and satiric pattern fundamentally unchanged, while tightening the structure of the Entertainment and reducing the amount of confusion-of-identity comedy. The thoroughness with which he originally worked out every personality and relationship involved in the exchange of bodies reminds us once again that his mind was essentially systematic and abstractive, while the balance of the "turns" for each performer foreshadows the care he took to insure that all roles in *The Gondoliers* "shall equal be."

Eyes and No Eyes

There are no significant changes from the license copy of this Entertainment in the version printed by Joseph Williams in 1896. *LC* preserves a fleeting indecision as to whether Clochette and Columbine should be Cassandre's nieces or daughters. The manuscript copy in the Reginald Allen Collection, however, has additional dialogue, and the Mallett libretto includes a song which does not appear in any of the other versions.

The Allen manuscript is in a hand resembling that most often used in the license copies of the other Entertainments and in the license copy of *Trial by Jury*. The play has been written into a copybook like those into which, later, cut-up galleys of some Savoy operas were pasted to make up license copies. Gilbert probably used this manuscript in staging *Eyes and No Eyes*, for brief stage directions have been written in in pencil and on two of the blank pages there are sketches of what looks like Alfred Reed in costume as Uncle Cassandre. Approximately two and one-half pages of dialogue have been crossed out in this manuscript and rewritten on the following pages in the form found in *JW*. The original passage makes much more of Cassandre's and Nicolette's pretense that they cannot see the cloak. They take it out of the basket, feel it, speculate about it, nearly — as in *JW* — give themselves away to each other while the girls laugh, and finally express a desire to see it. At this point an ingenious elaboration of one of the lines extant in *JW* takes place.

CASS.   Yes, but when one's paid for a cloak it's natural to want to see what it looks like — it's human nature.

NIC.   Cassandre, while you are true to me, you cannot see that cloak.

CASS.   No, but if I were untrue to you!

NIC.   Cassandre!

CASS.   If I allowed my thoughts to wander to another for one minute so that I may get one peep at it.

NIC.   Never! I won't hear of such a thing!

CASS.   But only for a moment.

NIC.   No.

CLO.   Oh, do, dear Aunt, let his thoughts dwell lovingly on another for half a moment.

COL.   He has been so true to you for thirty years!

NIC.   Well, but mind, she must be very ugly.

CASS.   She's loathsome.

NIC.   And only for half a moment.

CASS.   Only half a moment.

NIC.   Very well — now go!

(Cassandre shuts his eyes and allows his thoughts to wander)

CASS.   Oh, oh, oh, how my thoughts are wandering! Oh, how untrue I am to Nicolette just now to be sure *(opens his eyes and looks at cloak)*. Ha! ha! I can see it! I can see it!

NIC.   *(putting her hands over his eyes)* Now you've wandered quite enough. Dismiss her from your mind for ever!

CASS.   *(with an effort)* She's gone! and so's the cloak.

ALL.   Well, what was it like?

CASS.   A beautiful yellow trimmed with rabbit skin and silver lace with ten little gold buttons down the front.

Mallett omits the duet for the elderly lovers, "When you were eight and twenty," but gives Columbine a solo.

> As I was going along the road,
>   I met a curious party;
> He was tall and thin, as his costume showed,
>   And his manners were frank and hearty,
> His eyes were large, and round, and red,
>   And though the fact's unproven,
> On fire and smoke I'm sure he fed,
> He'd very big horns on the top of his head,
>   And both of his feet were cloven!

ALL.
> Gracious me, and goodness you!
> Here was a serious how-de-do!
> Large red eyes and horns! Dear me!
> Who in the world could the stranger be?

> He offered to sell me the cloak he wore,
>   The very thing I wanted;
> But he quite forgot to remark before
>   That the mantle was enchanted!
> He handed me over the velvet cloak
>   Of which I've just been telling,
> And laughing as though at a very good joke,
> He disappeared in fire and smoke,
>   With a horribly hideous yelling!

ALL.
> Gracious me, and goodness you!
> Here was a serious how-de-do!
> Fire and flame and smoke! Dear me!
> Who in the world could the stranger be?

This song was developed from Columbine's original prose speech, reverted to in *JW*:

I bought it of a tall grim man with great flashing eyes and beautiful big teeth, and great horns sticking out of his head; he had the very thing, so I asked the price, and as soon as I bought it he disappeared in a whirlwind.

Mallett also omits "This state of things . . . the Domestic Curse" in Nicolette's song and the last verse of the "coincidental infants" trio. There are the customary variations among the texts in punctuation, line allotment, and wording.

Appendix B

THE ENTERTAINMENTS OF CHARLES MATHEWS
AND MR. AND MRS. HOWARD PAUL

CHARLES MATHEWS' ENTERTAINMENTS usually consisted of songs, monologues, and short dialogues or playlets, in which he impersonated all
speakers. Some of the conversations were held between himself *in
propria persona* and himself in the character of some one else — or of
several someones. Presumably in these sketches he faced from side to
side to indicate change of speaker, but he also used quick costume
changes or modifications and dressed himself as a female when appropriate. He could flit behind a screen or large chair and emerge immediately "completely transmogrified" in "size, shape, complexion, dress,
face, figure, voice, accent and gait, representing a being of a different
age, sex, and nationality."[1] His style of comedy is well illustrated by
the "theatrical album": *Mathews at Home; Being the Entertainment of
Earth, Air, and Water; as Delivered by Him at Theatre Royal English
Opera House, Strand, and at Most Country Towns; Comprising the
Whole of his celebrated Comic Songs & Tales* . . . (London: Dun-
combe, n.d.).

In "The Margate Library" (comic song and spoken dialogue) he was
the singer, narrator, library keeper, lady wanting book, Sir Noodle
Numps, another lady asking for new novels, Mrs. Jeffery Muffincap,
Mrs. Allspice, Captain, Mrs. Shuffleton, Master Crochet, several anony-
mous persons, and possibly a monkey. Illustrations in another volume,
The London Mathews (London: William Cole, n.d.), show the actor
in the seven different costumes for his seven roles in "Master Charley's
Youthful Days": George Augustus Fipley, French Organist, Sir Shiv-
eram Screwnerve, Monsieur Zephyr, Ap Llywelyn Ap Llwyd Esq., Mr.
Mark Magnum, and Miss Amelrosa.

An excerpt from one of Mathews' prose sketches, "The Polly Packet,"

---

[1] *Gossip of the Century* (London: Ward and Downey, 1892), II, 294.

suggests his use of rapid-fire delivery and eccentric characters (Major Longbow, in this case).

Hot, what d'ye mean by hot? pho! I have been in climates where sala-manders have dropped down dead with the heat of the sun. I once dined with a gentleman and his wife at CALLIHAMMAQUACKA-DALORE, near CUDDERAPOO; after dinner as we were sitting drinking, a ray of the sun struck the Lady and she vanished from our sight, and nothing was left in her place but a heap of ashes. — I was rather surprised, but my friend who was used to these things, he called to his KIT-MA-GARS and CON-SU-MARS, HITHERATOO JUNTAH, which is in English, bring us clean glasses and sweep away your mis-tress, upon my life its true, what will you lay its a lie? — talking of lying, I'll look at the births [sic], what a little ship this is — birth, pho! three of 'em won't hold me. I was born in a berth, suckled by the ship's cow until she broke her back in a storm, and then it was inconvenient for her to be wet-nurse any longer — never mind, nothing hurts me, there's muscle. I was once on the maintop for three weeks and never came down, upon my life it's true. When I was in the West Indies I fought a duel with Major O'Feathersplit at Chilljellyput, the first fire the ball grazed right between my eyes, bounced off at right angles like a tennis ball, killed a Buffalo on the spot that was feeding 280 yards off — upon my life its true, what will you lay its a lie?

Mathews' comic song "Caleb Quotem"[2] foreshadows the autobio-graphical songs and plurality comedy of both Planché and Gilbert:

> I'm parish clerk and sexton here,
>   My name is Caleb Quotem —
> I'm painter, glazier, auctioneer,
>   In short, I am factotum,
> I make a watch, I mend the pumps —
>   (For plumber's work my knack is)
> I physic sell — I cure the mumps —
> I tomb-stones cut — I cut the rumps
>   Of little school-boy Jackies.
>   Geography is my delight —
>   Ballads, epitaphs I write —
>   Almanacks I can indite —
>   Graves I dig compact and tight.

And so on. Mathews' headlong facility expressed itself in tongue-twisting numbers such as "The Bill of Fare":

---

[2] Mathews did not originate this song, but borrowed it from *The Review; or, The Wags of Windsor* (1800), a ballad opera by George Colman the Younger.

Some say what can a man do,
'Mongst fifty one cannot please two:
But tell me your taste, and your price,
And I will suit you in a trice.

Mutton and mullet,
Turkey and pullet,
Melon and calabash,
Calapee and calapash,
German sour crout,
Salmon and trout,
Cormorant, quail,
Woodcock and trail,
Oysters and widgeon,
Lobsters and pigeon,
Soy, parmesan,
Ketchup, cayenne,
Soup, vermicelli,
Cabbage and jelly,
Syllabub, mustard,
Kidneys and custard,
Mince pie,
Lambs' fry,
Toad in a hole,
Flounder and sole,
Giblet soup,
Died o' the roup,
Bubble and squeak,
Garlick and leek.
Cakes,
Steaks,
Chops,
Slops,
Snipe,
Tripe,
Ducks,
Plucks,
Eel,
Veal,
Rice,
Spice,
Pease,
Cheese,
Salt, Malt,

Ham, Lamb,
Roast, Toast,
Boil, broil,
Bears, hares,
Figs, pigs,
Quince,
Mince.
Busy at Cookery, as crow in a rookery,
Old Madam Glass, was but an ass,
For Mingle's the man,
At tossing a pan.
Some say, &c.

Some portions of "Caleb Quotem" follow the same kind of pattern:

Squills —
Pills —
Songs inditing —
Epitaph writing —
Steeple sound —
Corpse to the ground —
Windsor soap —
Physic the pope —

It is apparent that this sort of patter has more in common with its archetype, Figaro's *"Largo al factotum,"* than with the Lord Chancellor's "Nightmare Song"; but Gilbert used short rhyming lines like these for part of "My name is John Wellington Wells" in *The Sorcerer*. Mathews' kind of patter song generally depended on accretion and juxtaposition, with lines getting progressively shorter, usually in three stages.

The entertainments which Howard Paul wrote for himself and his wife have little of Mathews' dexterity. In *"Patchwork:" Embroidered with Wit, Whim and Fancy* (London: Routledge, Warnes, and Routledge, 1858), Paul followed Mathews in having an "I" character converse with various comic personages, but without Mathews' multiplicity and virtuosity. Dialect was frequently used: German, Yankee, Negro. Some of the monologues were also in dialect, such as Major Jonathan Bang's "How I got Invited to Dinner," which bears a family resemblance to "American" English as conceived in contemporary issues of *Punch*. Mr. Paul also impersonated such humour characters as Mr. Shellingham Pease, the Vegetarian, and Captain Puppington Loll.

Almost all of Mrs. Howard Paul's impersonations were illustrated by a song. The following excerpt from "The Unprotected Female," sung by Mrs. Paul as Miss Selina Singleheart, is characteristic.

Oh, it's really shameful!
'Tis most scandalous!
The sorrows and the hardships poor females must endure!
If a woman is but single, and has lived some thirty years,
The world henceforth, for her, poor thing, is but a vale of tears!
And the sooner that she quits it, — why, the better 'twill befall,
For she's pushed about, insulted, and imposed upon by all!
Oh! it's really shameful! 'tis most scandalous,
The sorrows and the hardships poor females must endure.

Those dreadful cabmen!
Swear, swear, grumbling!
They never think of charging less than eighteen-pence a mile;
And when, all in a flurry, at the door they set you down,
You get a leaden shilling in exchange for half-a-crown.[3]

It is easy to see why, in spite of immediate enthusiasm ("The exertions of Mr. and Mrs. Paul were rewarded by incessant laughter and applause." *The Times*, April 2, 1858), *Patchwork* soon proved to be quite forgettable.

---

[3] This song was published by Metzler & Son, Marlborough Street, London.

Glossary and Notes

TO THE TEXTS OF THE PLAYS

British readers will, of course, find many of these notes unnecessary; but I trust that they will recognize their utility for "Our American Cousin."

No Cards

p. 57	*Interior of Mrs. Pennythorne's boudoir.*	The scene of *No Cards* was originally the "Exterior of Mrs. Pennythorne's marine villa," which accounts for Annabella's gardening (". . . I'm planting double stocks") and for Mr. Dee's wearing his hat in what has now become a room.
p. 57	*working*	Doing needlework.
p. 57	*Pickford's van*	Pickford's trucks can still be seen everywhere in London. Gilbert used their motto for a topical joke in *Iolanthe:* "He's a Parliamentary Pickford — he carries everything!"
p. 59	*"Robert toi que j'aime"*	Isabella's famous aria in *Robert le Diable* by Meyerbeer.
p. 59	*"three-cornered constituencies"*	A three-cornered constituency returned three members to Parliament.
p. 69	*pillar post*	A pillar-box; in America, a mailbox.
p. 69	*alum*	Some nineteenth-century bakers adulterated their bread with chalk or alum, a practice repeatedly satirized by the comic writers, for whom "the baker who adulterates," as H. J. Byron put it, was a stock topical allusion.

p. 69   *"Chump-chop*   Obviously a butcher's redaction of the pop-
       Charlie is my   ular song, "Champagne Charlie," written
       name"   by Alfred Lee. In 1867, two years before
        No Cards was produced, George Ley-
        bourne made a great music-hall success
        singing this song, and "Champagne Char-
        lie is my name" became a catchword.
        Punch parodied the *brindisi* in Thomas'
        operatic version of *Hamlet*, with "Cham-
        pagne Hamlet is my name" (LVI [July 3,
        1869], 270).

p. 75   *The Queen of Bab-*   Queen Emma of the Sandwich Islands
       betyboobledore.   visited England in the 1860's; in 1874, five
        years after *No Cards* was written, she lost
        an election to the throne. The idea of an
        Englishwoman becoming Queen of an In-
        dian island was also topical in 1869, since Sir
        James Brook, the "white raja" of Sarawak,
        had died the year before and his nephew
        had succeeded to the raj.

Ages Ago

p. 82   *Characters*   The list of monarchs in the last column
       shows the costume period. The Henrys are
       late sixteenth-century kings of France.

p. 82   *Tare and Tret*   "The two ordinary deductions in calcu-
       lating the net weight of goods to be sold by
       retail." Tret is a standard deduction; tare
       is "the weight of the wrapping, receptacle,
       or conveyance containing goods, which is
       deducted from the gross in order to ascer-
       tain the net weight." (*O.E.D.*)

Our Island Home

p. 107   *Our Island Home*   The title comes from Tennyson's poem
       "The Lotus Eaters," in which the Greek
       mariners sing, "Our island home / Is far
       beyond the wave; we will no longer roam."

p. 109 *upon that bad eminence*	"High on a Throne of Royal State . . . / Satan exalted sat, by merit rais'd / To that bad eminence. . . ." (*Paradise Lost*, Book II, ll. 1–5.)
p. 113 *oysters crossed in love*	"An oyster may be crossed in love" originally comes from Sheridan's *The Critic*. It was expanded into a famous pantomime duet which Grimaldi sang with a property oyster.
p. 114 *my Dolland*	Binoculars or perhaps a pocket telescope. The firm of Dolland and Aitchison still sells optical goods.
p. 115 *Burgess's*	Burgess's was a well-known fish-sauce shop in the Strand near the site of the future Savoy Theatre.
p. 115 *Francatelli*	Queen Victoria's *maître d'hôtel*.
p. 116 *Hurrah, a sail!*	This trio is reminiscent of the famous song "The Bay of Biscay": "A sail in sight appears, / We hail it with three cheers, / Now we sail, with the gale, / From the Bay of Biscay, O!"

A Sensation Novel

p. 130 *Alice Grey*	This character no doubt owes her name to the popular song, "Alice Gray."
p. 134 *Canning*	This British statesman (1770–1827) "had a taste for mystery and disguises, which he had shown at Oxford, and which did much to gain him his unfortunate reputation for trickery." (*E.B.*, 11th ed.)
p. 137 *"Black as a boot is he!"*	Rhoda Broughton had published a three-volume novel, *Red as a Rose Is She*, the preceding year (1870).

p. 137 *Nana Sahib*

Nana Sahib was a Mahratta leader during the Indian Mutiny. His motive for revolt was alleged to have been resentment that the British government refused to continue paying him a pension granted earlier to his adoptive father, the last Peshwa. He was responsible for the massacre at Cawnpore. The Victorian estimate of Nana Sahib may be gathered from an entry in C. E. Buckland's *Dictionary of Indian Biography* (London: Swan Sonnenschein & Co., Ltd., 1906), which begins: "The chief rebel leader in the mutiny, whose barbarous cruelty and treachery have never been forgotten. . . ." Dion Boucicault played Nana Sahib in his own drama *Jessie Brown*; or, *The Relief of Lucknow* (1858), revived in the early sixties.

p. 137 *a falsification of a baptismal entry*

The plot of Wilkie Collins' "sensation novel" *The Woman in White* (1860) involves a false entry in a marriage register, legitimating the villain, Sir Percival Glyde, at the expense of the legal heir.

p. 138 *Yes, you look more than twenty.*

Rockalda's age and coronet of hair recall those of Miss Gwilt, the beautiful villainess of Collins' *Armadale* (1866).

p. 140 *carte de visite*

These photographic portraits mounted on small cards were very popular in the mid-nineteenth century.

p. 143 *limekiln*

M. E. Braddon's Lady Audley committed her first murder in the Lime Tree Walk of her husband's estate. Limekilns figure in Dickens' *Great Expectations*, in which Orlick intends to dispose of Pip in a nearby limekiln, and in English adaptations of Erckmann-Chatrian's *The Polish Jew*, in which the murdered Jew *is* thus destroyed. Gilbert retained Dickens' kiln when he dramatized *Great Expectations* in 1871, which was also the year of *A Sensation Novel*. In the same year, Henry Irving made his great success in *The Bells*, Leopold Lewis' adaptation of *The Polish Jew*.

p. 149 *Bradshaw* — Bradshaw's railway guide was the subject of many Victorian jokes, almost all presenting it as unintelligible.

p. 151 *Belgrave Square . . . Seven Dials* — Gilbert was fond of this juxtaposition of the aristocratic and the lower class. Lord Tolloller in *Iolanthe* declares that "Hearts just as pure and fair / May beat in Belgrave Square / As in the lowly air / Of Seven Dials!" Seven Dials was (and is) the convergence of seven narrow streets at St. Martin's Lane.

p. 159 *Her bed shall be apple-pie* — The apple-pie bed, a favourite practical joke of adolescents, is so made up that one cannot lie full-length in it.

p. 159 *tally-man* — "The pedlar tallyman is a hawker who supplies his customers with goods, receiving payment by weekly installments, and derives his name from the tally or score he keeps with his customers. . . . the general routine of linen-draper's stock, as silk-mercery, hosiery, woollen cloth, &c. —is the most prevalent trade of the tallyman." (Henry Mayhew, *London Labour and the London Poor*, 1851.)

p. 160 *swarthy Ethiopian* — A blackface minstrel playing the "bones," as in the Christy Minstrels, who were also referred to as "Ethiopian serenaders."

p. 161 *Somerset House* — "The national beehive," as Needham and Webster call it (*Somerset House Past and Present*, 1906), licensed public conveyances — and almost everything else. Gilbert drew on the bourgeois associations of Somerset House, with its myriad government offices, for Grosvenor's "reformation" in *Patience*: "A Somerset House young man, / A very delectable, highly respectable, / Three-penny-bus young man."

p. 164   *Invent a process if you have it not.*   "Assume a virtue, if you have it not." (*Hamlet*, III, iv, 160.)

Happy Arcadia

p. 181   *Welcome, little stranger!*   This greeting, wrenched from its context of babyhood, was a cliché among Victorian burlesque writers. Mark Lemon's dramatic sketch bearing this title was performed at the Adelphi in 1857.

p. 187   *wide-awake*   Wide-awake hats had low crowns, wide brims, and no nap. Hence the punning name — a pun which was not original with Gilbert.

p. 192   *Friar's Balsam and nine oils*   Friar's Balsam was a popularly advertised embrocation. The nine oils figure in other works of literature: "The nine oils. . . . It's what our people always use, sir, when they get any hurts in the ring. . . ." replies Sissy Jupe to Mr. Bounderby's question in Dickens' *Hard Times*. The comic landlady in Tom Taylor's *The Ticket-of-Leave Man* refers to the nine oils "rubbed in warm."

Eyes and No Eyes

p. 204   *A Black-a-Moore-and-Burgess*   G. W. Moore and Fred. Burgess were the proprietors of a phenomenally successful minstrel troupe.

Selected Bibliography

À Beckett, Arthur William. *Green-Room Recollections*. Bristol: J. W. Arrowsmith [1896].

Adams, William Davenport. *A Book of Burlesque; Sketches of English Stage Travestie and Parody*. London: Henry and Co., 1891.

Allen, Reginald. *W. S. Gilbert: An Anniversary Survey and Exhibition Checklist with Thirty-Five Illustrations*. Charlottesville: The Bibliographical Society of the University of Virginia, 1963.

Baily, Leslie. *The Gilbert and Sullivan Book*. London: Cassell and Co., Ltd., 1952.

Bancroft, Marie and Squire. *The Bancrofts: Recollections of Sixty Years*. London: John Murray, 1909.

Barrington, Rutland. *Rutland Barrington: a Record of Thirty-five Years' Experience on the English Stage by Himself*. Preface by W. S. Gilbert. London: Grant Richards, 1908.

Blanchard, E. L. *The Life and Reminiscences of E. L. Blanchard, with Notes from the Diary of Wm. Blanchard*. Edited by Clement Scott and Cecil Howard. 2 vols. London: Hutchinson and Co., 1891.

Brough, William. *Ching-Chow-Hi*. London: J. Mallett, n.d.

———. *A Peculiar Family*. MS License Copy, British Museum.

———. *A Peculiar Family*. London: J. Mallett, 1865.

Burnand, F. C. (Sir Francis C.) *Cox and Box*. London: J. Mallett, n.d.

———. *Mildred's Well*. London: J. Mallett, n.d.

———. *Records and Reminiscences Personal and General*. 2 vols. London: Methuen and Co., 1904.

Dark, Sidney, and Grey, Rowland. *W. S. Gilbert; His Life and Letters*. London: Methuen and Co., Ltd., 1923.

Dibdin, Charles. *Professional and Literary Memoirs of Charles Dibdin the Younger*. Edited from the original manuscript by George Speaight. London: The Society for Theatre Research, 1956.

Disher, Maurice Willson. *Blood and Thunder: Mid-Victorian Melodrama and Its Origins*. London: Frederick Muller Ltd., 1949.

———. *Victorian Song From Dive to Drawing Room*. London: Phoenix House Ltd., 1955.

Fitzgerald, Percy. *The Savoy Opera and the Savoyards*. London: Chatto and Windus, 1894.

Gilbert, W. S. *Ages Ago!!* MS License Copy, British Museum.

———. *Ages Ago!!* London: J. Mallett, n.d.

———. *The "Bab" Ballads. Much Sound and Little Sense.* London: John Camden Hotten, 1869.

———. *Eyes and No Eyes.* MS License Copy, British Museum.

———. *Eyes and No Eyes.* MS in copyist's hand, The Reginald Allen Collection, Pierpont Morgan Library.

———. *Eyes and No Eyes.* London: J. Mallett, n.d.

———. *Foggerty's Fairy and Other Tales.* London: George Routledge and Sons, 1890.

———. *Happy Arcadia.* MS License Copy, British Museum.

———. *Happy Arcadia.* London: J. Mallett, n.d.

———. *New and Original Extravaganzas.* Edited by Isaac Goldberg. Boston: John W. Luce & Co., 1931.

———. *No Cards.* MS License Copy, British Museum.

———. *No Cards.* London: J. Mallett, n.d.

———. *Original Plays.* 4 series. London: Chatto & Windus, 1925–28.

———. *Our Island Home.* Typescript made from License Copy, British Museum.

———. *A Sensation Novel.* London: J. Mallett, n.d.

Goldberg, Isaac. *The Story of Gilbert and Sullivan; or, The 'Compleat' Savoyard.* New York: Simon and Schuster, Inc., 1928.

Gossip of the Century. 2 vols. London: Ward and Downey, 1892.

Grossmith, George. *A Society Clown: Reminiscences.* Bristol: J. W. Arrowsmith, 1888.

Hatton, Joseph. *Reminiscences of J. L. Toole Related by Himself and Chronicled by Joseph Hatton.* 2 vols. London: Hurst and Blackett, Ltd., 1889.

Hollingshead, John. *Theatrical Licenses. Reprinted from "The Daily Telegraph" and "Times."* London: Chatto and Windus, 1875.

Jacobs, Arthur. *Gilbert and Sullivan.* London: Max Parrish and Co., Ltd., 1951.

Layard, George Somes. *Shirley Brooks of Punch: His Life, Letters, and Diaries.* New York: Henry Holt and Co., 1907.

Lewes, G. H. Introduction to *Selections from the Modern British Dramatists.* 2 vols. in 1. Leipzig: F. A. Brockhaus, 1867.

Macqueen-Pope, W. *Ghosts and Greasepaint: A Story of the Days that Were.* London: Robert Hale Ltd., 1951.

Marston, Westland. *Our Recent Actors: Being Recollections Crucial, and, in Many Cases, Personal, of Late Distinguished Performers of Both Sexes. With Some Incidental Notices of Living Actors.* 2 vols. Boston: Roberts Brothers, 1888.

Morley, Henry. *The Journal of a London Playgoer from 1851 to 1866.* London: George Routledge and Sons, 1866.

Morton, John Maddison. *Box and Cox; A Romance of Real Life.* London: Samuel French, n.d.

Nicoll, Allardyce. *Late Nineteenth Century Drama 1850–1900.* Cambridge: University Press, 1962.

Pearce, Charles E. *Madame Vestris and Her Times.* London: Stanley Paul and Co., n.d.

Pemberton, T. Edgar. *The Kendals: A Biography.* New York: Dodd, Mead and Co., 1900.

Planché, James Robinson. *The Extravaganzas of J. R. Planché, Esq., (Somerset Herald) 1825–1871.* Edited by T. F. Croker and Stephen Tucker. Testimonial Edition. 5 vols. London: Samuel French, 1879.

———. *Recollections and Reflections . . . A Professional Autobiography.* New and rev. ed. London: Sampson Low, Marston & Company, Limited, 1901.

Price, R. G. G. *A History of Punch.* London: Collins, 1957.

Pulling, Christopher. *They Were Singing And What They Sang About.* London: George G. Harrap and Co., Ltd., 1952.

Purnell, Thomas ("Q"). *Dramatists of the Present Day. Reprinted from "The Athenaeum."* London: Chapman and Hall, 1871.

Rees, Terence. *Thespis: A Gilbert & Sullivan Enigma.* London: Dillon's University Bookshop, 1964.

Robertson, Tom. *A Dream in Venice.* MS License Copy, British Museum.

Rowell, George (ed.). *Nineteenth Century Plays.* World's Classics Edition. London: Oxford University Press, 1953.

Scott, Clement. *Thirty Years at the Play* and *Dramatic Table Talk.* London: The Railway and General Automatic Library, Limited, n.d.

Searle, Townley. *Sir William Schwenk Gilbert: A Topsy-turvy Adventure.* Introduction by R. E. Swarthout. London: Alexander Ouseley, Ltd., 1931.

Soldene, Emily. *My Theatrical and Musical Recollections.* London: Downey and Co., Ltd., 1897.

Sullivan, Herbert, and Flower, Newman. *Sir Arthur Sullivan: His Life, Letters and Diaries.* Rev. ed. London: Cassell and Company, Ltd., 1950.

Taylor, Tom. *Our Family Legend.* MS License Copy, British Museum.

Trewin, J. C. *Mr. Macready; A Nineteenth-Century Tragedian and His Theatre.* London: George G. Harrap and Co., Ltd., 1955.

Webster-Brough, Jean. *Prompt Copy (The Brough Story).* London: Hutchinson, 1952.

Williamson, David. *The German Reeds and Corney Grain: Records and Reminiscences.* London: A. D. Innes and Co., 1895.

Wilson, A. E. *Pantomime Pageant.* London: Stanley Paul and Co., Ltd., 1946.

VOCAL SCORES

Ages Ago. London: Boosey & Co., n.d.
Cox and Box. London: Boosey & Co., n.d.

SELECTED PERIODICALS

Reviews of the Gallery of Illustration and of Gilbert's other work may be found in the contemporary issues of the *Athenaeum, Daily Telegraph, Graphic, Illustrated London News, Illustrated Times, Morning Post,* and *The Times,* among others.

The comic magazines, *Fun, Punch,* and the *Tomahawk,* contain briefer notices as well as verse and prose by Gilbert, Burnand *et al.* These, together with the *Mask, Mirth,* and the earlier *Man in the Moon,* constitute a representative sampling of Victorian comic journalism. *London Society,* the *Era Almanack,* and *Dark Blue* contain contributions by Gilbert. The latter periodical also published, in 1872, a serious survey of contemporary theatre, written by Tom Taylor. For the later careers of Arthur Cecil and others see *The Theatre* in the nineties.

Index

Comic devices: baby-switching, 36–37; disguise, 23, 35, 37, 230; elderly baby, 23, 23 n.; identity, problems of, 8, 8 n., 15, 22–23, 24, 31–33, 34, 35–37, 39–41, 43, 48; impersonations (mimicry), 1, 5, 6–7, 253; Invasion Plot, 47; Lozenge Plot, 35–36, 39–42, 45, 47, 48; mock-orientalism, 15, 16–17, 50; multiple roles, 5–8, 22, 27, 31, 40, 250–51; plurality, 31, 48, 251; puns, 10, 50; stock devices, 23; thoroughness, 33, 44, 45–46; time-juggling, 8, 15, 27, 28, 33, 36, 41, 46; Topsyturvydom, 23, 23 n., 33, 39, 47; transvestism, 40, 40 n., 41, 41 n.; *see also* Farce; Parody; Satire

Comic stage business, 12, 21
Comic values, stock, 23
Commedia dell'arte, 45
Committed for Trial, 25 n.
Court Theatre, 13 n., 26 n., 39
Cox and Box, 11 n., 17–21, 22 n., 25, 26, 26 n., 30, 34, 39
Creatures of Impulse, 28, 36, 39, 40, 247
Croquefer; ou le Dernier des Paladins, 11 n., 16

Daily Telegraph, 9 n., 20; reviews Gilbert's German Reed Entertainments, 26, 231–32
D'Erina, Rosa, 17, 25, 30, 231–32
Dialect comedy, 253
Dibdin, Charles, Senior, 5–6
Dickens, Charles, 2, 4 n., 6, 6 n., 9 n., 17 n., 22, 43, 258, 260
D'Oyly Carte, Richard, 10 n.
D'Oyly Carte Opera Company, 17 n.
Dream in Venice, A, 8, 8 n., 15
Du Maurier, George, 18

Elliott, J. W., 24 n.
Elliott, Lionel, 24 n., 229
"Emperor's New Clothes, The," 45, 46
Engaged, 12, 31, 31 n.
Entertainments, 1, 5–9, 16, 250–54; *see also* Gilbert's German Reed Entertainments; Reed, Mr. and Mrs. German, Entertainment of

"Etiquette," 32 n.
Extravaganza, 3, 11, 12, 21–22, 41
Eyes and No Eyes, 2 n., 228; critical analysis of, 45–47; first production of, 44–45, 47; glossary and notes for, 260; manuscript copies of, 227, 228, 247; text of, 199–226; variations in text of, 247–49

Fairy comedies, Gilbert's, 13, 13 n., 24, 36, 36 n., 42, 46, 47, 50
"Fairy Curate, The," 28
"Fancy Fair, The," 7, 24 n.
Farce, 7, 10; characteristics of, 15, 18, 34
Featherstone, Isabella; *see* Paul, Mr. and Mrs. Howard
Fees, abolition of, 10, 10 n.
Foote, Samuel, 5
Fun, 9 n., 15 n., 24, 37 n., 44 n.; Gilbert's work for, 39 n., 46 n.; reviews *A Sensation Novel*, 38 n.

Gaiety Theatre, 39
Gallery of Illustration, 1, 2, 7, 7 n., 9–11, 11 n., 12, 13, 14, 15, 16, 17, 22, 24 n., 25, 31, 31 n., 39, 44, 47, 49, 50, 227, 228
Gentleman in Black, The, 30, 36, 39, 40 n., 41
Gilbert, W. S.: "Burglar's Story, The," 44 n.; censorship, troubles with, 13 n.; *Chapeau de paille d'Italie, Un*, adaptation of, 28 n.; *Committed for Trial*, 25 n.; compared with Shaw, 43; concept of comedy, 49–50; contralto roles in works by, 43, 48–49, 49 n.; contributions to periodicals, 10 n., 23 n., 235, 264; criticism of life, light opera a, 50; debt to mid-Victorian stage conditions, 50; *Engaged*, 12, 31, 31 n.; "English" nature of best work, 50; *Fairy's Dilemma, The*, 33 n.; *Great Expectations*, dramatization of, 258–59; hand-writing of, 229, 229 n.; *Happy Land, The*, collaboration on, 13, 13 n.; love, treatment of, 24, 37 n., 38, 46; meets Sullivan at the Gallery of Illustration, 22, 30; *Mountebanks,*

Paddington Pollaky, 233
Palace of Truth, 13 n., 36, 36 n.
Pamela Dibbs (character), 14, 18 n.
Pantomime, 10, 11, 41, 45, 48, 51, 257
Parody, 12, 14 n., 32, 36, 50, 256
Parody, Gilbert's, 32, 233–34, 260; of literary conventions, 35; of melodrama, 31–33, 36, 38, 45, 46; of sensation novels, 34–38; of stage rhetoric, 33
Parry, John, 1, 6–7, 8, 14 n.
Pascal, Florian, 2 n., 38 n., 45 n., 228, 228 n.
Patchwork, 8, 253–54
Patience, 25, 36, 42, 43, 45, 233, 241, 259–60
Patter songs, 29, 251–53
Paul, Mr. and Mrs. Howard, 8–9, 48, 253–54
Peculiar Family, A, 14–15
"Phantom Head, The," 39 n.
Phelps, Samuel, 2 n., 3, 4 n., 6, 8
Pinafore, H.M.S., xiv, 14, 15 n., 36, 43, 45 n., 50
Pinero, A. W., 26 n.
Pirates of Penzance, The, 29, 33, 36 n., 39 n., 41, 43, 47
Planché, James Robinson, 3, 7, 8 n., 11, 12–13, 13 n., 16, 24 n., 39, 45 n., 251
"Precocious Baby, The," 23, 231, 234, 244
Pretty Druidess, The, 24, 24 n., 49
Princess, The, 11, 21, 24, 49
Princess Ida, 24, 43, 49
Princess Toto, 30
Punch, 13, 13 n., 24, 34 n., 49, 253, 256; compares Gilbert and Sullivan operas to German Reed Entertainments, xiv, 13 n.; hostility toward Gilbert, 22 n.; reviews *Ages Ago*, 26, 26 n.
Purnell, Thomas, 22
Pygmalion and Galatea, 13 n.

"Q"; *see* Purnell, Thomas
Quaker, The, 6

Randall's Thumb, 36 n.
Reed, Alfred German, 9, 31–33, 41, 44, 45, 228, 247
Reed, Mr. and Mrs. German: compared with Mr. and Mrs. Howard Paul, 8–9; contribution to Gilbertianism, 47–51; Entertainment of, xiv, 1, 5, 6–17, 228, 229; habits of impersonation congenial to Gilbert, 48; play themselves on stage, 8, 8 n., 31–33; provincial tour, 1; repertory company a prototype of the Savoy's, 48; respectability of, 3, 5, 9, 11, 12, 49; retirement of, 31 n., 44–45; *see also* Gilbert's German Reed Entertainments
Reed, Mrs. German (Priscilla Horton), 13, 14, 241; career before marriage, 1–3; compared with Vestris, 3; creates role of Georgina Vesey in *Money*, 3; death of, 31 n.; improvises costumes for *Our Island Home*, 34; musical-mimetic monologuist, 1, 6, 7–8; physical description of, 3 n.; plays in Gilbert's Entertainments, 25, 31–34, 35, 38 n., 40, 42, 237, 238; plays in Planché's works, 3, 8 n.; sets pattern for Savoy contraltos, 31, 48–49; Shakespearian roles of, 2–3; versatility of, 7–8; voice of, 3, 3 n.; writes to a Gallery-goer, 9 n.
Reed, Thomas German: as actor, 17, 31–34, 38 n., 44, 44 n.; as composer, 2, 24 n., 34, 38, 44–45, 229, 232, 234; asks Sullivan to set *A Sensation Novel*, 22; death of, 5; early career of, 1–3; methods of attracting non-theater-goers, 5; produces *Cox and Box*, 17–18; produces *opera di camera*, 17; produces season of English Opera, 17
Rees, Terence, 25 n.
Robert the Devil, 11 n.
Robertson, Tom, 4 n., 8, 8 n., 15
Robertson, William, 4, 4 n.
Ruddigore, 17 n., 28, 33, 36, 43, 238

Sadler's Wells, 2, 4 n.
St. George's Hall, 9 n., 17, 24 n., 44, 47
St. Martin's Hall, 1
Satire, 12, 15–16, 21 n.
Satire, Gilbert's, 12, 15, 23, 28–29, 43, 50, 247; of character, 31; of decorum, 38, 46; of duty, 33; of fallacious definitions of "the good life," 42–43;